MW01124647

Thinking about Social Problems

SOCIAL PROBLEMS AND SOCIAL ISSUES

An Aldine de Gruyter Series of Texts and Monographs

SERIES EDITOR

Joel Best, *University of Delaware*

THINKING ABOUT SOCIAL PROBLEMS

An Introduction to Constructionist Perspectives

Second Edition

Donileen R. Loseke

ALDINE DE GRUYTER
New York

ABOUT THE AUTHOR

Donileen R. Loseke is Professor of Sociology, University of South Florida. A past president of the Society for the Study of Symbolic Interaction, she is the author of *The Battered Woman and Shelters: The Social Construction of Wife Abuse,* and coeditor (with Richard Gelles) of *Current Controversies on Family Violence.* Dr. Loseke also has served as coeditor of the *Journal of Contemporary Ethnography,* is on the Board of Directors of the Society for the Study of Social Problems, and is an Advisory Editor for *Social Problems.*

ALDINE DE GRUYTER
A division of Walter de Gruyter, Inc.
200 Saw Mill River Road
Hawthorne, New York 10532

This publication is printed on acid free paper ⊗

Library of Congress Cataloging-in-Publication Data

Loseke, Donileen R., 1947–
    Thinking about social problems : an introduction to constructionist perspectives / Donileen R. Loseke.—2nd ed.
        p. cm. — (Social problems and social issues)
Includes index.
    ISBN 0-202-30684-4 (pbk.)
    1. Social problems. 2. Social problems—United States. 3. Social perception. 4. Social perception—United States. I. Title. II. Series.
HN17.5 .L67 2000
361.1'0973—dc21

                                                                2002008305

Manufactured in the United States of America

10 9 8 7 6 5 4 3 2

to Spencer

*the love of my life
and my inspiration*

Contents

Preface to the Second Edition

While social constructionist approaches to social problems are popular among academic researchers in sociology, communication, public policy, and criminology, this perspective tends to be not adequately covered in popular social problems texts. There are several likely reasons why students often are not introduced to constructionist perspectives until they reach advanced undergraduate or even graduate work. For example, student interest often lies in understanding the very real problems in our world, but social constructionist perspectives focus on questions about how humans create the meaning of our world. At first glance, the questions of constructionists seem esoteric and perhaps even a waste of time in a world containing very real want and pain. In addition, social constructionism originally was posed as an alternative to other theoretical approaches examining social problems as objective conditions. This has led some people to argue that *either* you believe that social problems exist outside human awareness, *or* you believe that social problems are constructed. When given such a choice, many people choose to examine social problems as objective conditions because denying the existence of objective reality does not make sense to practical actors. Finally, at least part of the reason why social constructionist perspectives have not become popular at an undergraduate level is because there are few articles or books offering an accessible overview. The classic statement of this perspective, *Constructing Social Problems,* by Malcolm Spector and John Kitsuse, now is twenty-five years old. Its examples seem dated and the debates inspiring their arguments promoting constructionism now seem old. The more current literature also is not much help in offering an overview: It is not obvious how the case studies in the empirical literature relate to one another to form a coherent research agenda; theoretical writings in this perspective most often assume audiences of readers already familiar with the perspective.

That is why I wanted to write this book. In the course of teaching classes such as Social Problems, Introduction to Sociology, Family Violence, Deviance, and Women's Lives, I have become increasingly convinced that social construction perspectives help us make sense of our lives. The questions of constructionism—how do humans create, sustain, and change meaning—only sound esoteric. I believe in the power of social constructionism; I think it encourages a way of thinking that is distinctly sociological and, to use a trendy word, empowering, to those who use it. I also believe that the insights of constructionism do not depend on suspending all belief that a real world exists outside our understandings of it. I do not see constructionism as an alternative to other theoretical frameworks: I see it as an important addition. Different frameworks simply pose questions about different aspects of life—to deny the importance of any theoretical framework is to limit our understandings. We cannot afford to do this if we want to understand the perplexity and complexity of the human condition. I think social constructionist perspectives can help us do this.

Rather than writing for an audience of insiders who already are convinced that social constructionist perspectives are important, I wanted to write for an audience of intelligent people who know nothing about the perspective. What I wanted to do was to encourage readers to think about social problems and, along the way, to offer a general introduction to social construction perspectives.

I ended up writing two books contained within one cover. The first is the chapters themselves, which tell a quite breezy story in conversational prose. My goal here is to spark interest and encourage readers to think about how social problems are constructed and about what this means in our daily lives. I think of the second book as contained in the footnotes to each chapter and in the theoretical appendix. This is a shadow book containing the academic underpinnings for what I often gloss over in the chapters. I hope that readers wanting to pursue constructionist perspectives will read the footnotes, check the references, and ponder the questions and theoretical options posed in the appendix. My goal is to offer those interested readers a road map into a further study of social constructionism.

There are two primary changes from the previous edition. First, this edition includes attention to the "new social movements" emphasizing social change through identity transformation rather than through structural change. This edition also looks more closely at the importance of emotions in constructing public consciousness of social problems. Second, Joel Best and I felt that this short text would be a better teaching tool if there were an accompanying reader, so *Social Problems: Constructionist Readings* can be used by those who want empirical examples to demonstrate arguments made here.

High on my list of acknowledgments are my former students at Skidmore College and my current students at the University of South Florida. In this book I have used many of their insights about social problems; their questions and comments often are what have led me to believe in the very real power of constructionist perspectives. When I turn to debts owed to the community of social constructionist colleagues, I should simply direct readers to the reference list—what I primarily have done is attempt to interpret and synthesize the works of many people who have developed this perspective. Some colleagues, though, have been particular sources of encouragement and advice in this project. Although I fear I've taken too much of their time and done too little with their comments and suggestions, I owe debts of gratitude to Joel Best, Spencer Cahill, Jennifer Dunn, Jaber Gubrium, James Holstein, Kathleen Lowney, Bryce Merrill, and Gale Miller. Richard Koffler of Aldine de Gruyter and Joel Best, series editor, have been remarkable in their continued support. The people at Aldine de Gruyter have been a joy to work with.

I

Issues in Studying Social Problems

1

Examining Social Problems

It's 8:45 A.M., September 11, 2001. I'm thinking about examples of social problems to use in my class today while drinking coffee and watching the *Today Show*. This program is loaded with possibilities. Al talked about a tropical storm heading for my home in Tampa. Matt talked with a scientist about the health problems of elderly people who can't afford their prescription medications. Katie talked with a representative of a group trying to stop the government from opening up huge areas in Alaska for oil drilling. I've seen a commercial for an upcoming *Dateline* challenging the effectiveness of school vouchers in giving students better education. So many possible examples of social problems. But in the middle of a sentence quizzing Congressman Condit's lawyer about a missing congressional intern, Matt stops. The picture changes: a burning World Trade Center is on the screen. What are we watching? No one knows. I forget my thoughts about the social problems of hurricanes, medical insurance, environment, schools, unethical politicians. Horrified, I watch and by 11:00 A.M. I can't think. I feel only horror, panic, fear. We can't think about it until we make sense of what is happening.

This book is about social problems so I will begin simply with a question for you, the reader of these lines: What do you think are the ten most important social problems in the United States today?

Most certainly, since September 11, 2001, your list probably includes the multiple problems of war and terrorism. Your list also might include AIDS, crime, credit card theft, identity theft, child abuse, wife abuse, sexual abuse, alcohol abuse, drug abuse, animal abuse, homosexual rights, ability-impaired people's rights, laboratory animal rights, racism, sexism, ageism, anti-Semitism, homophobia, unemployment, poverty, increasing college tuition, welfare, affirmative action, global warming, acid rain, toxic landfills, sport utility vehicles that use too much gasoline, tires that fall apart when driven at high speeds, illegal campaign contributions, voting machines that don't work, corrupt politicians, divorce, men who don't pay child support, single mothers, teenage pregnancy, schools that don't teach, schools that don't have money to hire teachers or buy computers, a lack of affordable child care, housing or medical care, medical malpractice, smoking, drinking, Satanic cults, obesity, teens who gun down classmates.

There are four important lessons in this small exercise in naming social problems. First, what we call "social problems" is *not* a stable category. In my newspaper delivered early in the morning on September 11, 2001, there were many articles and opinion pieces about problems with the social security system, too costly medical prescriptions for the elderly, voting machines that don't work, crime, and school failure. My paper on the next day included nothing about any of these. The social problems of one day simply disappeared the next as all attention was riveted on terrorism, national security, and war. It is likely that by the time you read these lines the list of things we worry about will have changed. Today's worries are not necessarily tomorrow's worries.

Second, there seemingly is no end to conditions in America that might be called social problems. Granted, crime and poverty tend to remain on the public's and policymakers' lists of problems, and racial inequality often is called this country's most enduring social problem. But after these, the list is all but endless. Given time, you could think of more than ten problems confronting the United States today, and if you compared your list with those made by others, the number of items would grow. What we call social problems range from conditions isolated within one or another community (there tend to be large forest fires each year in Malibu, California; moose from the Adirondacks in Northern New York sometimes wander into small towns creating much havoc), to those affecting particular states (the budget problems in Florida because the state's economy depends on tourists who stopped traveling after the terrorist attacks), to those in particular regions of the country (flooding in the Midwest, migrant workers in California, Texas, and Florida), to problems found throughout the entire nation (AIDS, inequalities, lack of low-cost day care for children), to those crossing international borders (human rights, world hunger, refugees without homes, overpopulation). The list is seemingly endless, ever changing.

A third lesson from this simple exercise in naming social problems is that social problems are about *disagreements*. You might believe that some of the problems I offered are not social problems at all, or that I failed to mention others that are far more important. Or, you and I might be thinking about very different things even if we did agree to include something on a list of important problems. If there is a problem called "homosexual rights," for example, is this a problem of too many rights or too few? Is the problem of school prayer a problem of too much prayer or too little? Or, we might disagree on what, particularly, should be included in the problem. So, for example, we hear about the problem of "teenage pregnancy." A married nineteen-year-old college student *is* a "pregnant teen," but do we include such a woman in our worry? Or, we might agree that something is a problem, we might agree on what should be included in this problem, but still not agree about what causes it and therefore, what should be done to resolve it. Is the problem of teens who gun down their classmates a problem of schools? Parents? Mentally unbalanced teens? Peer pressure? A mass media saturated with violence? Guns? Social problems are about disagreements.

A fourth lesson from this simple exercise of naming social problems is that social problems are about conditions *and* they are about people in those conditions. A social problem called crime is about criminals and victims of crime. A social problem called poverty is about poor people. Terrorism involves terrorists. Whether explicit and obvious (the condition of unemployment and unemployed people) or implicit and subtle (the deindustrialization of America, which implies unemployed or underemployed workers), social problems are about conditions (some*thing*) and they are about people (some*body*).

Another important lesson about social problems is not obvious from this exercise because I started by asking you to list important problems in the *United States now*. A critical characteristic of social problems is that each is located in a particular time and place. Social problems in the United States change: People in the late 1600s worried a great deal about the problem of "witchcraft." We no longer have that problem but we worry about the problem of "mental illness." Likewise, social problems are located in particular cultures. For example, although the United States and Japan both are industrialized, urbanized countries, social problems in these places are not the same. Consider how children who refuse to go to school in the United States are believed to have a personal problem. This same condition, children refusing to go to school, is called "school refusal" in Japan and people believe it is the consequence of bad schools and bad teachers. Likewise, while the federal government in the United States has taken a major role in combating child pornography, the Japanese government has not taken on such a role.[1]

As another example, consider the behaviors of "uncivil and aggressive behavior in workplaces." We certainly have such behavior in the United States, but it is not generally accorded the status of a social problem. Yet in Great Britain such behaviors receive considerable attention and "bullying" is an important social problem. In brief, what is—and what is not—a social problem, and how the problem is responded to, depends on when and where the condition happens.[2]

Let me ask another question. Think of your list of the top ten American social problems. What do all of these conditions have in common? What do conditions as diverse as illegal drugs, unemployment, child abuse, and environmental ruin share? Stated otherwise, what *is* a social problem?

WHAT IS A SOCIAL PROBLEM?

While we rarely ask in our daily life what the term *social problem* means, studies conclude that Americans in general do have somewhat specific notions about the characteristics of conditions that should be categorized as social problems. There are four parts to this common public definition.[3]

First, we use the term *social problem* to indicate that something is *wrong*. In popular understanding, a social problem is *not* something like happy families, physically fit people, or schools that teach children to read. This is common sense: The name is social *problem* so it obviously refers to conditions evaluated as wrong because they create harm.

The second part of the definition of social problem sounds harsh and uncaring: To be given the status of a social problem the condition must be evaluated as *widespread,* which means that it must hurt more than a few people. If I lose my job, that is a personal trouble.[4] It is a problem for me but it is not necessarily a problem for you or for anyone else. But if something causes many of us to lose our jobs, then it is a social problem. I think Jeffrey Dahmer can illustrate how we use the term *social problem* to categorize conditions we think are widespread. Jeffrey Dahmer was a man who killed—and then ate—young boys. Certainly we all would agree that killing and cannibalism are wrong. But Americans never mention the problem of cannibalism when polled about the country's problems; cannibalism never is mentioned in social problems texts, it is not debated in the halls of Congress, we do not have social services to reform cannibals, we are not asked to donate money for the cause of stopping cannibalism. Why not? Because as hideous as it was that Jeffrey Dahmer killed and ate young boys, one cannibal among us is not enough to make cannibalism a social problem. Social problems are troublesome conditions we believe affect a *significant number of people.*

Third, the definition of social problem contains a dose of optimism. *Social problem* is a name we give to conditions we think can be *changed* by humans. Consider the condition of death. This certainly is a troublesome and widespread condition. But humans will die and that cannot be changed. Death is not a social problem. At the same time, there are many conditions associated with death that *could* be changed and therefore can be talked about as social problems: We could change *when* people die (disagreements about using medical technology to extend life or assisted suicide to end life) and *how* people die (the problems of care in nursing homes for elderly people, the problems of automobile and airplane crashes that cause early death). Likewise, earthquakes, hurricanes, and tornadoes are not social problems because nothing can be done to stop them. But there are many actual and potential social problems surrounding natural disasters such as the cost of insurance, failures of early-warning systems for disasters, and the response of officials to such disasters. Social problems is a term we use when we believe the troublesome condition *can be fixed.*

A social problem is a condition evaluated as wrong, widespread, and changeable. The fourth and final component of the definition is that social problem is a category for conditions we believe *should* be changed. This is very logical: If the condition is evaluated as wrong, if it occurs frequently, and if it can be changed, then it follows it should be changed. To say that something is a social problem is to take a stand that *something needs to be done.*

In our daily lives, we tend to use the term *social problem* to categorize conditions that we believe are troublesome, prevalent, can be changed, and should be changed. When I write *social problem* from now on this is what I mean.

With this basic definition, we can go on to the next question: What should we *study* about social problems? This question does not have a simple answer because social problems are about *objective* conditions and people (things and people that exist in the physical world) *and* they are about *subjective* definitions (how we understand the world and the people in it). Because it is not immediately apparent why the objective and subjective aspects of social problems can be separated, I will discuss each of them.

I begin with the commonsense framework of a type of person I will call a *practical actor,* a term I will use throughout this book to refer to a type of person like you or me in our daily lives. As practical actors, we go to school or work, we take care of our children (if we have them), and pay our bills (the best we can). Unlike scientists and other academics who study the world, we live in the world. While we might not have the education or intellect of a nuclear physicist we are logical and try to make sense of our world. Practical actors most often are concerned with social problems as objective conditions.

SOCIAL PROBLEMS AS OBJECTIVE CONDITIONS

When members of the American public use the term *social problems,* we most frequently are interested in these as objective characteristics of the social environment. "Objective" means real, tangible, measurable. Within this *objectivist* perspective, social problems are about things we can see; they are about measurable and widespread conditions in the environment and they are about the living, breathing people who are hurt by these conditions (people we evaluate as victims) or who create these conditions (social structures, social forces, or people we evaluate as villains). Within this perspective, poverty is a condition where people do not have enough money to live a decent life, while poor people are people living in this condition; drunk driving is a condition where people with a high blood alcohol count drive, and drunk drivers are the people who do this. A series of practical questions emerge when we think about social problems as real conditions and real people: Who or what causes the condition? Who is harmed by it? What harm do they suffer? What can be done to stop this harm?

When experts study social problems in this way, they rely on *objective indicators*. These indicators include statistics about the condition (such as the number of school children who cannot read, the number of crimes committed, unemployment rates) and the people in it (measures such as the age, ethnicity, or gender of people causing social problems or harmed by social problems). At times, objective characteristics of people appear as complex psychological profiles: people who commit crimes are given various psychological tests and a profile of "criminals" is constructed; tests are given to heterosexuals to measure their "homophobia;" women victims of "wife abuse" are given tests and, from this, psychological profiles of "battered women" are constructed, and so on.

Such objective indicators are the basis of discussions in most social problems textbooks. Such texts most often are arranged in a series of chapters with titles such as problems in the economy, problems in government, problems of inequality (poverty, ethnicity, age, gender), and problems of deviance (sexual behavior, drug use, crime). Each chapter in these texts tends to contain a more or less standardized treatment of the problem at hand. Readers see objective indicators describing the extent of the problem (how widespread it is), what types of people are victims or villains, and the consequences of the problem for the victims. Various theories are used to explain the causes of the problem and this leads to statements about what can be done to resolve it.

While it makes sense to examine social problems as objective conditions involving flesh and blood people, we cannot stop there because it is *not* enough. Social problems are about things and people we *worry* about, and when we talk about "worry" we go beyond objectivity into *subjective definitions*. But you might ask, so what? Don't Americans worry about things we should worry about? To answer this question we must leave the concerns of the commonsense practical actor in order to examine the confusions in this thing called social problems.

OBJECTIVE CHARACTERISTICS AND SUBJECTIVE WORRY

We cannot simply assume that we worry about things we should worry about, because there is *no necessary relationship* between any objective indicators (statistics, results of tests) of social problem conditions and what Americans worry about, what politicians focus on, or what television, newspapers, or magazines tell us about.[5] This means there is no necessary relationship between the measurable characteristics of any given condition or the people in it and a definition of that condition as troublesome. For example, there can be *objective conditions without subjective worry.* Earthquake experts, for example, often talk about the potential damage of earthquakes throughout the United States. Yet the condition of earthquakes typically receives notice by the public or social policymakers only for a brief time after there has been an earthquake, people continue to live in areas prone to earthquakes, and they often fail to even buy earthquake insurance. In this case, there are objective indicators that a condition exists, but there is little public worry. People's *ideas* about risk matter more than the actual risk measured by objective indicators.[6]

Conditions creating harm can exist without public worry. Americans also can start to worry about a condition when objective indicators seem to show that the *condition is not new.* For example, the historical record (an objective indicator) shows that what we now call child abuse always has been part of human existence. Indeed, the historical record can be used to argue that what we now call child abuse was much more common in the past than in the present. Yet the term *child abuse* did not appear in the United States until the 1960s. In this case, the behaviors now called child abuse are *not* new, the worry *is* new. Or, how long did slavery exist before it was called a social problem? In these examples, objective indicators about the troublesome nature of conditions were available long before there was any worry about them.

Likewise, Americans can begin to worry about something when objective indicators seem to show that the condition is actually *getting better.* For example, there was much public and political concern about poverty in the 1960s, but this was a time when objective indicators were showing rates of poverty were declining. Concern about poverty began as the objective condition of poverty was getting better. Or, we can begin to worry about something where there is *no objective indicator* pointing to the presence of a prevalent condition. For example, fear about the safety of children trick-or-treating on Halloween was based on very few incidents. Yet these few incidents led to a generalized fear that many children all over the United States were being victimized by Halloween sadism. In the same way, the condition of "crack cocaine" received incredible attention in the United States beginning in 1986. Yet at that time there were no objective indicators that the use of crack cocaine was widespread, nor did objective indicators support the image that this drug was "instantly addicting."[7]

In brief, it is not possible to argue that Americans worry about what we should worry about. It is not enough to examine social problems as objective conditions because there is no necessary relationship between what we worry about and what exists in the objective environment.

Experts, Objective Indicators, and the Postmodern World

There are responses to my observation that there is no necessary relationship between things we worry about and objective indicators of problems. Proponents of objectivist approaches argue that *experts* know when a social problem exists. According to this line of reasoning, when indicators show there *is* a widespread and troublesome condition although the public is not concerned, the condition is a *latent social problem.*[8] Latent means it is there, even if the public does not know it or does not worry about it. This line of reasoning continues: when the public evaluates a condition as a social problem but the objective indicators do not support this definition, the problem is *spurious.* Spurious means there is worry about nothing. In this line of reasoning, we have a social problem (even if it is unrecognized) when objective indicators show we do, we do not have a social problem when objective indicators say one does not exist. Within this view, practical actors can be ignorant or misguided and it is the experts who are given the privilege of defining what is—and what is not—a social problem.

Should we simply rely on experts to tell us what we should worry about? I think that would be unwise. Experts might know a great deal about what exists in the world but social problems are about *moral* evaluations because to name any condition as a social problem is to evaluate the condition as *wrong.*[9] Science can tell us what "is," but it cannot tell us what "should be." This is because of the *political, social,* and *moral fragmentation* in our world.

I want to call your attention to a characteristic of my presentation so far. Repeatedly, I have defined social problems in terms such as things Americans worry about, or what we consider troublesome. But what do I mean when I say "Americans?" Who is this "we" I write about? To evaluate a condition as a social problem is to take a moral stand (it is wrong, it needs fixing), but "we" are not a nation of people who agree with one another. Who has the power to define one or another condition as wrong? Wrong for whom? Wrong for what reason? These are complex matters.

Academics often use the term *postmodern* to describe the characteristics of the United States (indeed, the world) as we begin a new century. *Postmodern* is an important term in the study of social problems because it encourages us to be aware that we live in a time of political, social, and moral uncertainties. So, for example, the postmodern world is characterized by *political fragmentation.* Many Americans now routinely vote for a president from one party and senators and representatives from another; there is far less loyalty to political parties than in the past. So, too, terms such as liberal or conservative, political Left, or political Right can be relatively meaningless. It is primarily only politicians and other political experts who have full-blown political belief systems (called *ideologies*). As practical actors, most of us think about issues one at a time and it is not all that uncommon for us to be liberal on some issues and conservative on others.[10] Consider, for example, how some feminists agree with religious fundamentalists that "pornography" is a social problem that must be eliminated. Certainly these folks do not agree on much else.

Postmodern also means *social fragmentation*. We no longer are a nation of farmers more or less sharing similar experiences in life. We increasingly are *heterogeneous* (different) in our experiences. What experiences in life likely are shared by a young black man and an elderly white woman? What experiences likely are shared by people living in a New York City penthouse and those barely making a living on a farm in West Virginia? What about people who are very religious (but what *type* of religion, you might ask, because there are many) and those who are not religious at all? What about people who trace their ancestry to the earliest immigrants to the United States in the 1600s and those newly arrived here (but from what country, you might ask, because not all immigrants are the same). Do we all experience the world in the same ways? Of course not.

The postmodern characteristic of social fragmentation leads to *moral fragmentation:* Americans do not agree on what is moral or immoral. Yet moral judgments are *necessary* to name something as a social problem. Objective indicators can tell us what is, they cannot tell us what is right or wrong.

Objective Characteristics and Knowledge

When social problems are studied as objective conditions, we rely on knowledge of these conditions to chart our actions toward them. But how do we know what we know? Our world keeps getting larger, more complex, and more confusing. Because each one of us can directly experience very little (about the world in general, about social problem conditions and the people in them in particular), we must rely on others to tell us. Yet how can we trust these others? We might be very careful and trust only the most official sources of information, yet a bold headline in my newspaper last week announced "Pentagon May Release False News." The article was about a planned "disinformation campaign" to support the war effort. Obviously, there was much public uproar and several days later a new headline appeared, "Top Officials Back Off From Public Disinformation Plan." Which headline do we trust?

While we often rely on the mass media for the information we use in our daily lives, media also tend to blur differences between fact and fiction, truth and fantasy. When you watch an "infomercial" are you receiving information (factual) or a commercial (biased)? Is a "docudrama" a documentary (implying true) or a drama (implying fiction)? This blurring of fact and fiction is most confusing in so-called reality television, which blends actual (real) videotapes of a crime with reenactments (fiction). Indeed, examinations of programs such as *America's Most Wanted* and *Unsolved Mysteries* demonstrate how the apparent "reality" of these programs is achieved by producers who explicitly set out to make programs that will seem real to viewers. Such producers are successful—viewers sometimes call police departments to report seeing the *actors* who *portrayed criminals* on these programs.[11]

Of course, proponents of objectivist approaches to social problems argue that we cannot know the truth from the mass media but that truth *is* knowable through science. But this, too, might be challenged. First, we live in a time when experts of all types are routinely accused of being not so objective. Practical actors know that all too many experts can be paid to tell whatever story they are paid to tell. Second, scientific evidence needs to be interpreted and there can be different interpretations by equally thoughtful and highly skilled scientists. For example, one group of experts now says it is a social problem that *not enough* "women over 40 years old" receive yearly mammograms. They argue more women should receive such mammograms because this would prevent life-threatening breast cancer. Yet another group of experts believes that *too many* "women over 40 years old" receive yearly mammograms. According to them, mammograms are expensive, subject women to radiation, and are not medically necessary because there is no evidence that the chances of survival from cancer are better when women have yearly mammograms. Equally thoughtful and skilled scientists can offer very different interpretations of the meaning of scientific evidence. Whom do we believe?

Third, experts often change their minds and this can greatly change our beliefs about the world. For example, in 1993 the Centers for Disease Control changed its definition of AIDS to include more than it previously had included. When the number of AIDS cases immediately skyrocketed, many members of the public believed the condition was getting worse at an astounding rate. It was not—the numbers of cases increased because the definition of what was included expanded. Or, in June 1998, the National Heart, Lung, and Blood Institute lowered by five pounds the official standard for being "overweight." Millions of people who were not overweight suddenly were officially overweight because of this change. The problem instantly seemed far worse. On the other hand, the problem of "educational failure" was instantly not so much of a problem when professionals decided to recalculate SAT (Scholastic Aptitude Test) scores. By adding over one hundred points to each student's test, tens of thousands of formerly "low-achieving" students miraculously were not so low-achieving. Whom do we believe when experts keep changing their minds?

Clearly and most certainly, I am *not* trying to tell you that we cannot or should not study social problems as objective conditions in the social environment. I am also *not* arguing that we should ignore experts. What I *am* arguing is that if we confine ourselves to objectivist approaches we will miss other important issues; if we simply assume science can tell us what to think about the world we are giving too much power to one group of people who can tell us what "is" but not what "should be." If we want to understand social problems we also must examine how problems are subjectively defined and that is the topic for this book. I will begin with a brief introduction to a social construction perspective that also is called the problem definition perspective in public policy.

THE CONSTRUCTION OF SOCIAL LIFE
AND SOCIAL PROBLEMS

Social construction perspectives on social problems are applications of more general social construction theoretical perspectives. I have included an Appendix at the end of this book that more fully develops the theory and current issues in this perspective. Here, I will lay out in simple form the most basic points in this framework so that we can get on to the major topic of what kinds of questions it leads us to ask about social problems.

The Physical World and the World of Meaning

Objectivist approaches to social problems lead us to focus on the real, tangible physical world inhabited by humans. We do live in this physical world. In my immediate environment at this moment I see a desk, a computer, a clock, some bills to be paid, two cats, and so on. These are very real. But social construction perspectives are less concerned with the physical world than with how we *understand* this world. If I were a member of another culture, I might look at my desk and understand it as firewood for cooking dinner, I might look at my cats and see what to cook for that dinner, I might look at my computer and see the workings of Satan. For the clock on my wall to be meaningful, I must have a concept of time and this concept must be one where minutes (rather than merely night and day) are important, and so on. Social construction perspectives do not concern themselves with the objective world. Think of this as an academic division of labor: Others can concern themselves with the objective world. Constructionists focus on the *meaning* humans create in our world.

Social construction perspectives are called *subjectivist* approaches because they are concerned with social problems as *subjective definitions.* So, for example, we might be able to measure the number of calories people eat and medical science might be able to tell us whether or not this is enough for good health. We then could have an objective condition called "people not eating enough calories for good health." But this is not enough to make this objective condition into a social problem. For there to be a social problem we first need to make sense of this condition. What is it? Is it unavoidable hunger? Religious fasting? Anorexia? A trendy eating fad? Then, we must attached a particular meaning (troublesome) to this condition, and to do this we need to decide why it is troublesome. Or, consider the behavior of "spanking." While many Americans evaluate spanking as an acceptable form of punishment, others believe that spanking is a form of "child abuse," so parents who do this are "child abusers." The same behavior—spanking—yet it now exists for some people as a social problem because they define it in that way.[12] Any objective condition is not a social problem until it is named and given meaning. Likewise, any particular person is not a victim or a villain until someone classifies the person in that way.

This is why it is possible to argue that a *social problem does not exist until it is defined as such.* Conditions might exist, people might be hurt by them, but conditions are not social problems until humans categorize them as troublesome and in need of repair.

Meanings and Categorizations

A characteristic of all humans is that we *categorize.* The names we attach to objects in our world are labels for *types* of things or *types* of people. So, although each of my two cats is unique, both are members of the category of "cats" (as are lions and tigers). In daily life we see similarities among diversity. We can look at people living in very different places in very different ways yet still categorize them as living in poverty. Using what we call common sense, we categorize people in categories such as gender (women, men), race/ethnicity (such as Asian, African, Anglo, Hispanic), age (such as baby, child, teen), economic class (poor, middle class, rich), and so on. A primary characteristic of the way we understand our world is that we categorize.

In daily life our commonsense categories serve us well. Indeed, they serve us so well that once we learn many of them in childhood (children must be taught what food is, they learn to distinguish women from men, and so on), we do not even think about them. Only when we travel to a far different culture do we see that our particular categories and their particular contents are matters of *human definition* that do not flow necessarily from physical objects. This means that the categories and their contents are *socially constructed*, which raises all sorts of questions: What objects go in what categories? What are the meanings of the categories themselves?

The term "social problems" is a *name* for a *category* that contains those conditions Americans believe are widespread, wrong, changeable, and in need of change. So, just as critics often ask: What is art? We can ask: What is a social problem? More specifically, we can ask: What is "crime"? or What is "environmental ruin"? or What is "racism"? We can ask: What are "criminals," or "racists," or "sexually abused children"? The meanings of each of these goes far beyond the name on the container. For example, one social problems textbook defines racism as "a belief in the superiority of one racial group over another that leads to prejudice and discrimination."[13] To that, I say, fine, but then I want to ask: What is a "racial group"? What is "prejudice"? What is "discrimination"? How do we know these things when we see them? What kinds of behaviors and people are included and which are not? Social construction perspectives encourage us to look more closely at the categories we use to evaluate and make sense of experiences, conditions, and people.

Categorizations and Reactions

Social construction perspectives examine how we categorize the objects and people in our world. How do we decide that a particular person is an "alcoholic" or a "social drinker"? How many Americans must be "poor," and how "poor" must they be before we worry about "poverty"? Is the behavior of "spanking" a form of acceptable punishment or is it a form of unacceptable child abuse? At what point do individuals move from ideal weight to overweight to obese?

This is important because at the heart of constructionist perspectives is the belief that our categorizations are important because they *influence our behaviors*. So, for example, I have named my two cats Mel and Ella, and they reign as king and queen of my household. I can predict with utmost certainty that I will *not* eat them for dinner tonight. While in the physical world, cats (as well as dogs and grubs) are (objectively speaking) nutritious human foods, the meaning I have attached to the physical category of "cats" makes it impossible for me in my normal daily life to think of them as food. Humans react toward objects in terms of the meaning we give these objects.

What this means for the study of social problems is that it is important to know *how* we give meaning to objects in our environment because those meanings will encourage us to react toward those objects in particular ways. Think about the two sides in the abortion debate. Objectively speaking, abortion is a medical procedure, it does not have any necessary meaning. Yet the social problem of abortion certainly is filled with meaning. But what kind of meaning? One side of the debate about this medical procedure has chosen the label "pro-life," which encourages us to think of this medical procedure in terms of embryos. The other side has chosen the name "pro-choice," which encourages us to think of this *same* procedure in terms of women. The same condition can be given different names, and these different names encourage us to have different reactions. Names matter because they often carry with them associations. "Terrorism," for example, goes far beyond being a label for specific acts. It has a much larger meaning: safety, security, the future.

So, too, it can matter a great deal how individual people are categorized. To be categorized as "mentally ill" is far different than to be categorized as "eccentric." When we hear a word categorizing a person, the word can carry with it a set of associations. Consider the category "moron." Formally, this is a scientific term for a person with a specific score on a intelligence test. Yet the meaning of moron in daily life certainly is not scientific. Moron is used as an all-purpose descriptor to criticize behaviors evaluated as less than "intelligent," even when people doing those behaviors score very high on tests of intelligence.[14] In brief, when we categorize conditions or people as particular types of conditions or people our categorizations can bring with them varying kinds of associations, social evaluations, and reactions.

As a quick side note, you might have noticed my tendency to place quotation marks around some terms. When I put quotation marks around a word such as "pro-choice," I want to call your attention to the *word* itself. I want you to stop for a short moment and ask yourself, what *is* this? In daily life, we rarely ask one another to specifically define the words we are using. We use words like "poverty" or "obesity" without thinking. Constructionist perspectives encourage us to take words seriously because even the most simple words (*particularly* the most simple words) are categories for *entire systems of meaning*.

Categorizations and Typifications

Humans categorize conditions and people and this is important because it encourages us to react to these conditions and people in predictable ways. But there are two characteristics of the social world that make this a very complicated process.

First, each category is held together by an organizing device (what I will call a *frame*). To begin simply, the category of food contains "things to eat," so it contains liver, chocolate cake, pigs feet, and caviar. These are very different things sharing only the commonality that they can be categorized as "things to eat." This becomes more complicated when we talk about our categorizations of people: We categorize half the world's population as "women," and the other half as "men." While in daily life we most often do this (and uncountable other categorizations) without thinking, if you do think about it for just a moment, it is amazing. What are we looking at in order to see similarities? And, just as important, what are we ignoring in order to see similarities?

For example, how do we categorize the tens of thousands of children who cannot read at the level expected of them? Are such children stupid? Lazy? Learning disabled? Are their families dysfunctional? Are their teachers incompetent? Do their schools have the necessary resources to teach them? If we looked closely at many such students we probably would categorize some in one way, others in another way, still others in ways we did not expect. How, then, do we categorize and see similarities when real conditions and the real people in them are so multidimensional? This is the first complexity in understanding our world in terms of categories. Categories require us to see *similarities* among things, conditions, or people that are—objectively speaking—incredibly diverse.

The second complexity of understanding our world in terms of categories comes from the postmodern condition: Our world is far too big and complex for us to experience it all. Most of us do not personally experience most social problem conditions. And even if we do have such personal experience, this would be only ours and it might be far different from that of others. So, my sister and her family were homeless after Hurricane Hugo destroyed their home. Yet cushioned by home insurance, continuing income from employment, and living temporarily with my parents, their "homelessness" certainly was different than that experienced by people living on the streets because they are totally without resources.

Humans categorize and we often do this although we do not have personal experience. Think about what you know about the world and think about how little of what you know comes from what you have directly experienced. This leads me to the point that we categorize by *typification*.[15] Think of a typification as an image in our heads of typical kinds of things, be these cats, prostitutes, or ecological ruin. Because we cannot know all cats, prostitutes, or instances of environmental ruin, the best we can do is have an image of the *typical*.

My students often stop me at this point and complain that what I am calling an image or typification is really nothing other than a *stereotype*. In one way, they are correct: the concepts of image, typification, and stereotype have very similar formal meanings. All are about preexisting images of types of things or types of people. And none include much room for emphasizing the many ways that each thing or person is different from all others. Yet the problem with the term *stereotype* is that it has drifted into popular culture as a word used to condemn. We say, "You're stereotyping," when we believe others are denying complexity. We say, "That's just a stereotype" when we believe the typification does not match objective reality. But from social construction perspectives the issue is far more complex because we begin with the understanding that *we have no choice* but to use typifications in our daily lives. For example, if I asked you to describe what comes to your mind when I say "welfare mother," my hunch is that you would respond, even if you said something like, "Well, most people would say . . . but I don't agree." Yet if you could respond *at all* to this question, you would do so based on typifications—it is not possible to personally know the several million women in this particular category of "welfare mother."

My point is that our world is altogether too big and complex for us to refuse to use typifications. We can *not* know the individuality of each and every thing, condition, and person in the world. So, while the term *stereotype* is associated with only negative consequences, the terms *typification* and *image* should be understood as *social resources* to help us get through our days. While we will see as we go along that using typifications can have very negative consequences, typifications also have very positive consequences. After all, the only feeling we can have about events we do not personally experience and about people we do not personally know is through our typifications. Without these pictures in our head we would not be able to understand other than our own extremely limited personal experience. Without these images we would not know how to react to the countless others in the world of strangers we encounter daily. I can feel compassion for people I do not know, I can talk to my students about prisons and jails even though none of us have ever lived in one. Without typifications, our worlds would be very small because we could only think and feel about things we actually had experienced.

The Human Creation of Meaning

Social construction perspectives begin with the assumption that there is nothing in the world whose meaning resides in the object itself. A cat is an animal but it can be a pet—or food, the flag of the United States is a piece of cloth with colors and shapes arranged in particular ways but it can be prayed to or spat upon. "Suicide bombers" are people who kill themselves in the course of killing others but they can be understood as pathological or as heroic soldiers. Meanings do not come attached to people, conditions, or experiences. Humans give the world meaning.

This has been a very brief tour through some of the major points of social construction perspectives that are important in studying the construction of social problems. The major point is that this framework is concerned first, and foremost with the *subjective meanings* of social problems. At times, I will completely ignore questions about objective conditions: I will not talk about whether the condition exists in the real world. At other times, I might bring objective characteristics into a shadowy background. But even here, my concern will be with how objective indicators are used to create particular typifications of social problem conditions and the people in them. In brief, I will leave it to others to tell you about what social problems objectively exist in the world, about what causes them, about what should be done to stop the harm. My emphasis will be on examining *how* humans create the meaning of social problems; on *what* we think about the world, on *why* we think that way, on *what happens* because we think the ways we do.

SOCIAL CONSTRUCTION QUESTIONS
ABOUT SOCIAL PROBLEMS

There are a great many things that Americans *could* categorize as social problems, many things we *could* worry about. But at any one time only a small number reach the consciousness of any segment of the public; at any one time only an incredibly small number of harmful conditions become "celebrity social problems," a topic of attention for national media or politicians. Here are our primary questions:

- How is it and why is it that some conditions—and not others—are accorded the status of social problems?
- How is it that many members of the public more or less share particular typifications of social problem conditions and their victims?
- What are the consequences of the typical ways that social problems gain public support? How do subjective definitions of social problems change the objective characteristics and the cultural climates of our world?
- How do subjective definitions of social problems change the ways we make sense of our selves and those around us?
- How do these definitions influence the experiences of people who need help or rehabilitation because of social problems?
- What do constructionist perspectives on social problems tell us about the larger characteristics of our world?

I will use two concepts throughout this book because they will be useful in examining constructionists' questions about social problems. The first concept is *social problems work*.[16] This is the human activity of categorizing some—and only some—conditions and people as social problems. We will look at what people *do* to persuade others that a troublesome condition is at hand and that something must be done about it, and we will look at how people categorize particular experiences and people as instances of social problem conditions, victims, or villains. Social problems work is the human activity needed to construct social problems and to do something about social problems. Practical actors also do social problems work when we evaluate and categorize *unique* experiences, conditions, and people as instances of *types* of experiences, conditions, and people. The term *work* is good because it draws our attention to the constructionist belief that meaning is created by people.

The second concept for examining these questions is the *social problems game*. The *goal* of the social problems game is to persuade people to worry about a condition and to do something to resolve it, it is to persuade people to use particular categorizations when they are practical actors in daily life trying to make sense of their own experiences and the experiences of others around them. The social problems game is a set of *activities* (social problems work) and *players* who compete, and there are *competitions* and *strategies* for winning. The metaphor of social problems game is good because it draws our attention to power and politics. But I need to caution you to not push the game metaphor too far for two reasons. First, we often think of games as having few consequences. But the social problems game has very serious consequences. The *prize* for winning the social problems game is the power to lead social change, to change the objective world in which we live, to change the ways we make sense of ourselves and others. The social problems game is not a game played just for "fun."

Second, while a game metaphor might encourage us to think there will be one winner and the rest of the players will lose, the social problems game most often has much more complicated outcomes. At times, some players can win one round but then lose the next, a win can be partial and so can a loss, a win by some players can encourage others to become players in the next round, which will increase competition. Yet while winning and losing are far more complicated than in many games, it remains that even partial wins or losses in the social problems game can shape our world so these are important. In brief, when I write about the social problems game I want to encourage you to think about competitions, power, and politics. I do *not* want you to dismiss this as only a game, or to believe that it is a game that is "won" or "lost." It is a deadly serious game of creating and maintaining both social limitations and social possibilities, it is a game that is ongoing in social life.

After defining the key concepts of claims and claims-making, Chapter 2 focuses on the players in the social problems game. The first type of players are members of *audiences*. These are the people who hear or see social problems claims and who do the social problems work of evaluating the believability and importance of these claims. The second type of player is called *claims-makers,* the people who say and do things to persuade audiences that a social problem is at hand. While each of us in our daily lives can be social problems claims-makers, I will focus on the three most important types: social movement activists, scientists, and mass media.

Chapters 3, 4, and 5 examine the social problems work of persuading audience members that a social problem exists and that something must be done to eliminate it. In real life, this requires claims-makers to construct a *package of claims* including typifications of conditions, victims, villains, and solutions. In real life, persuading audience members to take a condition seriously can be achieved by appealing to audience members' understandings of the ways the world should work and / or by appealing to audience members' emotions. For presentation purposes, though, I have separated these claims-making tasks and strategies. Chapter 3 focuses on how claims-makers can construct social problem conditions in ways compatible with cultural themes, which are broadly circulating ideas about the ways the world should work. Chapter 4 turns to how claims-makers can construct images of victims and villains in ways compatible with cultural feeling rules that are broadly circulating ideas about what types of people deserve the emotion of sympathy or condemnation and their behavioral expressions of help or punishment. Chapter 5 examines how claims-makers can construct solutions involving changes in social policy and / or changes in the cultural climate.

Chapters 6 and 7 look at the outcomes of successful claims-making. When claims-makers are successful, they change the objective characteristics of the world around us and they change our understandings of that world. Chapter 6 explores how claims change our experiences in everyday life, including how we make sense of our selves and others. Chapter 7 turns to the "troubled persons industry," the organizations, programs, and groups attempting to help, rehabilitate, or punish victims and potential victims, villains, or potential villains in social problems.

Because my primary goal is to encourage you to think about social problems, Chapter 8 will summarize differences between objectivist and constructionist perspectives and then discuss what we can learn about our world, our lives, and ourselves by studying the construction of social problems.

AN INVITATION TO SOCIAL CONSTRUCTION
PERSPECTIVES ON SOCIAL PROBLEMS

From the perspectives of practical actors concerned with doing something about social problems, social construction perspectives might seem to focus on trivial questions. In daily life the most immediate issue is do-

ing something about the very real human suffering caused by social problems. Given this, it does not seem important to ask questions about how
we know what we know.

To this comment I would reply: Yes, there are many conditions that create human suffering and we need to know about these conditions. We need
to know about the social structures, social forces, and people who do this
harm. We need to know about the people who experience this harm. I also
would reply that I believe we can look at the construction of social problems while not denying or discounting social problems as objective conditions. So, I am *not* asking you to forget that poverty, crime, AIDS, racism,
and so on are very real in their consequences, I am *not* arguing that if we
stopped thinking about social problems they would go away. Yet I also *do*
believe that questions raised by constructionist perspectives are anything
but trivial and that to ignore these questions leads to a less than complete
understanding of social problems, which, in turn, hinders our abilities to
resolve them. Here I invite you to consider some of these questions:

- How do people create the meaning of our world that we then take for
  granted?
- Why is it that some conditions—and not others—become the focus
  of public attention?
- What kinds of claims likely will be successful in leading to social
  change?
- What are the relationships between successful social problems claims
  and our practical efforts to do something about troublesome conditions and the people in them?
- How is the world changed by how we think about it?
- How can what we think about the world change the way we make
  sense of our own lives and the lives of people around us?

I would like to encourage you to think about what you know about the
world and about how you know it. This is critically important as we go
through our daily lives as practical actors. We each often are members of
audiences for social problems claims. It would be best if we know how the
social problems game is played because, in the final analysis, we are the
judges and juries for these claims and what is done about social problems
depends on how we evaluate claims.

NOTES

1. Conrad and Schneider (1980) examine the changing constructions of mental
illness. Darsey (1991) explores how claims about homosexuality in the United

States changed in response to AIDS. Hufker and Cavender (1990) examine how immigration from Cuba in 1980 was constructed by the media in ways reflecting the historical and ideological contexts of Cuba-U.S. relations. Jenkins (1999) explores the political context that framed "antiabortion violence" as terrorism. Examples of international variations in social problems include several examinations centering on Japan such as antismoking campaigns (Ayukawa, 2001, excerpted in *Social Problems: Constructionist Readings*), "school refusal" (Yamazaki, 1994), the role of government in resolving the problem of child pornography (Suzuki, 2001), and juvenile delinquency (Ayukawa, 1995). Others have explored education in Nicaragua and Iran (Najafizadeh and Mennerick, 1989) and abortion in Sweden (Linders, 1998). Also, see Nichols (1995) for his discussion of the effects of international context on public and political understandings of social problems.

2.   Furedi (2001, excerpted in *Social Problems: Constructionist Readings*) explores why "bullying" is accorded the status of a social problem in Great Britain but not in the United States.

3.   See Stafford and Warr (1985) for an empirical examination of how people in the general population define "social problem."

4.   The distinction between "personal trouble" and "social issue" was made by Mills: "Troubles occur within the character of the individual and within the range of his immediate relations with others. . . . Issues have to do with matters that transcend these local environments of the individual and the range of his inner life" (1959:8).

5.   Downs (1972:39) argues that objective conditions typically are *worse* during a "pre-problem" stage than they are by the time general publics become concerned. Linberry (1981) demonstrated the discrepancy over time between the public's perception of poverty as a problem and official government statistics measuring poverty. Funkhouser (1973) examined relationships among public opinion (measured by Gallop polls), media attention (measured by the number of stories in three national news magazines), and objective indicators (measured by government statistics) on a wide range of issues in the 1960s. He concludes that while the extent of media coverage of an issue was clearly related to whether or not that issue was mentioned in Gallop polls, the extent of media coverage did *not* have a clear relationship to objective indicators. Warr (1995:298–99) examines trend data and concludes that public fear of crime seems to be independent of actual changes in crime rates.

6.   Stallings (1995, excerpted in *Social Problems: Constructionist Readings*) compares what experts say about the gravity of the earthquake threat with a lack of public concern about this threat.

7.   For an examination of relationships between objective indicators and a range of problems featuring child victims, see Best (1990). Reinarman and Levine (1995, excerpted in *Social Problems: Constructionist Readings*) examine United States government statistics and argue that when the drug scare about crack cocaine started in 1986 there were no objective indicators supporting the incredible attention and concern about this condition. Glassner (1999) examines a range of such worries (such as road rage, battered husbands, baby-killing mothers, suicidal teens) that are not supported by evidence that they are widespread.

8.   Merton made this distinction between manifest and latent social problems:

"Apart from manifest social problems—those objective social conditions identified by problem-definers as at odds with social values—are latent social problems, conditions that also are at odds with values current in society, but are not generally recognized as being so" (1971:806).

9. Waller wrote: "Various attempts to treat social problems in a scientific manner have proved useless because they have dealt only with the objective side of social problems and have failed to include the attitude which constituted them problems. The attitude, the value judgment, is the subjective side of the social problem and its existence renders meaningless any purely objective account of social problems" (1936:922).

10. The political belief systems of politicians tend to be much more elaborate and internally consistent than those of practical actors (Converse, 1964). Iyengar (1987) likewise argues that few citizens make sense of the world through ideological principles or clearly defined political preferences. Bellah and his colleagues (1985: especially Chapter 8) link a lack of political knowledge or involvement with increasing individualism.

11. Cavender (1998, excerpted in *Social Problems: Constructionist Readings*) examines the reality-producing techniques in *America's Most Wanted* and *Unsolved Mysteries*. Barak (1994) also examines this confusion in television portrayals of crime.

12. Davis (1994, excerpted in *Social Problems: Constructionist Readings*) explores how spanking is evaluated as a social problem by some people but is a taken-for-granted method of child discipline for others.

13. Coleman and Cressey (1996:567).

14. Spector and Kitsuse ([1977] 1987) discuss the social process leading to scientists naming varying levels of intelligence and how these originally scientific labels drifted into daily life in ways distinctly not intended by scientists constructing these categories.

15. Best (1995) more fully elaborates this term of typification. Yet because I often will explicitly argue, and always implicitly assume, that such images are socially created and more or less socially shared, Durkheim's (1961: especially 479–87) concept of *collective representation* could be substituted for typification. This is more fully elaborated in the Appendix.

16. The concept of social problems work was first proposed by Miller and Holstein as a term for "any and all activity implicated in the recognition, identification, interpretation, and definition of conditions that are called 'social problems.' Social problems work can be any human activity contributing to the practical 'creation' or understanding of an instance of a social problem" (1989:5). I will elaborate on this in the Appendix.

2

Claims-Makers and Audiences

I'm reading my newspaper, the *St. Petersburg Times.* There's a front page bold headline, "Fight Against Obesity Widens." I read how United States Surgeon General Dr. David Thatcher is urging sweeping changes to encourage Americans to exercise more and eat less. He quotes from a new scientific study showing that well over half of American adults are overweight or obese and this excess weight causes 300,000 deaths a year. According to him, this problem threatens to erase the health gains that have come from reducing Americans' blood pressure, cholesterol, and smoking. A director of a weight loss program is quoted: "We need to make this into a social issue, there is an obesity epidemic." This is front page news. On the fifth page of the paper there's an advertisement for pills leading to weight loss without diet or exercise. I glance at the television and a commercial tells me that the only thing better for women than a "little black dress" is a "littler black dress." This is followed by a commercial for McDonald's double bacon-cheeseburger, which can be supersized for mere pennies. I look at my exercise bike but decide to check what's in my refrigerator instead.

Social construction perspectives on social problems begin with the belief that people create meaning because meaning is not inherent in objects. In this chapter we start our tour through this world of constructing meaning by focusing on the people who make this meaning (*claims-makers*) and the people who evaluate the believability and importance of what claims-makers say (*audiences*). Before starting on that, I want to give you some basic definitions and examples of the key constructionist terms *claims* and *claims-making*. Making claims is the social problems work of claims-makers, evaluating the believability and importance of claims is the social problems work of audience members.

CLAIMS AND CLAIMS-MAKING

Constructing a social problem requires that audience members be persuaded that a condition exists, that it is troublesome and widespread, that it can be changed, and that it should be changed. As used in social construction perspectives, a *claim* is any verbal, visual, or behavioral statement that seeks to persuade audience members to define a condition as a social problem.

Let's start with verbal claims (which also can be called *rhetoric*).[1]

When I stand in front of my Social Problems class and say to my students, "Almost half of all households with a single mother have incomes lower than the poverty level," I am doing the social problems work of claims-making. If you write a letter to the editor of your local newspaper about the problems in your local school district, you're doing social problems work and the contents of your letter are claims. Lawyers arguing their cases in court are making claims; so, too, are politicians who try to persuade us that their plans and policies will solve social problems. You can understand the nightly news as a series of verbal claims, verbal claims about all sorts of social problems are the regular fare of television talk shows (Jenny Jones), radio call-in shows (Rush Limbaugh), and music (particularly rap music). Verbal claims are on flyers taped to the walls of staircases leading to college classrooms, they are in mailings to voters from elected officials, they are in textbooks and newspapers. These all are verbal claims constructing meanings through *words.*

Claims also are made through *visual images.* Indeed, a picture can be worth a thousand verbal claims. For example, a picture of a badly beaten child can be a powerful persuasion that child abuse cannot be tolerated, a picture of a dead or oil-drenched bird is an effective claim about environmental ruin. Because typifications of social problems are "pictures in our head," claims using visual images can be very powerful because they put these pictures directly into our head.

There also are *behavioral* claims where the social problems work involves *doing* something rather than saying something or creating a visual picture of something. These claims sometimes typify a social problem condition (war protesters carrying coffins in a protest march to dramatize that war leads to death), but often such behavioral claims seek rather to disrupt social life in order to persuade audience members to *listen* to verbal claims, to *see* visual claims.

There are clear examples of behavioral claims from the civil rights movement of the 1950s and 1960s. During this era, African-Americans sat in the front of buses and in segregated cafeterias where they were not allowed. Behavioral claims for other social problems include the activities of people who chain themselves to trees in order to make claims about the importance of preserving forests; behavioral claims are hunger strikes, labor strikes, protest marches, and the activities of people in the antifur movement who dump red paint or ketchup on mink coats worn by wealthy women. Behavioral claims include the dramatic and irreverent behaviors of people in ACT-UP (AIDS Coalition to Unleash Power) who stage "die-ins" and carnival-like performances to dramatize how Americans ignore the devastation of AIDS.[2]

Regardless of whether claims are verbal, visual, or behavioral, they are the social problems work of claims-makers who, if they are successful, persuade audience members to both think and feel in particular ways. Claims encouraging audience members to think in particular ways focus on constructing the logical (reasonable, rational) reasons why audience members should define a particular condition as troublesome. These claims might be in the form of statistics or scientific studies showing the magnitude of the condition or the kinds and quantities of harm the condition creates. This is the topic of the next chapter.

Yet, in addition to—or even instead of—appealing to logic, claims-makers can construct claims encouraging audience members to *feel* sympathy for social problem victims and/or to *feel* hatred for social problem villains. This is the topic of Chapter 4.

With the basic terminology of claims and claims-making, we can move to discussing characteristics of the players in the social problems game: audiences and claims-makers.

AUDIENCES

Although most academic research on the process of constructing social problems focuses on the characteristics of people who do the social problems work of making claims, I want to begin by emphasizing the importance of *audiences* for these claims. Audiences are critical because a social problem is created only when audience members evaluate claims as believable and important. In the metaphor of the social problems game: Who wins and who loses depends on how audience members vote.

When I write, "Audiences need to be persuaded," I am not arguing that each and every person must agree that a social problem exists before a condition is taken seriously as a social problem. We live in a complex world where differing experiences can lead to very different evaluations of the believability and importance of claims. Consider a social problem we might call "police brutality." One type of audience likely interested in this condition would be poor (especially minority) men who are the typical targets of something that could be called police brutality. Another type of audience might be members of police oversight committees charged with the responsibility of making sure the police do their job correctly. Obviously, these are different audiences who likely will be persuaded by very different types of claims. The claims made by rap music, for example, might be convincing to audiences of people experiencing something that might be evaluated as police brutality, but members of police review boards likely would not find the claims made in such music believable. Indeed, police review board members might construct rap music itself as a social problem.

Hierarchy of Audience Significance

The term *audience* rarely means all people also because of the *hierarchy of audience significance*. The social problems game is *not* like political elections, where we each have one vote and where each vote counts equally (that is, if voting machines manage to count them). The votes in the social problems game can be weighted with some worth far more than others. Indeed, it is possible to win the social problems game with a very small number of votes as long as they are from powerful segments of an audience. At times, power follows typical cultural patterns of inequality. For example, the evaluations of children most often count less than those of adults, just as the opinions of middle-class people all too often count more than those of poor people. At other times, power depends on the issue at hand. For example, if I believe that the social problem of "gang-related crime in schools" can be reduced by making all students wear uniforms, I *must* persuade school board members because they are the people who can make a rule that students must wear uniforms. I do *not* need to persuade students, their teachers, or their parents. In this case, audiences of parents, students, or teachers matter only if they start to make claims that uniforms are not good and school board members find their claims more believable and important than mine. So it goes with social problems in general. Convincing many people *can* yield a powerful claim ("Everyone agrees with me," "It's the public's wish to do this"), but this often is *not necessary:* Racial desegregation started in the South because of federal laws although many whites living in the South at that time did not agree. Convincing many people also can be *not enough:* the majority of Americans were against the Vietnam war for several years before the war ended.

When I say claims-makers must persuade audiences it is important to remember that "audience" does not necessarily mean the majority of people and that some people's evaluations of claims count more than others. We also cannot assume that audience members automatically believe what they are told or see. Consider the case of claims presented through the mass media. Contrary to images that people watch television and simply absorb televised visions of reality, practical actors evaluate claims and do not simply accept what they see or hear. Do you ever find yourself "talking back" to the television set, or sitting in class and silently challenging your instructor, or reading a book and thinking it is simply nonsense? Of course you do, because humans are practical actors who actively work to make sense of our lives.[3] Given this, we need to look more closely at the *social resources* audience members can draw upon to evaluate the believability and importance of claims they see or hear.

The Social Problems Work of Audience Members

Just as there is the social problems work of claims-makers who seek to persuade, there is the social problems work of people evaluating claims. Audience members seeing or hearing social problems claims do not automatically evaluate these claims as believable or important. Rather, audience members are practical actors who use our practical experience, popular wisdom, and general understandings of the ways the world *does* work and the ways the world *should* work to evaluate social problems claims.

Our *practical experience*, of course, is a resource we can use to evaluate claims. If I am or have been poor, for example, I can use my own experiences to evaluate claims other people make about poverty and poor people. If I have been a victim of crime, I might use that particular experience to evaluate claims made about crime and its victims. If I know a child who is "learning disabled," I might use that experience to evaluate claims about this type of person, and so on.

Because humans are social, it follows that some experiences can be more or less widely shared by members of particular *social categories* of people such as women, men, Hispanics, immigrants, and wealthy people. There are tendencies for people in certain social categories to be more or less likely to classify a particular condition as a problem. "Wealthy" people, for example, might complain about the problem of "finding reliable servants," while those "servants" might well see wages and the conditions of their work as a problem. As another example, white Americans holding racist views of African-Americans tend to more harshly condemn African-American welfare recipients and drug suspects than do white Americans not holding racist views. Also, people who have themselves been victims of crime tend to have more fear of crime than people who have not been victimized. The next time you see a public opinion poll about social problems, notice how the results of the poll often are tallied by social categories: We tend to see the world differently because of our practical experience and our practical experience can be influenced by our gender, race, age, economic status, and so on.[4]

Audience members can use their practical experiences to evaluate the believability and importance of claims and this practical experience tends to be shared by members of the same social categories. At the same time, this is only a tendency and we cannot predict practical experience from knowing an audience member is in one or another social category. The social category "women," for example, includes women who are young and not so young; rich and poor; Anglo, Asian, African, Hispanic; Muslim, Jewish, Catholic, Protestant, agnostic, and so on. People who are in the social category "immigrants" include highly skilled people whose native language is English as well as people with no formal education who do not speak or write the English language, and so on. So, while audience members can draw from their practical experience, and while practical experiences often are shared by people who share membership in a social category, claims-makers cannot assume that each and every audience member will be drawing from the same practical experience.

Popular wisdom is another social resource we might use to evaluate social problems claims. It is difficult to describe popular wisdom because it is our taken-for-granted ideas about how the world works: you reap what you sow, alcoholism is a disease, education is important for employment but being an excellent football player will pay more money, birds of a feather flock together, abused children become abusive adults, men and women are different, rich people are not like the rest of us, while bad things do happen to good people and while good things do happen to bad people it is more common for good things to happen to good people and bad things to happen to bad people. Popular wisdom cannot be fully elaborated—it is written nowhere but is everywhere around us. Audience members can use their understandings of this popular wisdom to evaluate the believability and importance of claims they see and hear.

Another form of popular wisdom is *cultural themes*, which are widely shared values and beliefs about the way the world should work. These are a topic in the next chapter and include such beliefs as the importance of freedom, families, patriotism, and individual responsibility.

Finally, audience members can use their understandings of *cultural feeling rules*. These are widely shared beliefs about how we should feel about particular types of people. They include general understandings of what types of people deserve sympathy and its behavioral expression of help and what types of people deserve condemnation and its behavioral expression of punishment. I will return to these feeling rules in Chapter 4.

In brief, audience members who see and hear social problems claims do not automatically evaluate these claims as believable, they do not automatically support claims-makers who argue the social problem condition must be eliminated. Audience members do the work of evaluating claims. Of course, my description is very general and certainly not enough to allow us to accurately predict how individual audience members likely will evaluate the believability and importance of any specific claim about social problems. Indeed, the postmodern characteristics of diversity and lack of agreement mean that claims likely will receive very different evaluations from different audience members. Claims-makers cannot assume that audience members will simply accept the claims they see and hear yet these audience members are the judges and juries for social problems claims.

I also have a very practical reason for emphasizing that audience members evaluate claims. In our daily lives we are all members of audiences for social problems claims. It is important for us to take the job seriously and not simply accept claims made by others. Yet taking seriously the work of being an audience member can be difficult. Social problems claims are all around us; we do not have the time to thoughtfully consider the believability of each one. And often claims about social problem conditions are in the form of statistics, which poses further problems because Americans in general have little understanding of the meaning of statistics. Because we do not understand them we tend to simply accept them, and when we do this we are likely to have very distorted images of social problems. I would argue that being a good audience member does not mean becoming an expert on statistics. It means only that when you hear claims you should ask questions about them rather than simply accepting claims as true.[5]

CLAIMS-MAKERS AND THE SOCIAL PROBLEMS INDUSTRY

The second type of player in the social problems game is called the claims-maker: the people who do the social problems work of claims-making. We will start with the *social problems industry*, a segment of the social world that produces, manages, and attempts to resolve social problems. In a most general sense, each of us is a part of this social problems industry because we often state our opinions on social problem conditions and when we do this, we are making claims. A bit more obviously, in daily life we can become a part of the social problems industry when we write letters to editors, sign petitions, or wear T-shirts or display bumper stickers on our cars that make claims about social problems.

More obviously, government and law are parts of the social problems industry. Indeed, the job of politicians (from the president of the United States to city council members in a local community) is to construct—and attempt to resolve—social problems. Government also includes political lobbyists who are paid by others to make claims about social problems to politicians. At times, these folks make claims to *create* social problems. So, for example, a lobbyist for the AARP (American Association for Retired People) might lobby (make claims to) congressional members that there *is* a social problem of elderly people who cannot afford their medical insurance premiums. At other times lobbyists make claims that a social problem does *not* exist: a lobbyist for the cigarette industry might claim that cigarette companies do *not* target young children in their advertising. So, too, lawyers can be active claims-makers. These people organize lawsuits claiming that one or another condition is a social problem and therefore should be illegal or that it is not a social problem and therefore should be legal.

The social problems industry also includes *organizational sponsors* for social problems. These organizations initiate considerable claims-making themselves and they also can lend their respected names, money, and organizational skills to the claims-making activities of others. The AMA (American Medical Association) sponsors many social problems surrounding issues of health, the American Cancer Society sponsors many problems surrounding that disease. Other common sponsors of social problems include the NASW (National Association of Social Workers), the AAUP (American Association of University Professors) the PHA (Public Health Association), and the NEA (National Education Association).

The social problems industry also includes people whose job it is to educate others about social problems. Teachers (especially those who teach courses in social problems), researchers who supply evidence for social problems claims, and authors of books on social problem topics (including me) most clearly are in the social problems industry.[6]

The social problems industry most assuredly includes many people who work in the mass media. This includes people who work for television or radio stations, those who write plays or music with social problems as themes, and those who write about social problems for newspapers and magazines. Indeed, we should include in the social problems industry many people whose job it is to *entertain* the American public. Jenny Jones, Montel Williams, Maury, Ricki Lake, and Jerry Springer would not have jobs without social problems. Social problems are the topics of movies, and the proliferation of shows such as *20/20, 60 Minutes, America's Most Wanted,* and *Dateline* is an indication of the American public's zeal to be entertained by social problems. There would be shocks felt throughout the entertainment industry if social problems went away.

Then there are the places in the *troubled persons industry.* "Troubled persons" are what social policy analysts call the *target populations* for policies to do something to resolve social problems. This troubled persons industry includes all the places designed to help victims and potential victims of social problems and to rehabilitate or punish villains and potential villains who create social problems. In the United States today, this includes everything from prisons and jails to foster care for abused children, from psychiatric hospitals to programs for children at risk, from methadone treatment centers to programs for teenage mothers and support groups for victims of rape or for alcoholics. Most clearly, these places do not share many characteristics. But what they *do* share is that each is in business because particular types of people have been constructed as troubled and in need of some type of assistance, rehabilitation, or punishment. The work of these places is the topic of Chapter 7.

Finally, the social problems industry includes the places that make products people buy because of social problems. There is a sign on a telephone pole on my way to work: "Buy two home security systems, get the third free, only $199 each and $19.95 a month monitoring charge." I wonder how much money is made from worry about the social problem of crime? Likewise, companies selling kits for parents to test their children for drug use would go out of business if we stopped worrying about the problem of children using drugs. There also is a segment of the population that depends on the continued existence of government programs attempting to resolve social problems: physicians make money from Medicaid and Medicare, grocers from food stamps, apartment owners from housing subsidies, and so on.

In summary, the social problems industry involves an incredibly wide variety of people and places that, in one way or another, construct social problems or attempt to resolve social problems. It is a huge industry in terms of the numbers of people it employs, the money it requires for its operation, and the money it generates.

Claims-Makers and Motives

Social problems work takes time and energy that could be used to do other things. This raises a question: Why do people do social problems work?

Subjective Values and Claims-Makers.   People sometimes become claims-makers because of their subjective values: They believe a condition exists that offends their moral values so much that they must work to resolve it. At times, personal tragedy leads to social activism. For example, the social change group called MADD (Mothers Against Drunk Drivers) was started by Candy Lightner, a woman whose own child was killed by a drunk driver. John Walsh (now the host of *America's Most Wanted*) originally became a social problems claims-maker for the problem of missing children after his son, Adam, was abducted by a stranger and brutally murdered. Christopher Reeve, the former Superman of movie fame, has become a primary spokesperson for Americans with disabilities because he, himself, now is paralyzed.[7]

At other times, people making claims might not personally experience the condition, yet they learn of it and are led to become active claims-makers. Each year, for example, there are a few students in my Family Violence class who are so disturbed by what they learned that they become claims-makers on behalf of abused children or battered women. Likewise, social problems claims-makers regularly appear on television talk shows such as *Oprah*. Often, at the end of these segments there is a number to call for more information. Some viewers will be recruited as new claims-makers because they are morally outraged about a condition that offends their values.

Objective Interests and Claims-Makers. People also can become claims-makers because of their objective interests. "Objective" means real and tangible, "interests" means what benefits us personally. The most obvious example, of course, is claims-makers who benefit economically from creating public concern. People selling alarm systems tend to make many claims about the increasing problems of crime in their sales pitch. The more people are worried about crime, the more alarms they will sell. A person owning a weight loss clinic might be active in making claims about the problem of obesity. Objective interests go much further than the obvious. For example, good health is important to each of us so I could argue we each have an objective interest in things leading to good health (such as a clean natural environment and good health care). We could say it is in the objective interest of women, minorities, and other disadvantaged groups to support claims about the importance of equal rights because if these claims are successful, the lives of people in these disadvantaged groups will be objectively better.

Community, Emotions, and Claims-Makers. While claims-making is work, at times it can be quite pleasurable. For example, unlike previous eras when people tended to identify strongly with their families, communities, religion, and so on, a characteristic of the postmodern condition is that many people now experience the disturbing feeling of being disconnected from others. Joining a group of claims-makers offers membership in a community of people working to achieve a social goal and this can be emotionally satisfying. Becoming a social problems claims-maker also can lead to a very positive sense of self. After all, claims-makers are taking their time and energy to promote social change and that is a reason to feel good about doing social problems work. Indeed, what might seem on the outside to be a high cost for claims-making—such as spending a night in jail after being arrested for participating in an illegal protest march—can be experienced as quite positive, a badge of honor to people identifying strongly with the claims-making goals. Finally, at times these activities can be downright fun, such as when college sororities and fraternities choose a cause to support and hold dances, raffles, car washes, and so on to earn money for that cause. Social problems work in such instances is accomplished (money is raised, publicity for the cause is generated), as claims-makers dance the night away. In brief, people might become claims-makers because it offers them a community, a way to feel good about themselves, and claims-making can be fun.[8]

The Problems in Examining Claims-Makers' Motives. While there has been considerable research on the question of why people become social problems claims-makers, this question is quite impossible to answer. First, it is not possible to neatly separate our objective interests from our subjective values. We tend to value things that are, objectively speaking, good for us; we tend to do things we more or less believe in.[9] So, for example, the man who sold me my home security system said he got into this line of work because a few years ago his own home was burglarized. He said he wanted to prevent this from happening to others. Likewise, people who work in the social problems industry do have an objective interest in encouraging continued concern about the problems their agencies are handling, but these people often begin working in these places because they deeply care about the problem. Objective interests and subjective values are difficult to separate. Second, and in the same way, people seeking a community (or fun) likely will be drawn to making claims about social problems conditions that are compatible with their objective interests and/or their subjective values, so these also cannot be distinguished. Third, we cannot assume that the reasons people are originally drawn to making claims are the same reasons why they remain claims-makers over time. We might enter a social problems game primarily because that is what our friends are doing but then start to deeply care about the social problem condition; we might begin by caring deeply about a problem but remain primarily because we have developed social relationships with others in the group or because our employment in the troubled persons' industry depends on continued public concern.

What I am arguing is that it is not possible to say that individual claims-makers have one or another specific reason for the social problems work they do. But now I will claim that when we are interested in the social problems game itself it does not matter why people do social problems work. What matters is the extent to which their claims are *believed by audiences*.[10]

Claims-Makers and the Hierarchy of Credibility

So far, I have argued that the goal of claims-making is to construct claims that audience members evaluate as believable and important. An alert reader might well wonder: What about the *truth*? Notice that the term *claims* conveys *no* meaning about their truth. Social construction perspectives do not lead us to focus on the truth because interest is in which claims are *believed* to be true. So, the truth *does not matter* in the social problems game. What matters is what audience members *believe* is true.

But evaluations of truthfulness are complicated in our postmodern world, where we often have little in the way of practical experience with the condition and must rely on others to tell us about it. Whom do we believe? Audience members often tend to begin their evaluations with preconceived notions of which claims-makers can be believed somewhat automatically and which claims-makers can be ignored somewhat automatically. Just as the evaluations of some audience members can matter more than the evaluations of others (the hierarchy of audience significance), there is a *hierarchy of credibility* among claims-makers.

At the top of the hierarchy of credibility are scientists. Notice when you see or hear claims how the speaker's academic credentials and institutional affiliation most often are explicitly mentioned. Title matters because *who* makes claims matters.[11] Scientists enter the social problems game with the distinct advantage that audience members tend to believe their claims. It's like starting a game of Monopoly with more money than the other players.

In going down the hierarchy of credibility a bit we find a range of professionals who also can enter the social problems game with distinct advantages. People called urban planners, for example, are powerful claims-makers in questions about development; the claims of "relationship experts" of television talk show fame rarely are challenged (even when their professional credentials are, shall we say, somewhat questionable). But these are localized positions of power. Stated otherwise, scientists *always* are at the top of the hierarchy of credibility, various categories of professionals *might* be at the top. The hierarchy of credibility in the middle can depend on the specific case in point.

At the bottom of the hierarchy of credibility we again can make generalizations. The question of why some conditions *fail* to be evaluated as social problems sometimes has a simple answer: claims are made by people low on the hierarchy of credibility. The story is predictable: the categories of people whose views and opinions are ignored or discounted in general are the categories of people at the bottom of the hierarchy of credibility in the social problems game.[12]

For example, children rarely are allowed to make their own claims. Social problems involving children typically are constructed by adults speaking on behalf of children. The claims of poor people (especially members of minority groups) rarely are heard by middle-class audiences or politicians unless these claims are important to more powerful claims-makers (such as politicians, social workers, or teachers). I began this chapter by arguing that claims are all around us in our daily life, so we need to ask why we hear so few claims. Those we actually hear and take seriously typically are made by the kinds of people audience members are prone to believe. People on the bottom of the hierarchy of credibility do make claims but these claims are not heard, they are silenced.

The social problems game is very complex. People who make claims include you and me in our daily lives, people trying to sell us things, politicians, authors, social activists, and so on. Many people make claims but we tend to hear only some of them, we tend to evaluate some claims as probably more truthful than others based on who is making the claim rather than on our thoughtful evaluations of the claim itself. I want to continue by examining more closely three important types of claims-makers: social activists, scientists, and people in the mass media.

SOCIAL PROBLEMS ACTIVISTS AS CLAIMS-MAKERS

Obviously key actors in constructing social problems are social activists. These are people who organize into social change groups or social movements for the precise purpose of persuading audience members that one or another condition is a social problem. There are countless such groups. Many churches and synagogues, for example, are social change organizations with active agendas. Indeed, the success of the civil rights movement depended on the prior organization and importance of African-American churches.[13]

There are many groups that now are well-known and have long histories in the United States, such as NAACP (National Association for the Advancement of Colored People), NOW (National Organization for Women), ACLU (American Civil Liberties Union), and AARP (American Association of Retired Persons). There are countless other groups such as SOS (Save Our Schools), SADD (Students Against Drunk Driving), ACT-UP (AIDS Coalition to Unleash Power), NRA (National Rifle Association), NORML (National Organization for Reform of Marijuana Laws), PETA (People for the Ethical Treatment of Animals), NAAFA (National Organization to Advance Fat Acceptance), VOCAL (Victims of Child Abuse Laws), GLARP (Gay and Lesbian Association of Retired Persons), CURE (Christians United for Reformation), and PAWS (Progressive Animal Welfare Society). You no doubt can think of many others. Because such groups are organized specifically for the purpose of claims-making it is not surprising that they are responsible for a considerable amount of claims-making activity.

People in these groups do the multiple kinds of work necessary to persuade audience members to evaluate a condition as a social problem and to support social change. For example, consider a relatively new social problem called "hate crimes" or "bias-motivated crimes," which are crimes targeting disadvantaged minorities because they are minorities. Although there is no indication that these behaviors are new, the type of crime—hate crime—is new. This new consciousness is the consequence of many groups of people who banded together such as those in the Anti-Defamation League of B'nai Brith, the Center for Democratic Renewal, the National Gay and Lesbian Task Force, and the National Coalition Against Domestic Violence. People in these groups worked together and separately in order to compile statistics, lobby politicians, and educate the public. They were successful in that we now have a new category of crime.

In the same way, people in Oregon organized into the Death with Dignity movement to make demands to allow physician-assisted suicide for terminally ill patients capable of making the decision that this is what they wanted. Efforts of this group included voter education and a blizzard of media appearances to encourage public concern. They, too, were successful because voters approved a Death With Dignity law. Of course, not all claims-makers are so obviously successful. For example, activists in the Size Acceptance Movement have engaged in protests and picketing of organizations they claim discriminate against fat people, they have produced brochures and books for large people, they have held workshops and supported letter-writing campaigns. While these social activists have done a great deal of social problems work they have had relatively little luck in achieving their goal to increase the social evaluation of overweight people.[14]

In brief, while we should not underestimate the power of individual claims-makers—Candy Lightner single-handedly organized MADD—the effectiveness of claims-making can be increased when people act together. Banding together furnishes social activists with a group of like-minded others that is associated with a feeling of belonging to a community. People might continue claims-making because they value membership in this community.[15] Furthermore, the chances of successfully persuading audience members to take a condition seriously increase when claims are heard repeatedly. The more people making claims, the better. Still further, and a topic in Chapter 5, it often takes considerable time and resources to obtain social change. Social change groups (such as NOW and ACLU) can offer the organizational and financial resources necessary to pursue long-term claims-making.

SCIENTISTS AS CLAIMS-MAKERS

The American public in general tends to believe claims made by scientists. As we know from our practical experience, at times this faith is misplaced. Not all scientists are competent, seemingly scientific credentials can be purchased over the internet at little cost, sometimes scientists charge a considerable amount of money to offer their claims as expert testimony, so we can wonder if their objective interests might be clouding their scientific findings. Also, because scientists are at the top of the hierarchy of credibility, it is not surprising that audiences can be told that claims are based on scientific evidence when no such evidence exists.[16] While these are obvious points about scientists in the social problems game, there are more interesting topics.

Science is at the top of the hierarchy of credibility because the ideal of science is that it is an objective search for knowledge, we think that what scientists do has nothing to do with what scientists as people believe in. But remember that social problems are about moral evaluations. Issues of moral evaluation *always* and *necessarily* lie behind any claims, including claims supported by scientific research. Scientists make many moral distinctions when they design their research.

For example, how many women are victims of "date rape"? The answer depends on how "date rape" is defined. It can be defined broadly to include instances where women were intoxicated before the sexual encounter and therefore unable to legally give their consent, it might include instances meeting the formal legal definition of rape even though a woman might not categorize herself as a victim. If we used this broad definition we would find almost one in three college women to be victims of "date rape." However, we could more narrowly define "date rape" to include only women who categorize themselves as victims and we could argue that women giving consent while drunk nonetheless did give consent so they should not be included. If we used this narrow definition, of course, we would find far fewer instances of "date rape" than if we used the broad definition. My point here is that neither one of these definitions is "right," neither is "wrong." They are both the result of *moral reasoning* about what is—and what is not—a problem and therefore what should—and should not—be measured in research. This is one reason why equally good scientists can design equally good research that nonetheless yields far different findings.[17]

While scientists can disagree among themselves, they often seem to form a united front to the public. There can be a vast difference between science as we see it performed on the "front stage" for general audiences and science as it looks on the "back stage" populated by scientists themselves. The apparent public agreement among scientists most typically is *socially constructed* in ways leading audience members to believe that science is somehow above the world of politics and individual ambition while the actual process of doing science is not so uncontaminated by the real world.[18]

Consider, for example, the *Diagnostic and Statistical Manual* (*DSM*). This is perhaps the most important book in psychiatry / psychology because it contains the *official* listing and *official* descriptions of psychiatric disorders. This book is incredibly practically powerful because it contains the diagnoses that can be used in courts of law as well as by people wanting insurance companies to pay for treatment. The *DSM* also is symbolically powerful because specific behaviors and characteristics in this book have the *official* stamp of "disorder." Yet while members of the general public might assume the contents of this book represent the currently accepted "scientific truth" about psychiatric disorders, the final contents of any edition of the *DSM* are the consequences of social and political back stage processes that rarely become public knowledge. So, for example, "homosexuality" in past eras was listed as a disorder in the *DSM* but no longer is. If we had access to the back stage where the contents of the *DSM* were debated, we would see that this change was not due to changes in knowledge, it was due to a changing social climate and successful claims-making. My point: the scientific construction of knowledge is a social process.[19]

Most certainly, I am *not* arguing that we should not believe claims made by scientists or that claims made by scientists can be ignored because science is contaminated. That would lead to less than thoughtful audience work because claims would be simply dismissed rather than evaluated. What I *am* doing is challenging the often taken-for-granted belief that scientists should always be at the top of the hierarchy of credibility simply because they are scientists. I am also encouraging you to keep in mind the typical differences between science as understood by scientists themselves and claims-making referencing science. As audience members we have the responsibility of doing the social problems work of evaluating claims and it is unwise to simply accept claims made by anyone, including those made by scientists and those referencing science.

MASS MEDIA AS CLAIMS-MAKERS

Social activists are people who explicitly set out to construct social problems and scientists are people whose claims tend to be believed by audience members. The third major player in the social problems game is the people in the mass media. While widely used, the term *mass media* is unfortunate because it disguises incredible diversity: Mass media is a term for *any* form of information / entertainment that is available to a large number (mass) of people. Technically, mass media include the books you can buy through Amazon.com or at Borders Books, movies shown at your local theater, newspapers and magazines delivered to your home or purchased at the grocery store, radio, music, and, of course, television. If you pause for just a moment and think about it you will understand how the term *mass media* is very vague. Magazines, for example, include the *National Inquirer* and *Business Week*; music includes Christian rock and gangsta rap; television includes network stations, PBS, Public Access, and hundreds of cable channels. Network television includes talk shows, news shows, docudramas, comedies, movies; talk shows include *Oprah* and *Jerry Springer,* and so on. In brief, be careful about making general statements about the "mass media" because this is a term disguising incredible diversity.

That said, people working in the mass media become claims-makers in two ways. First, they can be *primary claims-makers.* Reporters searching out information and writing a story are taking the same role as social activists in constructing social problems. Second, and more commonly, people working in the mass media are *secondary claims-makers:* their social problems work is that of translating and packaging claims made by others (politicians, social change activists, academic researchers).[20]

There are three major reasons why people in the mass media are important social problems claims-makers. First, while fragmentation and proliferation in the mass media means there is much more competition than in the past so audiences tend to be smaller than previously, the "mass" in "mass media" continues to signify that many people potentially can see or hear claims made in these sites. The mass media are important because these sites offer claims-makers the largest possible audiences.

The second reason why mass media are important is that as our world gets larger (because of the mass media) we must rely on these media to tell us about it. I can know what is happening in New York City or Afghanistan only if I watch television or read newspapers or magazines. So, while it is important to remember that audience members do not necessarily believe what we see or hear, it remains that an increasingly important source of information is the mass media. Indeed, peoples' ratings of specific conditions as a "problem important to society" depend more on the coverage they have seen on television than on their personal experience. What is presented through mass media, in other words, is what people *can* think about.

Third, while we should not push this too far because audience members actively think about what we are seeing, hearing, or reading, it is logical to argue that claims presented through the mass media will influence audience members' understandings of social problems. For example, there seem to be attitude changes among people who read experts' opinions in the *New York Times,* people who watch a great many television shows about crime tend to be more worried about crime than are people who do not watch these programs.[21] It makes sense that claims presented through the mass media will influence public opinion for no reason other than the fact that this is now our primary source of information about the world around us.

People interested in relationships between mass media claims and social problems have studied a variety of topics. For example, some have examined the social and economic organization of the mass media and have

noted how claims-makers introduced as officials or scientists are the preferred sources for news stories, how ownership of mass media outlets in-
fluences what appears, and how the demands of advertisers leads mass
media outlets to produce images that will not be offensive to advertisers.
Others have been interested in how media create particular images of social problems, such as how magazines and newspapers construct the social
problem of AIDS, how popular magazines written for pregnant women
construct pregnancy as a social problem, how movies negatively construct
Latinos and Latinas, how newspapers and magazines construct the missing children problem, how television talk shows construct Satanism, how
mass media constructs a culture of fear, and so on.[22] While such studies examine social problem construction in a range of mass media outlets including magazines and newspapers, there is particular interest in social
problem construction on network television.

Claims-Makers on Network Television

We know a great deal about claims-making on network television. These
stations are in the business of making a profit from advertising revenue so
they must seek as large an audience as possible. More precisely, television is
concerned with attracting particular *target audiences,* which are people in specific categories (age, gender, income, and so on) most likely to purchase the
products advertised on the programs. And while Americans rely on television as a source of information, this information must be presented in ways
audience members find *entertaining.* It has been some years since television
news divisions were allowed to be unprofitable and see their work as a public service. News divisions now must sell advertising and be profitable.[23]

Television becomes particularly important as a social problems claims-
maker when claims are presented as "factual" (news) or as "based on fact"
(reality programs) because these programs encourage viewers to evaluate
claims as truthful. But these programs also must attract large audiences of
particular types of people and this requires entertaining them. Given this,
it is not difficult to anticipate characteristics of the claims about social problems we likely will see. I will use two quite different examples to illustrate.

The first example is television talk shows such as *Montel Williams, Jerry
Springer,* or *Jenny Jones.* If you have cable, you could see these shows vir-
tually around-the-clock because they are played and replayed throughout
the day and night. Networks appreciate these shows because, unlike situation comedies, which have casts of highly paid actors, talk shows are inexpensive to produce. There is much about these shows that is intriguing.
For example, while the audiences for these shows are, relatively speaking,
quite large in the daytime hours, few people will admit they watch these
programs. Also, while the often bizarre nature of guests and their problems

can lead practical actors to wonder whether, indeed, the people and their problems are "real," these shows are promoted as containing real guests with real problems. These shows probably are most intriguing because, while they are routinely criticized as offering an immoral view of the world, a close examination of their contents reveals they promote a distinct morality. In the typical format, guests, hosts, and audience members alike combine to condemn sin and preach redemption. These shows produce images of a range of social problems and they promote very conventional moral codes.[24]

The second example seems far different, the news on network television. What *is* the "news"? On any given day there are an infinite number of events that potentially are important, but only some become the topic of news shows. Day by day, television producers decide what is—and what is not—news, and they decide how to package the stories in ways that will be interesting to audience members. Very complex stories often are not covered at all or are reduced to "sound bites" because there is not sufficient time to cover complexity, stories with visual components are preferred because audience members quickly tire of listening to reporters. Stories that are unusual and unexpected are entertaining and therefore tend to receive more coverage than their objective newsworthiness warrants. Furthermore, in the search for large audiences, claims on the news will not offend important audiences. Television claims-makers *do* go against rich and powerful people, they *do* challenge the corporations that give them advertising dollars. Yet it remains that on a day-to-day basis there are predictable biases in what is, and what is not, presented on the news and how those stories are packaged.[25]

RELATIONSHIPS AMONG CLAIMS-MAKERS

Any particular social problem such as AIDS, obesity, or poverty might have a variety of claims-makers. Some claims about any one particular condition can be made by activists and others by scientists; mass media sometimes are primary claims-makers and at other times mass media are secondary claims-makers packaging and transmitting claims made by activists or scientists. We need to look at relationships among activists, scientists, and mass media.

Social Activists and Scientists

At times, scientists *are* social activists. There are social change groups such as FAS (Federation of American Scientists) or PSR (Physicians for Social Responsibly) specifically organized by scientists who believe it is important to use science to resolve social problems. Scientists also can directly enter the social problems game when they offer expert testimony that supports one or another claim about social problems. So, although we tend to think of science as an objective search for truth and social activists as perhaps not so objective, science and social activism can be the same.[26]

Also, because scientists are at the top of the hierarchy of credibility, science is very useful to social activists. If a scientist actually makes the claim, this is a powerful tool to gain audience support. But even if a scientist is not the person offering the claim, activists can emphasize that scientific research supports the claim. Not surprisingly, the claims made by scientists might be interpreted by social activists in ways scientists did not intend or perhaps even support.

Social Activists and Mass Media

Because media often are secondary claims-makers who transmit and package social problems claims made by others, media personnel need social activists.[27] Such activists might tie themselves to trees, block the entrances to buildings, disrupt meetings, take over the offices of elected officials or college presidents. Media personnel can package these claims-making activities as entertaining stories. In turn, social problem activists need the media. Media coverage allows activists to enlarge the audience of people who hear their claims and therefore might become supporters or even new recruits to the cause. Media coverage also can add credibility to claims because coverage means at least someone in the media thought the cause was important enough to receive attention.

While social activists and media are dependent on one another, social activists typically need the media more than the media need them. Social activists are only one of many possible media sources, so media have more power over activists than activists have over media. Furthermore, social activists often find there are costs to receiving media coverage. Media personnel sometimes translate claims in ways not promoted by activists, "sound bites" selected by media personnel can misrepresent the major themes of activists' claims, claims that are very critical of mainstream institutions and cultural values might not be transmitted by the media at all. The relationship between media and social problem activists often is very tense: activists need the media yet the claims and interpretations of claims entering public consciousness through the media might be less than satisfactory from activists' perspectives.

Science and Mass Media

When general audiences hear claims based on science we often hear these claims through the mass media. Often the claims actually made by scientists are transformed in the process of translation for mass audiences. For example, television and newspapers have made many claims about the mapping of the human genome. Typically, this reaches the public as a very optimistic story. We hear how gene mapping, synthetic genes, and so on promise a rather easy solution to a range of social problems such as identifying genetically damaged fetuses and identifying people who likely will become alcoholics or who likely will suffer from various diseases, which allows preventive measures. Yet the many claims of successes and promises made through the mass media are far different from the story of failures and unknowns and hesitancies as told through the actual scientific reports on which media claims are based.[28] Media present science on the front stage to general audiences and this can be far different from the back stage claims scientists make among themselves.

SOCIAL PROBLEM CLAIMS-MAKERS AND AUDIENCES

In this chapter we started our tour through the social process of constructing social problems. Beginning with the social constructionist belief that meaning must be created by humans because it is not inherent in objects, we looked at the people who create meaning and those who evaluate the believability and importance of the meaning created. Now we will go to the next topic: the kinds of social problems work that needs to be done by claims-makers if they are to persuade audience members that a condition exists, that it is common and troublesome and must be resolved. We need to look at the kinds of meanings that must be created in order for claims-makers to be successful in the social problems game. The topic for the next three chapters is how claims-makers construct images of conditions, people, and solutions in ways that are logically and emotionally persuasive.

NOTES

1.   The term *rhetoric* is a good substitution for the term *claim* because both have the characteristic that they seek to persuade.

2.   Christiansen and Hanson (1996) explore how the comedic antics of ACT-UP members are meant to shock, which will encourage audience members to understand how AIDS is devastating yet typically ignored.

3.   A burgeoning field of inquiry is called audience reception studies. These studies examine how people actively negotiate the meaning of claims they see and hear, especially those presented through mass media. See, for example, Edelman (1977), W. Gamson et al. (1992), Gans (1993), and Tuchman (1993) for some of the theoretical issues in examining how audience members evaluate claims. Some ex-

cellent empirical studies on how people negotiate meaning include how women make sense of the meaning of romance novels (Radway, 1984) and television (Press, 1991), and how patrons at a bar make sense of the television programs they are watching (May, 2001).

4. Peffley, Hurwitz, and Sniderman (1997) examine relationships between racial stereotypes and political views; Dull and Wint (1997) examine relationships between personal victimization and fear of crime.

5. Best (2001a, excerpted in *Social Problems: Constructionist Readings*) examines the use of statistics in social problem claims and the tendencies of audience members to be less than thoughtful in interpreting them.

6. The subset of experts (scientists, academics, other professionals) is increasingly important as our world becomes more complex and knowledge more specialized. Baumgartner and Jones (1994:56) offer several examples of how major changes in public policy surrounding problems of divorce, drug use, and mental illness have been the consequences of "quiet and often unnoticed changes in professional norms." This is back-stage claims-making.

7. Not all claims-makers for Americans with disabilities want Christopher Reeve as their spokesperson. While we might appreciate his relentless activities to "get better," there is concern that audiences of nondisabled people will believe that disabled people should "get better" rather than demanding changes in the social environment that make disability easier to live with. Such disagreement among claims-makers is a topic for the next three chapters.

8. While scholars traditionally have focused on the material and value-oriented benefits of claims-making, the benefits of claims-making to identity currently are receiving much attention. See, for example, Jasper (1997: especially pp. 108–15, "The Emotions of Protest"), Hunt and Benford (1994), Melucci (1989), Taylor and Whittier (1992), and the articles in the book edited by Stryker, Owens, and White (2000).

9. For an extended example of the impossibility of separating subjective values and objective interests, see Luker's (1984) examination of "pro-life" and "pro-choice" abortion activists.

10. Of course, the question of motivations can matter a great deal when audience members simply dismiss claims because claims-makers have an objective interest in the issue. The most obvious example is that audience members often dismiss claims made by scientists working for the tobacco industry that the harm from cigarettes is not as great as often believed. Within popular wisdom, such research was "bought and paid for" by the tobacco industry and therefore is not to be believed.

11. This finding that news anchors emphasize the academic credentials and institutional affiliations of claims-makers appearing on television comes from Roth (1998), who examined a range of television news programs such as *Nightline, Meet the Press*, and *MacNeil/Lehrer News Hour*.

12. L. Miller (1993) discusses "claims-making from the underside." She explicitly critiques the common practice among social constructionists to focus attention on claims made by politicians and social movement activists. Miller argues that this bias leads us to ignore unsuccessful claims, many of which are made by marginalized categories of people.

13.   The importance of African-American churches in the civil rights movement is widely acknowledged among observers of social movements. See, for example, Morris (1984).

14.   Jenness and Broad (1997, excerpted in *Social Problems: Constructionist Readings*) examine the groups and activities leading to hate crime becoming a social problem; Sobal (1999, excerpted in *Social Problems: Constructionist Readings*) explores the activities of the Size Acceptance movement; Hillyard and Dombrink (2001) examine the Death with Dignity movement in Oregon.

15.   Some observers now argue that this sense of community leads individual claims-makers to construct a personal identity that in and of itself is fulfilling, regardless of any social change that might come from successful claims-making.

16.   Rios (1997) examined the creation of a commonly cited statistic that "gay teenagers are approximately three times more likely to commit suicide than heterosexual teens." Although this statistic came from the U.S. Department of Health and Human Services, and therefore was given the status of "scientific," Rios argues it was not the result of research at all but rather was generated by social activists. See also Best (2001a) for how seemingly scientific statistics often are a social product of activists and media rather than of scientific study; Stacey (1999) and Furstenberg (1999) for relationships between social science research and political advocacy; Schram (1995) for the distinctly political nature of social policy research on poverty.

17.   We could extend this line of reasoning by noting that differences in research findings also are associated with other research designs. See Best (2001a) for a wide variety of examples. For the "date rape" controversy see Koss and Cook (1993) and Gilbert (1993); see Lynch (1996) for a general discussion of how estimates of the social problem of rape vary depending upon the research design. Margolin (1994, excerpted in *Social Problems: Constructionist Readings*) argues that there are many problems in research on "gifted children" because comparison groups are not used.

18.   Knorr-Cetina (1981) and Aronson (1984) elaborate this constructionist nature of science. Gusfield (1981) examines the rhetoric of science in the social problem of "drunk driving" and the type of person known as a "drunk driver." He argues this rhetoric disguises myriad disagreements and distinct lack of evidence. Hilgartner (2000) conceptualizes science as a "public drama" and examines the differences between the front stage agreements and the back stage arguments among scientists doing research on diet, nutrition, and cancer. See also *Commoner* (2002) for differences between front stage and back stage claims about cloning.

19.   Kirk and Kutchins (1992, excerpted in *Social Problems: Constructionist Readings*) and Figert (1996, excerpted in *Social Problems: Constructionist Readings*) examine the back stage social and political process surrounding constructing *DSM III;* Pawluch (1996, excerpted in *Social Problems: Constructionist Readings*) explores relationships between the pediatric profession and claims about children; Trent (1994) examines the social processes leading to the social category of "mental retardation."

20.   The distinction between primary and secondary claims-making is more fully elaborated by Best (1991) who used the empirical example of the 1987 "freeway shootings" problem in Los Angeles to argue that mass media can be a primary claims-maker.

21.   Jordan (1993) examines how expert opinion quoted in the *New York Times* is associated with the social policy preferences of readers; Barak (1994) claims that people who watch many crime programs develop what he calls a "mean world" view.

22.   This certainly is an incomplete list of attention to mass media claims. The examples taken here are of the social and economic organization of the mass media (W. Gamson et. al., 1992), AIDS (Albert, 1989), pregnancy (Gardner, 1994, excerpted in *Social Problems: Constructionist Readings*), Latinos/Latinas (Rodriguez, 1998), culture of fear (Glassner, 1999), missing children (Best, 1990), Satanism (Lowney, 1994). There also are edited collections containing several empirical examples of how various forms of mass media construct social problems: Mann and Zatz (1998), Ferrell and Websdale (1999), Fishman and Cavender (1998). Interest in mass media constructions of social life in general also can be found in the field called cultural studies such as Kellner (1995).

23.   Campbell (1991:3) claims that *60 Minutes* perfected the style of packaging news as entertainment. He quotes Don Hewitt, the producer of *60 Minutes*, as saying, "If we package reality as well as Hollywood packages fiction, I bet we could double the rating."

24.   Lowney (1999, excerpted in *Social Problems: Constructionist Readings*) argues that the format and content of these television talk shows combines the format and content of religious evangelical revivals and the carnivals of the nineteenth century. See also J. Gamson (1998) for how these same talk shows have been important claims-making sites for the social problem of "deviant sexualities."

25.   Attention to how the news is packaged for television include Gans (1979), who studied how producers and editors decide what is "news" and Campbell's (1991) examination of how the television news program *60 Minutes* is constructed. How the news constructs political meaning is explored by Neuman, Just, and Crigler (1992); Katz (1987) examines what makes crime "news." Cavender (1998, excerpted in *Social Problems: Constructionist Readings*) describes how television produces construct "reality" television.

26.   Epstein (1996) examines the work of gay and lesbian activists/scientists who do research on HIV/AIDS; Scott (1993) describes the "research wars" among scientists interpreting the Agent Orange studies.

27.   In this section I am summarizing the claims made by Gamson and Wolfsfeld (1993) on relationships between social activists and media.

28.   See Conrad (1997) for an examination of what happens when scientific claims about human genes are filtered through the media, Furstenberg (1999) for a similar account of what happens when scientific studies about "families" are filtered through the media, Stacey (1999) for relationships between social scientists and the mass media.

II

Constructing Packages of Claims

3

Constructing Conditions

I awake with a start at 2:30 A.M. when a DC-3 flies fifty feet above my house. I remember that aerial spraying of Malathion to kill medflies continues. My newspaper yesterday contained reports, summaries of meetings, editorials and letters to the editor from the State Department of Agriculture, the Environmental Protection Agency, farmers, CRAM (Citizens for the Responsible Application of Malathion), and independent citizens. Those supporting continued overhead spraying say a billion dollar a year citrus crop is at risk: consumers don't want worms in their oranges. Canada won't import Florida citrus until the medflies are gone. The economic health of the community is at stake. Anyway, they say, a hundred scientific studies prove that Malathion is safe. Those against the spraying, though, say Malathion isn't safe. They have a hundred scientific studies proving it. And citizens are saying they're finding dead birds and fish; old people and people with asthma are reporting health problems. We're selling out our environment, our health, and the health of our children for the citrus industry, they say. And why are taxpayers footing the bill?

We know from the previous chapter that claims-maker is a term for people in the social problems industry. It includes you and me when we make claims in our daily lives, social movement activists, scientists and other professionals, researchers, mass media, teachers, social workers, people trying to sell us things to protect us from social problems or cure us of the consequences of social problems. What all these people share is the goal of persuading audience members to define and respond to particular conditions as social problems. We know also that the term *audience* disguises much variability: claims-makers might be trying to persuade politicians, the public in general, or some segment of the public in particular, not all audience members are equally interested in claims, the opinions of some audience members are more highly valued and needed than others.

The goal of the social problems game is to persuade audience members, and the claims-making cause will be helped if claims-makers also manage to recruit new people to make claims.[1] This persuasion takes two forms. First, audience members can evaluate a condition as a social problem when

they are persuaded by *logical reasoning* that the condition violates their beliefs about the ways the world should work. That is the topic of this chapter. Second, audience members can be persuaded to take a condition
seriously when they are *emotionally moved* by the plights of victims. That is
the topic of the next chapter.

THE SOCIAL CONTEXTS OF SOCIAL PROBLEMS WORK

These claims-making tasks take place within the social contexts of competitions and complexity of practical experience. It is important to consider
these contexts of social problems work.

Competitions

The social problems game is about competitions. But unlike board
games, where competition is only among players, the social problems
game involves multiple competitions. Successful claims are those evaluated as more important than their competitors.

Audience Carrying Capacity.   Audiences for social problems claims are
not similar to audiences of people attending a movie, concert, or football
game. Most people in those audiences have chosen to attend and therefore
have an interest in the activity at hand. Much social problems claims-
making rather takes place in daily life, where audience members might—
or might not—be attentive. While some observers argue that Americans
have become too inner-focused and therefore simply do not care about
harm experienced by others, there is another very practical reason why we
are not always attentive to social problems claims we hear in our daily
lives: Claims-makers ask us to take conditions seriously, to worry about
them, perhaps to give them our money so that conditions can be resolved.
And, when they try to recruit us to become claims-makers ourselves, they
also are asking for our time. But how much worry, time, and money do we
have to spend on social problems? Social problems compete with activities
of daily life (going to school and work, doing our laundry, fixing our cars)
and with our personal concerns (about our own health, our own relationships, our own futures, the well-being of people we care about). In the terminology of social constructionism, individuals have a limited *carrying
capacity* for social problems. Claims-makers must persuade audience members that the condition is important enough to take time, worry, and perhaps money that otherwise would be spent on the personal concerns of
daily life.

Likewise, social problems claims compete with the rest of life in *public arenas,* such as government, the courts, and mass media. Each of these places also has a limited carrying capacity. Newspapers and magazines contain only so many inches of space, Congress has only so much time for debate, and so on. Social problems compete with everything else in public arenas. If claims-makers want mass media attention or need the support of people in law or politics, they must persuade these audiences that the condition at hand is more important than other demands for time, attention, and resources. In brief, unlike board games where players face competition only from other players, the social problems game involves competition between social problem and everything else.[2]

Competitions among Social Problems. At any one time, there are countless possible social problems, so only a limited number can be the subject of attention. Because the carrying capacities of practical actors and of specific public arenas are limited, social problems compete among *themselves.* When members of Congress are spending their time on the problems of terrorism, they are not attending to the problems of education, medical insurance, or the environment. When I give a donation to my local humane society, that is money I do not give to the food pantry. Claims-makers therefore must persuade target audiences that their problem is as important as—or more important than—others.[3]

Competitions within Social Problems. Another type of competition is among claims-makers who seemingly are concerned with the same condition yet nonetheless construct very different claims. Social movements, for example, can be accompanied by *countermovements:* There are social activists who argue that "global warming" is a social problem and there are others who argue that it is not a problem (they claim that global warming is not happening, or that it does more good than harm, or that the cure would be worse than the problem). At other times, social activists construct very different visions of morality. For example, some people claim that cohabitation outside marriage is immoral and should be condemned while others claim it is good and should be promoted. In the same way, some people claim it is wrong for mothers with small children to be employed while others claim it is best for children when their mothers are employed, and so on.[4]

Consider the problem of "crime." Americans worry a great deal about crime, yet claims made by social activists, academic researchers, and mass media certainly do not agree on what crime is, what causes it, or what should be done to resolve it. Some claim that crime is a consequence of blocked opportunities leading people to turn to crime, others claim it is about racism, still others focus on how mass media present so many images of crime that it has become normalized, expected, and therefore not deviant. Still other claims-makers focus on how social institutions such as family and religion have lost their power to control, or how our criminal justice system is too lenient, meaning that there are few costs for criminal activities. So, while people making all these various claims are claims-makers constructing the problem of crime, they are not offering similar constructions. They compete among themselves.[5]

Competitions among claims-makers also can be found within organizations or groups of people who often appear united on the front stage of social problems claims-making. For example, movement activists claiming we need increased rights for gays nonetheless disagree among themselves about the extent to which the rights of transsexual and bisexual people should be a part of the agenda. On the front stage of social problem construction these folks seem united, but on the back stage—when they talk among themselves—they are not. In the same way, proponents of nuclear disarmament disagree on the extent to which movement activists should turn to behavioral claims of civil disobedience (disrupting social life) in order to get attention. There also are many disagreements among social activists in the women's movement in the United States about relationships between women's rights and the needs of particular categories of women such as lesbians, poor women, and women of color.[6]

Social problems work involves persuading audience members that a particular social problem is more important than all other demands on our time, worry, and resources; it involves persuading audience members that a particular set of claims about a particular social problem is more believable and important than other sets of claims constructing that problem.

Complexity and Diversity

In the first chapter I talked about the importance of typifications and I need to emphasize this. Especially in our complex world, social life depends on typifications—the images in our head of *types* of things, conditions, and people. Each child is different but we have a typification of "children," each tree is unique but we have a typification of "trees" (and subcategories such as oak and spruce), and so on. Our need to use typifications is especially true for social problems because we use the term *social problem* to talk about conditions harming *many* people. It is simply not possible for each of us to rely on our own practical experience. Even people who work daily with the problems in the "inner city" cannot know the detailed characteristics of every such place and the characteristics of each and every person in such places; it is not possible for any one person to visit each and every prison to know from personal experience what each of them is like, and so on.

It is important to always keep in mind the incredible diversity in our world. Consider the example of "child abuse." What specific real-life experiences would you include in this category? In real life, all too many children are brutally killed by their parents, all too many are severely physically injured. Likely all audience members would evaluate these as specific instances of a social problem called child abuse. But is it "child abuse" if a parent "spanks" a misbehaving child? When a parent roughly "yanks" a wandering child out of oncoming traffic? When a father "slaps" his seventeen-year-old son after the son took the family car without permission and wrecked it? You no doubt could add many other kinds of experiences that you think should be called child abuse; and you might have read one or another example on my list and thought "This clearly is not an example of child abuse," or "This might not be good, but it isn't an example of child abuse." That is my point: social life is complex, so each word such as "homelessness" or "illiteracy" or "drunk driving" can be used to categorize many very different kinds of specific experiences and unique people. Social problems work is the work of constructing images of *typical* conditions and *typical* people, it is the work of constructing simplicity out of incredible complexity.

Surviving competitions and typifying complexity must be done if claims-makers are to be successful. Our next topic is how claims-makers typify conditions in ways leading to this success. In real life, this is accomplished by constructing images of conditions *and* people, by persuading audience members through appeals to logic *and* to emotion. I will start with how claims-makers typify social problem conditions in ways encouraging audience members to logically evaluate these as widespread, harmful, and wrong.

SOCIAL PROBLEMS WORK: CONSTRUCTING GROUNDS

Most audience members are interested in social problems as *objective* conditions. As such, practical actors want to know "facts" about social problems: What is the condition? What harm does it create? How many people are harmed? Claims-makers construct the *grounds* of a social problem condition when they define it, and when they specify the harm and the number of victims it creates.[7]

For example, we often hear about the problem of "drug abuse," but what are "drugs"? Do we include prescription drugs? Marijuana? Weight loss pills sold at the grocery store? Steroids? What specific instances are included in the condition constructed as a social problem? Do we include nineteen-year-old married women in the social problem of teenage moms? Do we count college students economically struggling through Harvard Law School among the poor? Claims-makers construct the parameters of the condition when they define what is included in it.

Because a social problem is a condition creating harm, claims-makers also must specify the harm. What is the harm of "obesity"? Is it limited to physical problems of people who are overweight or do we extend the notion of harm and include problems such as the low self-esteem of people who are overweight in a country prizing thinness? Or, how do we measure the harm of "drug use"? Do we define harm narrowly as the physical problems experienced by people who use drugs, or do we expand our definition of harm to include crimes committed to get money to buy drugs? Do we include harm experienced by the families and friends of people using drugs? People in their communities? Society at large?

Here is the major point: The number of people constructed as harmed by a condition will depend on how the parameters of the condition are constructed and it will depend on how harm is defined. The more included in the definition of the condition and in the definition of harm, the more harm will be found. An example is "child abuse." From time to time scientific studies claim that "nine out of ten American children are victims of child abuse." This is a "true fact," generated by defining the condition of child abuse to include *any* physical punishment done at least *one* time. With this definition, a child who is "spanked" once in her childhood is a victim of child abuse, because that is how "child abuse" has been defined.

Claims-Making Strategies

Out of the complexity of social life, claims-makers construct the grounds for social problems conditions. Some claims-making strategies are associated with encouraging audience members to evaluate a condition as a social problem. These are the characteristics of claims often shared by many very different social problems that have been successful in persuading audience members.

Typifying Stories as Implicit Definitions. If we started talking about what specifically should be included in any particular social problem condition we likely would get into many arguments. Some people, for example, evaluate the "recreational" use of marijuana as very different from cocaine or heroin use, others believe that marijuana is no different than cocaine or heroin. Good claims-makers know they can avoid these disagreements by not explicitly specifying the condition. That is, they often do not say something such as, "When I say racism, this is what I mean . . ." Rather, a claims-making strategy is to use one or two examples and then allow audience members to "fill in the blanks." So, for example, claims-makers constructing the missing children problem often begin with a story of a child kidnapped and then killed by a stranger. Audience members tend to take such typifying stories as specifying the condition at hand. Claims-makers then continue by quoting the *total* number of missing children. Claims-

makers have not lied, they never said that the typifying story described
the most common experience, but audience members are encouraged to
think that almost a million children a year are kidnapped and killed by
strangers. In this case, the objective reality is that the overwhelming majority of missing children are teens who run away from their homes or children taken by noncustodial parents after divorces.[8] While these certainly
are problems, I would argue they are problems of a different sort than children kidnapped by strangers. Yet from the perspective of claims-makers
it makes perfect sense to emphasize the particular problem of children kidnapped by strangers because this is the type of "missing children" that
most likely will encourage audience members to evaluate the condition as
intolerable.

Of course, this strategy of casting a wide net for victims has its limits, because audience members evaluate the believability of claims through their
practical experience and popular wisdom. A claim such as "One in six
women are victims of rape" might be effective in convincing audience
members that the condition is frequent, but a claim such as "All women
are victims of male violence" likely is convincing to a much smaller audience. Audience support can be lost when claims-makers cast a net of victims that is evaluated as too large to be credible.

Constructing Extreme Consequences.   This strategy follows from that of
using typifying stories rather than explicit definitions to define conditions.
We know from our practical experiences that the objective consequences
of specific experiences included in social problem conditions will range
from the "inconvenient" to the "pretty bad" to the "horrifying." Yet a
claims-making strategy is to construct grounds dramatizing *extremely horrifying* consequences. This makes sense because when we hear about social
problems they often are described in strong language—they are a "crisis,"
or a "disaster." Claims about the social problem of poverty, for example,
focus on people having much more than a "rough economic time." Claims
tend to dramatize the most *extreme* poverty with the most *devastating* consequences imaginable. Likewise, claims about drunk driving emphasize
the most extreme consequence—when such drivers kill others, the image
of "childhood obesity" becomes that of a three-year-old weighing three
hundred pounds.

A more specific claims-making strategy for constructing harm is to construct conditions as containing *only* horrifying consequences. So, for example, if I am making claims about the condition of teenage parenting, it
would not make sense for me to talk about the possible ways in which
young mothers might be better than older mothers in developing friend-
ships with their children. Such claims would not encourage audience
members to define teenage parenting as an intolerable condition. Or, if I
wanted to convince you that "unemployment" is a social problem it would

not make sense for me to talk about how some people who lose their jobs use the opportunity to gain new skills and get into more enjoyable work. Indeed, if you were listening to my claims about the terrible nature of unemployment and asked about its possible positive consequences it would make sense for me to deny the possibility of other than great harm.[9]

Claiming at the Right Time.   Audience members are motivated to listen and take claims seriously when claims are made at the right time. This strategy has two components. First, and most obviously, claims are not effective when audience members literally do not see or hear them. I think about the many social problems in my local newspaper on the morning of the terrorist attacks: there was considerable concern about the presidential election (many votes were not counted), the environment (government officials were talking about selling leases to drill for oil in Alaska), the economy (technology stocks had lost over half their value in the preceding year), school failures (American children were falling farther behind children in other countries), the high cost of prescription drugs (elderly people forced to choose between buying their prescriptions and buying food). While these were important problems one day, they simply disappeared the day of the terrorist attacks. There was no reason to make claims for almost two months—media would not have reported them, audience members would not have been interested because all conditions other than war and terrorism seemed trivial and unimportant.

This strategy to claim at the right time is not limited to national emergencies. Seasoned claims-makers know not to hold a rally or protest march on Super Bowl Sunday because no one cares. Likewise, they know their behavioral claims, such as protest marches, often will receive more media attention on weekends than weekdays, but then again, relatively few people watch the news on weekends so it is a trade-off. Successful claims-makers also know that audience members are more attentive to problems of poverty (especially the problems of poor children) during December, claims about homelessness are more effective when made in the winter than in the summer.

Second, claims are most effective when the world offers a *real-life example* of the condition at hand. The most recent example (at the time I am writing this) are the terrorist attacks. Claims-makers now regularly appear on television saying, in effect, "We told you so." They are claiming they warned the American public about problems with national security, they say they warned us that the public health system was in shambles and could not effectively respond to biological or chemical warfare, they say they made these claims throughout the 1990s—but no one listened. Claims about national security and public health now are taken very seriously. We are worried about these because we have graphic immediate experience (yet, by the time you read this, the experience of the terrorist attacks might not seem so immediate). Likewise, when Princess Diana of Wales died in an automobile crash, her death quickly led to increased claims-making about the conditions of drunk-driving and celebrity stalking. Also, the O. J. Simpson murder trial was accompanied by increased claims-making about wife abuse, and claims about global warming were ineffective until the especially hot summer of 1988.[10]

At times, the real world supplies an experience so incredibly troublesome that it leads to a *moral shock.* These are times when audience members actively seek out claims-makers because the meaning of the world is challenged.[11] In the United States in recent years, the Columbine High School massacre, the Oklahoma City bombing, and, of course, the terrorist attacks are such moral shocks. During such time public attention is riveted on the condition so claims-makers encounter audience members who are actively seeking ways to make sense of what originally seems only nonsense.

Claims about social problem grounds construct the "facts" of the condition. They answer the typical questions of audience members: What is the condition? What harm does it create? How many victims are there? But it is not enough to construct the facts, because facts in and of themselves are meaningless. Claims-makers must give meaning to the facts by constructing a *social problem frame,* which has several components.[12] The *diagnostic frame* constructs the meaning of the condition. (What type of a problem is it? Who or what causes the problem?) The *motivational frame* constructs the reasons why audience members should evaluate the condition as intolerable. (Why should audience members care?) The *prognostic frame* constructs the solutions to the problem. (What should be done?) Claims-making in practice involves simultaneously constructing typifications of conditions *and* people, problems *and* solutions, in ways motivating audience members to think *and* to feel in particular ways. For purposes of presentation, though, I will continue this chapter by focusing on the social problems work of constructing conditions (rather than people or solutions) in ways appealing to logic (rather than emotions). Chapter 4 will turn to the work of constructing images of types of people in ways appealing to emotion, and Chapter 5 then will focus on the social problems work of constructing images of solutions.

SOCIAL PROBLEMS WORK: CONSTRUCTING DIAGNOSTIC FRAMES

Claims-makers must construct a condition as a particular type of condition and this, in turn, constructs blame and responsibility.[13] This is called the *diagnostic frame.*

For example, in the United States in the 1990s we heard a great deal about the social problem of "welfare." What *kind* of a problem is this? The diagnostic frame could construct this as a problem of lack of jobs for women, of women who would like to be employed but who lack job skills or who lack someone to care for their children, or of women who lack the desire to be economically self-sufficient. We have one condition, one "fact" called welfare, but this can be constructed within several different diagnostic frames. Each of these frames constructs welfare as a particular type of condition, and in doing this, each constructs blame and responsibility for this condition.

While there are multiple ways to construct diagnostic frames of any given condition, these can be categorized in two broad types. First, frames can construct *social* causes of a condition. These include *social structure* (such as the ways family, the social welfare system, schools, or the economy are organized) and *social forces* (such as ageism, prejudice, racism, homophobia). Second, causes can be constructed as being inside *individuals* (such as behavior, personality, or beliefs).

The problem of "school failure," for example, can be framed as a *structural* problem and we could blame a lack of funding for schools, low-paying jobs leading parents to work too many hours and therefore be unable to supervise their children, or poverty that creates children unable to learn because they are hungry. The condition of school failure also can be framed as a problem of *social forces* and we could blame the too many activities that compete in a child's life with education, or we could claim our country does not really value education except as it is associated with employment. School failure also can be framed at the *individual* level and we could blame parents who do not care about their children or children who do not care about their education.

As another example, consider the problem of "crack babies," who are babies born to mothers who have used crack cocaine during their pregnancy. What creates this problem? We can look at these women and note they primarily are poor, the school system has failed to educate them, the employment market offers them no opportunities, as poor women they likely have not received adequate medical attention or medical education during their pregnancy. This is a structural diagnostic frame. We also can construct a frame blaming social forces such as racism, sexism, or classism that hurts women's chances of having the material resources to be "good mothers." These frames constructing social causes compete with an individual-level diagnostic frame that blames such women for their irresponsible and immoral behavior of using drugs during pregnancy.[14] Just as the grounds for social problems can be constructed in multiple ways (various constructions of what is included in the condition and the harm it creates), any social problem condition can have multiple diagnostic frames.

Claims-Making Strategies

Diagnostic frames answer audience members' questions about how to understand the meaning of the condition and what causes it. Specific claims-making strategies can answer these questions in ways encouraging audience members to evaluate claims as important.

Constructing Simple Diagnostic Frames. Throughout this book I have been encouraging you to keep in mind that our real life experiences are complex and multidimensional and that claims-makers must typify these experiences. But an effective claims-making strategy is to ignore this complexity and construct very simple (sometimes downright simplistic) diagnostic frames. For example, some claims-makers offer a simple diagnosis of the problem of "school failure" by claiming that the problem of schools is the lack of money, while commonly heard counterclaims construct the problem of schools as due to the failure of parents to support their children's teachers. Such claims might be effective because they seem to offer an easy route to resolution of the problem—simply give schools more money or encourage people to become better parents. While such claims are compelling in their simplicity, they most certainly ignore the real-life complexity. I would claim that schools fail to educate all too many children because they do not have enough money *and* because parents often do not take an active role in their children's education, *and* because curriculum often is not interesting to children, *and* because adult Americans tend to value education only as a route to gain job skills rather than as a route to becoming knowledgeable, and . . . and . . . and . . . You can fill in the blanks and that is my point: effective claims tend to offer simple diagnostic frames. It is primarily in college classrooms, on PBS television, and in magazines with small audiences that you will see complex diagnostic claims.

Constructing Familiarity. Although we tend to think of social problems one at a time—there is the problem of poverty and a problem of abuse and a problem of school failure—effective claims-making often links problems in ways making newly constructed problems seem nonetheless familiar to audience members.

The first specific strategy for linking social problems is called *piggybacking*, which is when a new problem is constructed as a different instance of an already existing problem.[15] The most obvious example would be the modern-day social activists organized to promote equal rights. Historically, the civil rights movement to gain equal rights for African-Americans was the first equality movement after World War II in the United States. These social activists were doubly disadvantaged in gaining support for their claims. First and most clearly, racial inequality had been a part of the

American social landscape from the beginning of this country. In popular wisdom, this inequality was not challenged, it was simply "the way things are." The second disadvantage was related: When activists started making claims in the late 1950s, the word *equality* was in the constitution of the United States, yet Americans in general did not tend to think about it. Claims made by people fighting for racial equality introduced into daily life the cultural theme of equality. This made it easier for claims to use the equality theme to fight for the rights of other types of people such as women, students, gays/lesbians, and disabled. In social constructionist terms, these claims have been piggybacked onto claims about equal rights for African-Americans.

The second specific strategy for linking social problems is called *domain expansion*, where the contents of a previously accepted social problem category are expanded. The condition of slavery, for example, began as a very narrow category including only people who were *physically* prohibited from leaving the condition. More recent claims have greatly expanded this category to construct immigrant labor as slavery and women prostitutes as slaves to their pimps. A law requiring welfare recipients to work at low-wage jobs has been constructed as slave labor. Another example of domain expansion is the category of attention deficit-hyperactivity disorder. This category started as a way to categorize *children*, but it now has expanded to include *adults*.[16]

Piggybacking and domain expansion are effective claims-making strategies for two reasons. First, a practical problem faced by claims-makers is called *audience saturation*, which happens when audience members become bored with repeatedly hearing the same claims. New claims can spark renewed interest.[17] Second, piggybacking and domain expansion are effective strategies because claims-makers can build upon the successes of previous claims-makers by linking a problem constructed as new to a problem that already has achieved some level of audience acceptance.[18]

While piggybacking and domain expansion can be effective strategies, there are limits to their use because expansions must make sense to audience members. For example, there have been recent attempts to include smoking on the list of "disabilities" covered in the Americans with Disabilities Act. If this were to occur, then employers would be mandated to offer people who smoke "reasonable accommodations" (such as smoking breaks or a place to smoke). Not surprisingly, this expansion is meeting resistance. So, too, a six-year-old boy recently was suspended from school for kissing a six-year-old girl on the cheek. Although some claims-makers classified his behavior as "sexual harassment," many Americans rather evaluated this as an indicator that claims-makers had gone too far, as "too far" is evaluated through popular wisdom. Claims-makers must be careful: Expanding the contents of a category can spark interest in claims, but expanding categories too far can backfire because audience members might stop listening to all claims about the category.

In summary, claims-makers construct the grounds (the facts of the condition) and diagnostic frames (the meaning and cause of the condition). Claims also must persuade audience members that the condition cannot be tolerated and must be changed. These constructions are called *motivational frames*. These frames seek to persuade audience members that a condition is intolerable, so they answer audience members' question, "Why should we care"?

SOCIAL PROBLEMS WORK: CONSTRUCTING MOTIVATIONAL FRAMES APPEALING TO LOGIC

There are two methods of persuasion: logic and emotions. The next chapter turns to how claims can be emotionally appealing to audience members and here we will look at how claims appeal to logic.

Cultural Themes: Evaluating the Acceptability of Conditions

People in audiences for social problems claims are members of a particular social order. Successful claims often are those that more or less appeal to audience members' understandings of *cultural themes*, which are beliefs about how the world should work.[19] Here I will focus on these themes in the *United States at the present time.*

I emphasized the "United States at the present time" because these general ideas about how the world should work are historically and culturally specific. Constructing problems in particular ways might be highly successful in one country at one time yet be totally unsuccessful in the same country at a different time or in a different country at the same time.[20] In the United States, for example, there was a social problem of "women attending college" in the late 1800s. The problem then was fear that too much "stimulation of the mind" would hurt women's reproductive capacity. While many audience members in the late 1800s evaluated such claims as believable and important, such claims now are easily dismissed as a joke. Cultural themes are *historically* specific.

So, too, themes are *culturally* specific. Consider the condition of "smoking cigarettes," which has reached the status of a taken-for-granted social problem in the United States. Yet the same condition is *not* a social problem in Japan, although Japanese people smoke *more* cigarettes than Americans. We can understand this by looking at political and cultural differences between these two countries. For example, in the 1980s the United

States threatened to impose severe trade sanctions on Japan unless they started to import more cigarettes from the United States. At a very practical level, this meant that the Japanese government could not become an antismoking claims-maker, nor could the government support antismoking claims-makers by such trade sanctions because this would have led to severe economic problems. Also, the Department of Health in the United States is in charge of all smoking-related issues but issues surrounding smoking in Japan are controlled by the Ministry of Finance, which promotes *increased* sales because the cigarette tax money is needed by federal and local governments. In brief, the meaning of cigarettes is not the same in Japan and the United States. Also, because Japanese people respect hierarchy and value harmony, people who are offended by cigarette smoke do not wish to offend others with their complaints. This means there have been very few efforts to ban smoking from workplaces.[21] How audience members likely will evaluate claims depends on the social and political culture in which claims are made.

Claims-makers can encourage audience members to support their cause by constructing conditions as violating one or more cultural themes, which are generally accepted ideas about how the world should work, and these themes are culturally and historically specific. Furthermore, claims-makers in the United States still cannot assume that their audience members will agree with one or another cultural theme even though claims-makers and audience members live in the same time and place. That is the postmodern condition: Americans are not united in our visions of how the world should work.

There are countless cultural themes in the United States at the present time. Americans, for example, often talk about the "importance of children," we hear a great deal about the "importance of health," we believe in "progress" and "technology." The following are some examples of more-or-less enduring cultural themes. I hope you will read my list, add themes of your own, and perhaps disagree with some of my themes. These are simply broadly circulating themes but clearly and most certainly not all people agree with them.

Individualism.   A primary cultural theme in the United States is the belief that individuals are important. Individualism is a theme stressing the importance of individual *freedom* and individual *responsibility*. Individualism is a cultural theme that is far more common in the United States than in any other country. It is the theme for all problems involving individual freedom (the rights of smokers / the rights of people who do not smoke, the rights of criminals / the rights of victims, the rights of students / disabled people, and so on) and individual responsibility (the responsibility to be economically self-reliant and care for the self).[22]

Nationalism. Nationalism is another word for patriotism. This is a cultural theme of the importance of devotion to the United States. Nationalism obviously is a cultural theme constructing the many social problems associated with terrorism and war. The theme of nationalism is incompatible with the theme of individualism: nationalism places the welfare of the country first, individualism places the welfare of individuals first.

Capitalism. From its beginning, the United States has had a particular kind of economic system called capitalism, which is the belief in the goodness of private property, private profit, and a free market for goods and labor. The cultural theme of capitalism also tends to lead Americans to believe that goods and services produced through private companies are better than goods or services produced by the government. The cultural theme of capitalism is constructed in a variety of problems such as unemployment and poverty; we see it in questions about privatizing the prison or education systems. The theme of nationalism is compatible with the theme of capitalism: a sign on my way to work proclaims "Celebrate Freedom! Get Up, Get Out, Go Shopping!" Appealing to patriotism also is a theme of American companies facing foreign competition who tell consumers to Buy American. Capitalism also is compatible with individualism (the belief that individual hard work leads to economic success).

Family. Although many current families certainly differ from those of the past, the importance of family remains a commonly held cultural theme and "family values" (although constructed in very different ways) remain a staple of political campaigns. Family (focusing on the good of a group of people) is incompatible with the cultural theme of individualism (focusing on the good of individuals) but family is commonly linked with nationalism ("Strong families make a strong nation") and capitalism ("A strong economy is good for families," "The economy needs strong families"). Family is a common cultural theme for problems of divorce, family violence, child day care, single mothers, teenage pregnancy, deadbeat dads (fathers who do not pay child support).

Fair Play. The cultural theme of fair play is the belief that the basic workings of the American social order should be fair to citizens. Included here are specific themes stressing the importance of *equality of opportunity* and *equality under the law.* Fair play is the cultural theme for conditions such as racism, sexism, ageism, anti-Semitism, homophobia. Fair play also is the primary theme in the "father's rights" movement, which is a group of men who argue they are discriminated against in cases of child custody.[23]

The theme of fair play always is compatible with the theme of individualism and it is theoretically compatible with the cultural themes of nationalism, capitalism, and family. The theme of fair play, though, can be used to challenge the actual workings of nationalism ("All citizens are not treated equally"), capitalism ("All workers are not treated equally"), and family ("Husbands have too much power over wives," "Parents have too much power over children").

Religion.   Religious themes define the secular world in terms of sacred texts. While there are many kinds of religion, all constructions referencing a religious cultural theme share two characteristics. First, we know they are religious themes because they construct morality as a judgment *not* made by humans: A higher order tells us that something is right or wrong. Second, while there often are claims competitions about interpretation, religious morality is contained on the pages of particular books such as the Bible or the Koran. Religious themes often are found in claims about conditions such as school prayer (constructed as good), pregnancy outside marriage or abortion (constructed as not good). Signs or bumper stickers saying "God Is On Our Side" combine nationalist and religious themes; religious themes easily can be combined with themes of families, but are incompatible with individualism. Some specific religious themes are compatible with the cultural theme of fair play ("All men are brothers," "Do unto others as you would have them do unto you") and others are incompatible ("Men and women are governed by different rules and different expectations").

Claims-Making Strategies

Claims-makers must motivate audience members to evaluate a condition as intolerable, and one way to do this is by constructing conditions as violating cultural themes. There are three claims-making strategies associated with effective motivational frames constructing cultural themes.

Constructing Multiple Cultural Themes.   Although some cultural themes are incompatible, many are compatible.[24] Motivational frames can construct *multiple* cultural themes violated by a condition and this is an effective claims-making strategy. Equivalent to the strategy of domain expansion where the content of claims about a condition's grounds is expanded, claims-makers can expand the number of cultural themes constructed as violated by a condition. For example, diagnostic frames about the problem of wife abuse have expanded over the past twenty years from emphasizing how wife abuse violates the theme of fair play (equal rights for women) to how it violates the theme of family, to how it interferes with women's employment (capitalism), to how the extent of such abuse in the United States poses a problem for the entire social order (nationalism). Because individual audience members might not personally believe strongly in any one cultural theme, constructing multiple themes—reasons why the condition is harmful—increases the chances of support.

Consider the much different example of "factory farming," which is a condition where animals are bred and raised for food in inhumane environments. How might claims-makers convince audience members that this condition cannot be tolerated? Obviously, there is a possible theme of "animal rights" (the inhumane treatment of animals). Yet in a country dominated by people who eat meat, there is not widespread support for this theme. Claims-makers might gain more audience support by constructing the environmental problems associated with large-scale factory farming. Yet while more Americans support a cultural theme of the importance of the environment than the importance of animal rights, environmental themes still are not the major concerns of many Americans. Claims-makers, however, might construct the health problems associated with "eating meat." This might gain them far more support because the importance of "health" is one of the currently dominant themes in the United States.[25] Critically, it really does not matter *why* audience members are motivated to evaluate claims as important. Hence, a claims-making strategy is to construct diagnostic frames to include several cultural themes; the more cultural themes constructed as violated by the condition, the more likely at least one of them will appeal to audience members.

Constructing Popular Worry. Recall that claims-makers often link claims about conditions (piggybacking) and this encourages audience members' interest and builds upon the success of previous claims-makers. Likewise, claims can construct new conditions as violating the same cultural themes as previous conditions. Each newly constructed violation of the same theme can add a sense of urgency to all conditions constructed within similar motivational frames. Consider, for example, the multiple discrete problems violating the cultural theme of the importance of family. Over the past years various groups of claims-makers have constructed problems such as divorce, single-parent families, fathers who do not pay child support, family violence in its many forms, decreasing parental authority, parents who do not sufficiently supervise their children, increasing cohabitation outside marriage, and poverty as violating the cultural theme of the importance of family. Each one is a problem, yet as the number of discrete problems increase, so too do evaluations that the family is threatened.

Constructing Conditions as Symbolic. Claims linking several problems can be effective in expressing cultural worries that are difficult to address directly. As such, successful claims sometimes are about far more than they appear to be on the surface. Such claims are *symbolic*. Consider, for exam-

ple, the multiple fears about children beginning in the 1960s. First, claims-
makers constructed the problem of child abuse, then, piggybacking on to
these claims, there was a rapid succession of claims constructing problems
such as adolescent prostitution, child pornography, tainted Halloween
candy, and missing children. In the case of child victims of many sorts, the
statistics (indicators of objective reality) do *not* easily support the claim that
each of these conditions was new (in the case of child abuse) or that they
were widespread (in the case of tainted Halloween candy, missing children, and adolescent prostitution).

We can understand why claims about threatened children have been so
successful by thinking about the more diffuse cultural worries in the
United States. In particular, the 1960s to the present have been a time when
Americans in general have been worried about the future of the country.
The Vietnam War, student demonstrations, loss of faith in the government
(Watergate, Iran-Contra, Travelgate, illegal campaign contributions, sexual
affairs between politicians and student interns, and so on) as well as perceived failures in traditional institutions such as family and education, and
now terrorism have led to an uneasiness among the general population.
There also have been major changes in relationships between women and
men, between Anglo- African- Hispanic- and Asian-Americans, between
people whose families immigrated here a hundred years ago and those
newly arriving. The postmodern condition has changed the social landscape and created an incredibly diverse population and this has shifted political power and led to new concerns and demands for social change. But
claims-making about wars, student rebellions, government and family failures, and changing relationships among people are difficult to make. Each
of these can be constructed in many different ways. Because they are complex conditions leading to competing evaluations it is difficult to obtain
significant support from audience members. But Americans in general—
regardless of our many disagreements—*can* unite around worry about
children.

This theme of "endangered children" is symbolic of more diffuse fears
that are difficult to discuss. Likewise, when audience members hear constructions about the problem of "street crime" they also can be encouraged
to think about more general fears about race and social class. The specific
problem of street crime therefore is symbolic of the larger, and more difficult, problem of race and class. In the same way, the problem of "pedophile
priests" is symbolic of more diffuse fears about children and sexuality. It
also is a way for claims-makers to criticize the Catholic church, which has
been unwilling to listen to claims made by a variety of people about the
need for changes in the church. In each of these instances, audience members can be persuaded to worry about the specific condition when that condition becomes symbolic of larger, more diffuse worries.[26]

Cultural themes are socially circulating and widely held ideas about the ways the world should work. Successful claims can construct images of conditions as violating one or more of these themes. Yet because our post-modern world is characterized by a lack of agreement, claims-makers cannot assume that all audience members will support particular themes. This is why it is social problems *work*.

SOCIAL PROBLEMS WORK: CONSTRUCTING SOCIAL PROBLEM OWNERSHIP

Constructing conditions in ways leading audience members to evaluate them as social problems is what claims-makers must do if they are to win the social problems game. Yet recall that this game never is completely "won" or "lost" because social life is ongoing. Audience members can change their minds or be persuaded by later counterclaims; conditions in the objective world can change, which calls into question the believability or importance of earlier claims. Claims-makers who apparently win at one time or in one place must maintain their win and this means keeping audience support. This work is far easier when a group of claims-makers obtains social problem ownership.

Social problem ownership happens when one particular social problem diagnostic frame becomes the taken-for-granted frame for that problem.[27] Claims-makers constructing the taken-for-granted frame become the accepted authority on that problem, they are high on the hierarchy of credibility. They *own* the problem so to speak, so their claims are given more attention than are claims constructing alternative frames.

Consider the example of the social change group called Mothers Against Drunk Driving (MADD). These claims-makers had several possibilities in constructing a social problem condition involving the components of alcohol, cars, roads, and people who drive these cars on these roads after drinking alcohol. They could have constructed this as a problem caused by cars that allow even the most sober drivers to travel at unsafe speeds, they could have constructed this as a problem caused by roads that twist and turn and are in such poor condition that they challenge even the most sober of drivers, they could have constructed this as a problem caused by the lack of public transportation that gives people—drunk or not—few alternatives to driving cars. And, of course, they could have constructed this as a problem of alcohol because, without alcohol, the problem would go away. But claims-makers in MADD constructed "drinking-driving" as a problem of *people* who drink and drive. Over time, this has become the taken-for-granted construction of this problem. Claims constructing drunk *driving* as a problem caused by drunk *drivers* will tend to succeed, claims offering alternative definitions have a more difficult time gaining audience support.

In the same way, alcoholism now is constructed as a disease rather than as a defect of character; learning disabilities is constructed as a biological problem of students, not a problem with the ways schools are organized. Social problem ownership is a powerful component in the hierarchy of credibility because a particular frame often is simply assumed to be the truth. Such accepted constructions have the possibility of becoming a part of popular wisdom. Because audience members evaluate the believability and importance of claims in part through popular wisdom, social problems ownership is power to influence the likely effectiveness of future social problem claims.

THE SOCIAL PROBLEMS WORK OF
CONSTRUCTING CONDITIONS

Within social constructionist perspectives, what we call social problems are a consequence of human activity. People do things and say things to persuade others that a condition is at hand, that it is morally intolerable, that something must be done. Clearly, because our world and our experiences in it are complex, claims-makers must typify. Out of the complexity of lived reality, they must construct images of particular types of conditions, they must construct these typified conditions as having particular types of meaning, and they must motivate audience members to evaluate these conditions as intolerable and therefore in need of change. This is social problems work. Yet encouraging audience members to *think* in particular ways about social problem conditions is not always sufficient, indeed, it is not always even necessary. Successful claims can be organized around encouraging audience members to *feel* in particular ways and this is accomplished by constructing images of the suffering of victims and the evil of villains. That is our next topic.

NOTES

1.   Although gaining new recruits to a social movement involves more than convincing them that a condition exists and that something needs to be done (for example, Snow and Benford, 1988, 1992; Gamson, 1988), my focus here is on how social problems can be constructed in ways that are successful in persuading audience members to evaluate the claims as believable and important.

2.   According to Hilgartner and Bosk (1988), limited carrying capacities is the most important reason why most potential problems do not gain attention at all and why many that do get initial attention do not hold it for long.

3. This competition for our time, concern, and money is increasing as our world becomes increasingly available to us through proliferating mass media and the World Wide Web. In an analysis of forty years of "Gallop Poll Most Important Problem" questions, McCombs and Zhu (1995) found evidence of an increasing diversity of problems and an increasing lack of public agreement on what important problems are. This, in turn, leads to a faster rate of issue turnover.

4. For examples see Smith and Windes (1997) and Fetner (2001) for "progay" and "antigay" claims; McCright and Dunlap (2000) for the global warming controversy; Williams and Williams (1995, excerpted in *Social Problems: Constructionist Readings*) for the fathers' rights movement as a countermovement of feminism; McCaffrey and Keys (2000) and Vanderford (1989) for the abortion controversy.

5. Sasson (1995, excerpted in *Social Problems: Constructionist Readings*) examines crime frames and their sponsors.

6. Such disagreements among activists often remain back stage and are not a part of public claims-making activities. See J. Gamson (1997) for disagreements among one group of gay rights activists and Benford (1993) and Kubal (1998) for disagreements among proponents of nuclear disarmament.

7. This terminology is from an analytic framework advanced by Toulmin (1958) and used by Best (1990) in his examination of claims-making about endangered children. In this framework, arguments (of any type) have three components: *grounds*—which are the basic "facts," *conclusions*—what should be done (equivalent to prognostic claims in the Snow and Benford (1988) framework which is a topic in Chapter 5) and *warrants*—why something should be done (equivalent to motivational claims in the Snow and Benford (1988) framework).

8. See Best (1989) for an empirical example of the importance of, and problems with, statistics used to construct the missing-children problem.

9. For this tilt in social problems claims toward dramatizing extreme conditions leading to extreme harm see Johnson (1995, excerpted in *Social Problems: Constructionist Readings*) for child abuse, Best (1990) for missing children, Loseke (1992) for wife abuse.

10. For the examination of relationships between claim success and objective indicators that can be understood as indicating global warming, see Ungar (1992). Also, Paul (1994) claims that the social problem condition of sexual harassment was successful because Anita Hill, the "Tailhook" affair, and Senator Robert Packwood's "indiscretions" supplied a constant source of real-life happenings that easily could be constructed as graphic instances of the condition of sexual harassment.

11. For further clarification of moral shocks see Jasper and Poulsen (1995). Moral *shock* can be related to moral *panic* when conditions elicit much more than what might be called a reasonable fear. See Best (1999, excerpted in *Social Problems: Constructionist Readings*) for moral panic surrounding random violence, Litt and McNeil (1994, excerpted in *Social Problems: Constructionist Readings*) for the moral panic surrounding crack babies, Ungar (1990) for moral panics and the military-industrial complex, Zatz (1987) for moral panics about Chicano youth gangs, Goode and Ben-Yehuda (1994) for relationships between moral panics and categories of deviance, Welch (2000) for moral panic and flag burning, Jenkins (1992) for moral panics in Great Britain.

12. Originally developed by Erving Goffman (1974), frame as defined by W.

Gamson and his colleagues (1992:384) is a "central organizing principle that holds together and gives coherence and meaning to a diverse array of symbols." Snow and Benford (1988:137) define frame as "an interpretive schemata that simplifies and condenses the world 'out there' by selectively punctuating and encoding objects, situations, events, experiences and sequences of action within one's present or past environment." See Snow and Benford (1988) for an elaboration of the contents of diagnostic, prognostic, and motivational frames.

13.   According to social policy analyst Deborah Stone (1989), the very foundation of social policy lies in claims-making that assigns cause, blame, and responsibility for the problem to be resolved.

14.   Litt and McNeil (1994, excerpted in *Social Problems: Constructionist Readings*) discuss these varying diagnostic frames for the problem of "crack babies."

15.   The concepts of piggybacking and domain expansion were developed by Best (1990). I also draw from Hilgartner and Bosk (1988), who examined the principles of selection for attention to social problems in public arenas.

16.   Conrad and Potter (2000) examine this expansion of ADHD to include adults. Jenness and Broad (1997, excerpted in *Social Problems: Constructionist Readings*) discuss how the civil rights frame has expanded over time.

17.   Audience members also become bored and inattentive when proposed solutions to social problems are tried but yield less than successful consequences (Downs, 1972).

18.   Hilgartner and Bosk (1988) advance a series of theoretical propositions for which social problem claims will receive public attention. Among other principles of selection are: saturation with redundant claims dedramatizes problems, and new symbols or events must continually renew the drama or concern with the problem will decline.

19.   There are many alternative terms and frameworks for discussing such cultural evaluations. For example, Waller (1936) talks of "mores," Merton (1971) of "social values," Fuller and Myers (1941) of "social norms" or "cherished values," Linde (1993) of "cultural coherence systems." W. Gamson (1988:220) defines cultural themes as "frames and related symbols that transcend specific issues and suggest larger cultural views. It is a concept akin to such terms as ideology, values, belief systems, and *Weltanschauung*." He focuses on cultural themes such as "technology is good" and "self-reliance is important." In other theoretical frameworks, Ibarra and Kitsuse (1993) discuss the importance of "rhetorical idioms" such as the rhetorics of loss, entitlement, endangerment, unreason, and calamity. Williams (1995) focuses on different ways to construct "the public good." See also Lowney (1999, excerpted in *Social Problems: Constructionist Readings*) for her examination of how television talk shows construct morality and Schneider (1984) for a discussion of how morality is a proper and important topic for social constructionist examinations.

20.   For example, Linders (1998) looks at abortion as a social problem in the United States from 1840 to 1880 and in Sweden from 1910 to 1940. She found that although claims-making in both countries shared similarities, it yielded very different social policies: abortion in the United States was criminalized, in Sweden it was legalized. Nardi (1998) compares European countries with America and argues that claims supporting the acceptability of homosexuality are easier to make in Eu-

rope. Soesilo and Washburn (1994) examine differences in American and Indonesian media accounts of the "crisis in the Gulf." Nakagawa (1995) offers a summary of differences between the social construction perspective as practiced in the United States and in Japan. Also, see Note 1, Chapter 1.

21. See Ayukawa (2001, excerpted in *Social Problems: Constructionist Readings*) for this examination of smoking in Japan. For a comparison, Troyer and Markle (1983) discuss the antismoking social movement in the United States. Furedi (2001, excerpted in *Social Problems: Constructionist Readings)* examines why "bullying" is a social problem in Great Britain but not in the United States.

22. Bellah and his colleagues (1985) offer a thorough examination of the cultural theme of individualism; Lowney (1999, excerpted in *Social Problems: Constructionist Readings*) explores the cultural themes of individualism and family in the recovery movement.

23. See Williams and Williams (1995, excerpted in *Readings in Thinking About Social Problems*) for their analysis of the cultural theme of equality in the fathers' rights movement.

24. For an empirical example of competing themes see Coughlin's (1994) analysis of the "individualist" and "communitarian" themes in the social policy debate about the problem of traffic congestion. For how themes can be combined see Loseke's (1997) examination of the construction of "charity."

25. Kunkel (1995, excerpted in *Social Problems: Constructionist Readings*) examines the expanding diagnostic frame in claims about factory farming as a social problem.

26. See Jenkins (1995, excerpted in *Social Problems: Constructionist Readings*) for the symbolic value of pedophile priests; Cavender (1998, excerpted in *Social Problems: Constructionist Readings*) for the symbolic value of crime on reality television; Berger (2002, excerpted in *Social Problems: Constructionist Readings*) for the symbolic value of the "Jew" in Nazi Germany; Best (1990) for the symbolic value of the child victim; Scheingold (1995) for the symbolic value of street crime; Stein (2001) for the symbolic value of homosexuals in a small community struggling with problems of social change.

27. The concept of social problem ownership was developed by Gusfield (1981:10): the "concept of ownership of public problems is derived from the recognition that in the arenas of public opinion and debate all groups do not have equal power, influence, and authority to define the reality of the problem. The ability to create and influence the public definition of a problem is . . . 'ownership.'" For a complete examination of the drinking-driving problem, see Gusfield (1975, 1976, 1981).

4

Constructing People

Halfway through my Family Violence class today I realized that many students weren't really listening. Indeed, one woman was taking the opportunity to catch up on her sleep. Obviously, they were bored. I was talking about how Americans tend to ignore behaviors such as slapping, pushing, and shoving and worry only when violence seems very extreme. My students didn't buy my argument that we should take this violence seriously. To them, slapping, pushing, and shoving were normal, they were no big deal. I needed to get their attention. I told them a true story of a woman named Gloria who had been a nurse. One day, her husband became very angry with her because, while cleaning their apartment, she had moved his plants around and had dropped his favorite marijuana plant and several of its stems had broken off. He slapped her. Gloria was a small woman and he was a large man and his slap was so strong that she lost her balance and fell into a bookcase. The bookcase fell on her and her spine shattered. She'll never walk again. But the judge in the case ruled that the husband wasn't guilty of a real crime because, after all, it was just a "slap." Gloria's injury, he ruled, was caused by her bad luck to be standing next to a bookcase that wasn't stable. My students now were awake and interested. They wanted to know what happened to Gloria, they were very troubled that something with such horrible consequences could be categorized as not a crime.

Within a scene of competition, social problems claims-makers must persuade audience members that their claims are important. In the previous chapter I focused on how claims-makers construct grounds (the "facts" of the condition) and diagnostic frames (the meaning and the cause of the condition). I also discussed how motivational frames (why audience members should care) could be constructed by claiming the condition violated one or more cultural themes (general beliefs about how the world should work). That chapter focused on how claims might encourage audience members to *think* about *conditions* in particular ways. This chapter looks at other kinds of social problems work: the work of constructing images of *people* (victims and villains), which simultaneously is the work of encour-

aging audience members to *feel* the moral outrage associated with evaluating conditions as social problems.

SOCIAL PROBLEMS WORK: CONSTRUCTING
MOTIVATIONAL FRAMES APPEALING TO EMOTION

While claims-makers can construct motivational frames encouraging
audience members to evaluate a condition as a social problem because it
violates cultural themes, this type of frame might not be enough. Indeed,
while I argued in Chapter 3 that claims-makers might gain increased support by *expanding* motivational frames to include more than one cultural
theme, it also is possible to construct effective motivational frames that *ignore* these themes and appeal only to emotion.

The importance of motivating audiences through emotional appeals
makes sense for at least three reasons. First, a characteristic of the postmodern condition is a lack of agreement about cultural themes. So, while
most Americans believe that capitalism is moral and good, others believe
it is immoral and bad. While many Americans believe that families are
critically important for the well-being of people, others believe family is
a relic of the past that should be discarded. Some Americans believe we
need more individual rights while others believe we already have too
many rights. Also, given the multiple questions about the social process of
doing science, claims supported by the logic of scientific research can be
challenged and criticized. The first reason why it makes sense for claims-
makers to motivate audience members through appeals to emotions is that
they are less risky appeals than those encouraging audience members to
think in particular ways. Claims encouraging audience members to feel in
particular ways are less likely to be challenged.

Second, Americans seem to be increasingly concerned with how we feel.
Questions like "How should we *think* about this?" now often are replaced
with questions like "How should we *feel* about this?" National political campaigns, for example, now revolve as much (or more) around our emotional
reactions to the "personalities" of candidates as our logical evaluations of the
strength of candidates' plans and platforms. Encouraging audience members' emotional reactions to social problems claims is in keeping with this
larger social trend of focusing on feeling rather than thinking.

Third, the category of social problem is as much about how we feel as
about how we think. Most obviously, we take conditions seriously when
we fear them, we can experience anger or outrage about the harm done by
social problem conditions. Other emotions are associated with our reactions to victims and villains: we can *feel* sympathy when we *think* about social problem victims, we can *feel* anger or hatred when we *think* about social

problem villains. How we think and how we feel about social problems are inextricably related. Therefore, appeals to logic might not be sufficient—indeed, appeals to logic might not be even necessary—if claims successfully appeal to emotion and persuade audience members to be fearful about the condition and/or to feel sympathy for victims and/or anger toward villains.[1]

This focus on emotions first leads us to examine how motivational frames can be constructed using *humanitarian themes.* What humanitarian themes share is their appeal to a human desire to make the world a better place, to help those in need, to stop pain and suffering. There was a segment on the news yesterday about the 343 firefighters who died saving the lives of others after the terrorist attacks. That segment contained very little information, there were few "facts," it did not try to persuade me to think about these people. Yet it was a effective claim about the evils of terrorism because it made me feel sad about those who lost their lives and their family and friends who continue to grieve. Humanitarian themes focus on victims and their suffering. We can be motivated to evaluate a condition as a social problem by our feelings of sympathy, compassion, or pity for victims. These humanitarian themes appeal to the noble side of people—our capacity to care about others.

But second, a focus on emotions also leads us to understand that not all social problems claims are so uplifting in their appeal to the noble side of people. Claims encouraging feelings at times can appeal to our human capacity to hate and to seek revenge. These appeals can be accomplished through constructions of villains, the causes of the harm experienced by victims. When we *think* about social problem villains we can be motivated by *feelings* such as hatred, revulsion, hostility, or loathing, we can *feel* the need to seek revenge for the harm they created.

Claims-makers therefore can construct motivational frames encouraging audience members to feel in particular ways. This is possible because, although we tend to think of feeling as something very personal, each culture nonetheless contains *feeling rules,* which are general conventions surrounding how we "think we should feel."[2] Motivational frames can be successful if they make good use of these cultural feeling rules, which surround both the sympathy associated with social problem victims and the hatred associated with social problem villains.

SOCIAL PROBLEMS WORK: CONSTRUCTING VICTIMS DESERVING SYMPATHY

Who or what is victimized by a social problem? While nature or animals can be constructed as a victim, victims most often are constructed as *peo-*

ple: there are crime victims, unemployed workers, people without medical care, and coal miners with black lung disease.[3] Victims also can be constructed as *future* people such as in claims about environmental ruin, nuclear war, an insolvent Social Security system, or a too-high federal budget deficit. Constructions of victims might be of people in general such as in claims that "crime reduces the quality of life for us all."

Now, it would be fairly easy if claims needed only to construct victims as people harmed by a social problem condition. Claims constructing the social problem grounds do that when they construct the number of people harmed. But the meaning of the word *victim* in popular understandings as well in the social problems game, is far more complicated because of cultural feeling rules. First, I must be clear that in discussing these rules I am certainly *not* claiming they are good or beneficial. On the contrary, I personally would argue these cultural feeling rules surrounding sympathy are very rigid and lead to denying sympathy and assistance to many people who are greatly harmed. Yet despite this, the rules remain.

Cultural Feeling Rules: Sympathy and Help

Not all people experiencing harm are evaluated as "victims" because Americans tend to categorize a person as a "victim" only when we believe the person *deserves sympathy*. The status of victim and the emotion of sympathy go hand in hand. So, we need to examine the feeling rules surrounding sympathy. What are the characteristics of people typically judged as worthy of sympathy?[4]

First and foremost, Americans generally believe that people who are *not responsible* for the harm they experience are worthy of sympathy. This is a consequence of the cultural theme promoting the importance of individual responsibility. Consider an example of the social problem of rape. Rather than asking why men rape, audience concern often is with the characteristics and behaviors of women victims. Audience members often ask questions such as: Where were these women when they were raped? What were they wearing? Did they try to stop their attackers? The underlying question is about victim *responsibility*. What audience members really are asking is: Did women do something to cause the harm they experienced? Within cultural feeling rules surrounding sympathy, if the answer to this question is yes, then a woman experiencing rape is responsible for it. While she has been harmed, she is not given the social status of victim because she is evaluated as not worthy of sympathy.

Constructing victims as not responsible for the harm they experience is necessary for audience members to feel sympathy. But this is not enough, because American audiences tend to give a victim status to, and feel sympathy toward, people who also are evaluated as *moral*. Of course, different audience members will have different evaluations of what is and is not moral. But in general, think about all the ways Americans construct social categories of people as moral (or as not moral). We categorize individuals into social categories such as "hard-working guy" or "no-good jerk," "dedicated mother and wonderful wife" or "slut." While we could quibble about the details, and although you personally might not agree, a social category such as "nun" often is much higher on a hierarchy of social morality than a category such as "prostitute." In general, audience members feel sympathy for, and therefore are more apt to assign victim status to, people in *higher moral categories*.[5] Harm to people in higher moral categories is, in general, given more attention than the same harm experienced by people in lower moral categories. Because audience members use their understandings of cultural feeling rules surrounding sympathy to evaluate claims, constructing victims as moral and as not responsible are important claims-making tasks.

Third, Americans tend to feel sympathy toward people who are in *very* troublesome conditions, and we tend to evaluate troublesome by comparing others' troubles to our own. What this means is that if you are struggling to live on $15,000 a year it is unlikely you will feel much sympathy for a person losing a $200,000 a year job who must now must live on a mere $150,000 a year.

Fourth and finally, the feeling rules surrounding sympathy link this emotion with a behavioral expression of *help*. In our daily lives we offer help (or at least believe help should be offered) to people we evaluate as worthy of sympathy. When claims motivate audience members to feel sympathy toward a social problem victim, they simultaneously motivate audience members to support claims that victims must be helped.

What we have here is very complicated: Claims must persuade audience members that a social problem condition leads to victims but cultural feeling rules surrounding sympathy are anything but straightforward. We tend to reserve the status of victim for people we feel sympathy toward and we feel sympathy when our evaluations lead us to conclude that *morally good people are greatly harmed through no fault of their own*. Such constructions are motivational frames when they construct humanitarian themes. Why should audience members care? They should care because good people are unjustly harmed.

Claims-Making Strategies

These feeling rules surrounding sympathy lead to some predictable claims-making strategies for constructing typifications of victims. Technically, these are strategies for constructing social problem grounds because they establish the "facts" of the case by describing the characteristics of victims. Yet they do far more because they simultaneously are motivational frames encouraging audience members to feel that an injustice is being done that must be stopped.

Constructing Victims as Suffering Horribly.   Because successful claims about grounds often construct very horrifying conditions, it follows that victims are constructed as suffering horribly. We do not hear about the "crack babies" who grow up healthy, we do not hear about couples who manage to stop violence before it becomes the terrible violence of "wife abuse," we do not hear about previously "poor single mothers" who now are college graduates with good jobs and good children. Recall that one strategy for convincing audience members to evaluate a condition as intolerable is to cast a wide net and claim that the condition produces a great many victims. There is a related strategy: the more victims are constructed as suffering, the more effective claims tend to be in motivating audience members. The more victims suffer, the more we worry and feel sympathy.

Constructing Potential Victims as Anyone.   We saw in the previous chapter how successful claims tend to magnify the extent of conditions. At times, claims include almost everyone as a victim. Such claims simultaneously construct anyone as a *potential* victim. We hear claims, for example, that any woman is a potential victim of rape or wife abuse, that anyone might contact the HIV virus, that unemployment might strike anyone, that the next terrorist attack might be anywhere. Such claims construct social problems as equal opportunity conditions because we cannot predict who will become the next victim. When a condition is constructed as victimizing everyone or anyone, claims are constructing victimization as *random*. Such constructions of random victims are multiply beneficial for claims-makers. For example, they encourage audience members to evaluate victims as worthy of sympathy because if victimization is random then nothing victims do or have done leads to their victimization. It also encourages audience members to believe they have an objective interest in stopping the condition: If anyone can be a victim then audience members or their loved ones are potential victims. Such claims encourage audience members to be fearful for their own selves and fear is a powerful motivation to take claims seriously.[6]

More subtly, there are other benefits to constructing conditions as producing random victims. Consider the problem of "crime." Objectively speaking, there are clear racial and social class characteristics associated both with being a criminal and with becoming a crime victim. But racial and/or social class constructions are risky in America, where all too many audience members evaluate claims through racial and/or social class biases. Claims likely will be more successful if race and social class are ignored and this can be done by constructing conditions as producing random victims.[7]

Constructing Victim Purity. Cultural feeling rules emphasize that sympathy should be felt for innocent and morally worthy people, so effective claims therefore emphasize that victims are in no way responsible for the harm they experience. For example, the American public in general did not worry about the devastation created by AIDS when the condition was constructed as harming homosexual men and intravenous drug users. Powerful middle-class and heterosexual audiences could evaluate victims as responsible for the harm they experienced. The condition of AIDS started receiving attention when claims linked it with sick children who contracted it from tainted blood transfusions, and innocent women who contracted it from their wandering husbands. In other words, AIDS began receiving widespread attention when victims were constructed as worthy of sympathy as this worthiness is evaluated through cultural feeling rules.[8]

Constructing victim purity also is an issue when victims are members of devalued groups. Prostitutes, for example, are constructed by some claims-makers as "pools of contagion," villains responsible for the spread of AIDS into the heterosexual population. Yet social change groups advocating for the rights of prostitutes (such as COYOTE, Call Off Your Old Tired Ethics) construct prostitutes as victims of discrimination and as women who are *better* than nonprostitutes in using the methods of safe sex. It is not surprising that there is considerable claims-making competition surrounding constructing the "purity" of victims. If victims are evaluated as responsible for their plights or as morally suspect then they are not deserving of sympathy and assistance.[9]

Constructing Cultural Biases in Sympathy Evaluation. The American social order contains multiple biases for—and against—offering sympathy to particular types of people. For example, while audience members certainly differ in their personal evaluations, there are general *positive* biases for feeling sympathy toward, and offering assistance to, elderly people and children. These types of people are easier to construct as victims than are adults. There also are many *negative* biases against types of people constructed as deviant—it is far more difficult to construct prisoners or prostitutes as worthy of sympathy than it is to construct to construct "hard-working folk" as victims. Furthermore, among the most powerful middle-class audiences in the general public, there are biases against offering sympathy to poor people. Constructing victims of crime as middle-class people, for example, tends to be more successful in encouraging sympathy than claims constructing poor or minority victims. Therefore, we can understand why claims about social problems such as wife abuse, rape, and crime tend to focus on victims who are white, well-educated, and middle-class. While such people certainly can be victims, it remains that social problems of all types are more likely to produce victims who are far less privileged. So again, despite the objective reality of who becomes victimized, typifying victims as similar to people who constitute powerful audiences (race, social class) is a good claims-making strategy.

Personalizing Victims. While American audiences want to know how many people are affected by a social problem condition, it is not enough for claims-makers to construct grounds that include only statistical estimates of the number of victims. Big numbers and the scientific studies on which they are based do not easily spark emotional reactions. We seem to want to know the details of how conditions affect people and such details can be found only in *narratives,* which are personal stories of individual lives. In Chapter 3 I talked about the importance of typifying stories because they could lead audience members to conclude that the typifying story was the "average" story. These stories, though, can do more because they are a way to encourage audience members' feelings of sympathy.

Personal stories can be about regular people who might seem similar to audience members and therefore encourage them to support the social problem because "this might be me." The semifictional characters of Francine and Miki Hughes in *The Burning Bed* are claims about a condition called wife abuse and about the categories of people called the battered woman and the abusive man. *Adam's Story,* a movie about a child abducted and brutally killed by a stranger, constructs the missing-children problem and the missing child as a special category of victim. Rodney King was just a regular guy until a home video captured images that were used to construct a graphic and detailed image of the condition of "police brutality."

This strategy of personalizing social problem conditions also works well when it uses stories of celebrities. Many Americans are fascinated with the stories of celebrities and these stories also serve to emphasize how *anyone* can be victimized by a social problem condition. For example, the life stories of Rock Hudson, Magic Johnson, and Greg Louganis have been used repeatedly in making claims about the social problem of AIDS; the death of basketball star Len Bias in 1986 of a cocaine overdose led to a flurry of claims and the beginning of a "war against drugs"; Michael J. Fox's is the most common story currently told about Parkinson's disease; and so on. Read celebrities' stories such as those in *People Magazine,* or as told to Oprah, as claims about the horrid consequences of social problems conditions.

In conclusion, there are claims-making strategies in constructing typifications of social problems victims that are associated with persuading audience members that victims deserve sympathy and its behavioral expression of help. These all are sensible given socially circulating cultural feeling rules. Claims constructing victims tend to appeal to humanitarian themes. Audience members should feel sympathy, they should evaluate claims as important because good people are greatly harmed through no fault of their own.

SOCIAL PROBLEMS WORK: CONSTRUCTING VILLAINS DESERVING CONDEMNATION

Victims are people harmed by the condition, *villains* are the things (social structure or social forces) or people constructed by diagnostic frames as responsible for the condition. Within cultural feeling rules, blame and responsibility should be accompanied by the emotions of hatred or condemnation and this should be accompanied by the behavioral expression of punishment. But as in the case of evaluating the sympathy worthiness of victims, complicated reasoning can surround assigning blame, and feeling rules do not necessarily promote condemnation even when blame is assigned.

Cultural Feeling Rules: Blame, Hatred, and Punishment

We begin again within the logic of everyday life. Do we blame all things or people who do harm? Of course not. Just as we ask a series of questions about victims, we want to know details about villains before we are comfortable evaluating them as things or people who can be blamed, and then we have further questions before we evaluate them as things or people who should be hated and punished.

First, we tend to assign blame only when we believe that things or people who do harm *intended* to do harm. So, we have a general term called "accident" to categorize conditions where harm was created but where we evaluate the harm as not intended. This can make it very difficult to blame social structures (such as the economy) because "intent" implies conscious action and social structures and social forces are not capable of that. This tendency also can make it difficult to assign blame to individuals when they offer a believable counterclaim that the harm they created was an accident.

We therefore tend to assign blame only when we believe the thing or person creating the harm intended to create this harm. Yet assigning blame does not necessarily mean we will feel the emotion of hatred. We continue by making another evaluation: Was there a *good reason* for creating harm? Our economy, of course, creates much harm—jobs that pay less than a living wage, business cycles creating recession, unemployment, and financial need; there are many problems when factories move to where labor is cheaper and towns simply vanish because the work is gone. This *is* harm, it *does* create victims. Because people often intend to do this harm (such as when the chairman of the Federal Reserve raises interest rates making it difficult for people to buy homes), we can *blame* the economy for these conditions. But many audience members will not go the next step and feel hatred because the cultural feeling rule encourages feeling hatred only when the harm is done for "no good reason." The cultural theme promoting the goodness of capitalism can define harm as done for a "good reason" and therefore something that cannot be condemned. I also think of when my sister called me and said she felt like a "child abuser." She had taken her children to their doctor because they suffered from terrible allergies, but the allergy tests required that they be stuck numerous times with needles. Was she a "child abuser"? Few people would say yes, even though she did sit and watch as they experienced pain and even though her children blamed her for taking them to the doctor's. But because she did it for a "good reason," I assured her she was not a "child abuser," who is a person who hurts children "for no good reason."

When we look at how audience members evaluate "good reasons" for harm, we find many problems in our postmodern world because what is a "good reason" for one person might not be evaluated as a "good reason" by another. Some men, for example, batter their wives claiming that something these women did or said was intolerable (in other words, they claim the women were responsible) and so there was a "good reason" to hit. Some absentee landlords say they charge outrageous prices because tenants destroy their property and the money is needed to fix it, some industrial polluters say this cannot be changed—the costs of modifying their equipment to stop pollution would force them out of business and all their workers would lose their jobs.

Our cultural feeling rules surrounding hatred and condemnation are very complex. It can be difficult to assign blame when we have the alternative category of "accident." We feel hatred only when we evaluate the harm as done for "no good reason." This means that constructing blame is risky for claims-makers because there are many opportunities for claims competitions.

Complexity in these feeling rules is magnified because while Americans have a tendency to prefer diagnostic frames blaming individuals (rather than social structures or social forces), we also believe that experiences in childhood often shape adult behavior. So, for example, we often hear the claim that "abused children become abusive adults." Despite what child abusers do, how can we hate them when we believe they act so terribly only because they, themselves, were victims in the past?

Claims-Making Strategies

This leads to a claims-making problem: While encouraging emotional reactions is a powerful claims-making tool, diagnostic claims constructing blame might lead to counterclaims; it is difficult to construct a typification of a villain that will encourage audience members to feel hatred and condemnation. Yet there are claims-making strategies to construct diagnostic frames typifying villains.

Do Not Construct Villains.   Perhaps because as practical actors we know the causes of social problem conditions are complex, audience members in the United States tend to be drawn far more to claims about victims than we are to claims about villains. Because of this, and because of the complexity of constructing persuasive claims about villains, it is not surprising that successful claims-makers often pay far more attention to the social problems work of constructing victims than to the work of constructing villains. Although MADD, for example, is about the villain of the drunk driver, notice that when these social activists make claims they most typically focus on the *victims* of drunk driving. Notice also how you hear many more claims about the problems and characteristics of abused children than about abusive parents, how you hear much more about rape victims than rapists. One claims-making strategy is to focus on constructing victims and minimize constructions of villains. Rather than encouraging audience members to blame and feel hatred toward villains this strategy places all the emphasis on encouraging audience members to feel sympathy for victims.

Constructing Villains as Dangerous Outsiders.   Claims-makers at times do construct diagnostic frames that clearly blame individuals and encourage audience members to feel hatred. Such claims can be effective if they construct grounds of *extremely horrifying consequences* and *extremely pure victims* (an elderly woman raped in her own apartment by a man who broke a window to enter, or a child kidnapped, mutilated, and killed by a drug addict). Claims also must construct images of *extremely evil* villains. Such constructions are of villains as dangerous outsiders, as not one of us, as somehow less than human. They can be effective in constructing types of people such as "terrorists," "serial murderers," or "child sexual molesters."[10] These are types of people Americans in general are willing to blame, hate, condemn, and punish.

Yet clearly, not all people who do harm can easily be constructed as such dangerous outsiders. Categories of potential villains such as the "absentee landlord" who charges too much rent, the "out of control teen," who defies authority, the college student who "talks his date into having a sexual encounter," and the "fourteen-year-old father who doesn't pay child support" are difficult to construct as dangerous outsiders. Yes, such people do harm, and yes, such people can be blamed for the harm they do, but audience members might not be persuaded that such people are evil to their cores. Indeed, on a case-by-case basis audience members might identify with the villain and evaluate the condition as "unfortunate, but understandable." We might hate what such people do but we feel uncomfortable in hating or condemning them.

Deflecting Blame and Condemnation.   One way to circumvent this problem is to deflect blame onto someone or something else. Every claim that a villain is a product of a dysfunctional family, a poor school, or a terrible neighborhood deflects blame from the person doing harm. The most typical kind of blame deflecting is accomplished through the *medicalization of deviance,* which is a tendency in the United States to construct physical or mental illness as the cause of troublesome individual behavior.[11] The medicalized diagnostic frame simultaneously constructs individuals as the cause of the problem while releasing these people from responsibility and blame.

Within commonsense reasoning, when people do something because they are ill then they are not responsible. If they are not responsible they are not villains because by definition, villains are people who intend to do harm. Consider the most common example of "alcoholism." Historically, alcoholism was constructed as a sin or as caused by a "weak character." Within this construction, alcoholics were people choosing to drink so they could be blamed, condemned, and punished for what their behaviors did to others. But alcoholism now most often is constructed as a disease, so that people with this disease are not responsible. The medicalized diagnostic frame constructs their disease, not them, as responsible for the harm.

There are many other examples of the medicalization of deviance, and new ones appear quite regularly. In recent years, for example, we have seen constructions of many "addictions" such as those to gambling, shopping, shoplifting, love, food, and the internet. The problem of disruptive students is framed as a medical problem of "attention deficit-hyperactivity disorder." A few years ago American psychologists proposed that some men suffer from a "propensity to rape," meaning that their actions are not under their control so they are not responsible.[12] In addition, women who have been victims of wife abuse and who kill their abusers can offer a legal defense of the "battered woman's syndrome." If this defense is successful, women are judged as not responsible: their actions are constructed as a result of the psychological trauma of abuse. In each of these instances we *do* have a construction of individual people who create harm but, simultaneously, diagnostic frames construct these people as *not* responsible for the harm they create.

Another example of the medicalization of deviance is Pre-Menstrual Syndrome (PMS). Some women experience physical indicators of the female menstrual cycle such as bloating and cramps. These most certainly are medical. But PMS now also is associated with a range of other characteristics such as irritability and "mood disorders." These disorders can create troubles for the woman experiencing them and they also can create troubles for family members and coworkers who find such women to be unpredictable and somewhat less than cheerful. Are such "mood disorders" medical in their origin? Although both the medical *and* the "mood disorder" components of PMS now commonly are constructed as a medical problem (in other words, PMS is owned by medicine), the evidence is not so clear that the "mood disorders" associated with PMS are clearly medical in their origin. On the back stage of social problems claims-making, scientists disagree and the evidence is contradictory. Yet the "mood disorders" components of PMS did become established in the *Diagnostic and Statistical Manual,* so they are officially medicalized.[13]

Many observers have criticized the consequences of the trend of medicalizing deviance because it makes medicine too powerful, stops us from examining both individual responsibility and social structure, and has unintended consequences. For example, individual women might evaluate the medicalization of PMS as positive because troublesome behaviors of irritability and unpredictability can be forgiven as a consequence of a "disease" that is not under individual control. Yet medicalization is not all positive because, in the popular imagination, the image that PMS controls all women once a month and makes them "crazy" is not an image associated with achieving the cultural theme of equality between women and men.

Yet despite criticisms, medicalized diagnostic frameworks remain popular in no small part because deflecting blame is a good strategy to encourage audience support of claims. Medicalized diagnostic frames encourage audience members to hate the sin but love (or at least not hate) the sinner. Hence, audience members can condemn the condition yet not feel the unpleasant emotion of hatred toward people doing harm.

Furthermore, when the diagnostic frame of a social problem is medicalized, we no longer need to consider the perplexing problems of "punishment." On a case-by-case basis, punishment can raise many troublesome questions: What if it really was an "accident" as the troublemaker claims? Should we punish people who act badly because they themselves were victims in the past? Does the behavior justify the well-known horrors of prison? These are serious questions and likely at least some audience members will offer counterclaims on a case-by-case basis that punishment is not justified. Yet audience members need not worry about unjustly punishing people when diagnostic frames are medicalized. Within cultural feeling rules, people who are ill are not punished: they are ill and therefore deserve sympathy and help. Audience members who support claims-makers can feel good about their support because "help" appears very compassionate.[14]

SOCIAL PROBLEMS WORK: PACKAGING
CLAIMS AS STORIES

This chapter and the previous one together considered how claims-makers do the social problems work of persuading audience members that their claims are believable and important. These are the tasks of appealing to logic and to emotions, of constructing grounds, diagnostic, and motivational frames. But my discussion in these chapters has been very "textbook-ish" for three reasons. First, I arbitrarily separated appeals to logic from appeals to emotion when in real life we experience these simultaneously; claims-makers construct grounds, diagnostic and motivational frames in ways appealing to both logic and emotion. Second, while I talked about different claims-making strategies, many of these strategies are linked. For example, when claims construct the extreme harm created by a condition (I covered this in constructing grounds in Chapter 3), they simultaneously construct almost "anyone" as a victim as well as construct great victim suffering (I covered these in this chapter). Or, the importance of typifying stories (Chapter 3) assumes personalizing victims (this chapter).

Third, I constructed the strategies for claims-making in both chapters by looking at what often is shared by successful claims about many types of social problems. These strategies do not come from a "claims-making rule book" that you could buy at Borders Books. Granted, groups of claims-makers can talk among themselves about the best way to present claims, but they do *not* say to one another, "We need to construct the condition as producing random victims," or "Let's medicalize the condition so we don't have to blame people."[15] Indeed, terminology I have been using (grounds, frames, cultural themes, feeling rules, and so on) is the terminology of academics who study social problems—it is *not* something claims-makers talk about (or probably even know about). While experience can lead seasoned claims-makers to learn what kinds of claims are effective, claims-makers are best understood as *practical actors* who use their own understandings of the world to persuade audience members.[16]

We need to pull together everything from this chapter and the previous. We need to think of all the types of social problems work and all the strategies together. A good way to do this is to examine how all the various types of work by all the types of claims-makers together produce what audience members see, hear, and evaluate as a *package of claims* that produce a *story*.

It might seem odd that I am arguing that we can understand packages of social problems claims about conditions and people as stories. After all, claims-makers can offer statistics, charts, lists of events, or scientific research to support their claims, and these certainly do not seem to be stories. Yet numbers and research results do not have any meaning. A claim such as "One in four children is living below the level of poverty" is merely a number until audience members are persuaded that children living in poverty suffer, that this suffering cannot be tolerated. A claim such as "Research shows 50 percent of women raped by an acquaintance suffer low self-esteem" has no meaning until audience members are persuaded that "low self-esteem" is harmful, that women are pure victims not creating their harm, that this harm is so great that it cannot be tolerated. Numbers and research must be given meaning and it must be meaning that will persuade audience members to evaluate the condition as intolerable.[17]

While I discussed claims-making strategies one at a time, think of them now as all combined to create a *narrative,* a story with a plot and characters, and a point for being told.[18] These plots and characters might be constructed through various combinations of statistics, research results, and/or personal stories, and they might be constructed by many claims-makers (activists, scientists, mass media) who each construct only parts of the story. Yet we can look at how the packages of claims construct a *social problems formula story.*

Social Problems Formula Stories

Social problems formula stories are narratives about types of experiences involving distinctive types of characters. A social problems formula story is a general *type of story* that, with minor modifications, can be the story of conditions as diverse as unemployment, school failure, obesity, rape, welfare, or teens who gun down classmates.

The Plot of Social Problems Formula Stories. Every story has a plot and the plot of social problems formula stories is extreme harm. This plot might be constructed through claims made with statistics, research, or personal stories. Whether these stories are about the harm of crime, poverty, racism, unemployment, or anorexia, claims construct the plot of social problems formula stories as one of extreme devastation. There are two particular characteristics of the typical plot of social problems formula stories.

First, the plot is very narrow. In daily life, we have our ups and downs, good days and bad days; we experience some aspects of our lives as positive, others as not so positive, and others as negative. In comparison, the social problems formula story contains only those elements of life constructing the condition and constructing the harm. So, for example, the social problems formula story of "school failure" contains only the ways schools fail, the social problems formula story of "nursing homes" contains only the ways in which these places fail their residents. The plot of social problems formula stories is tightly confined to the plot of extreme harm created by the condition.

Second, this plot includes notions of cause and effect: The victim suffers because of the social problem condition. While in daily life we know that things can happen (or not happen) for many reasons, the social problems formula story is one where the condition leads to the harm. So, for example, the story of "drunk drivers" does not include any mention of bad roads or bad cars that might lead to car crashes. Likewise, children in single-parent homes are constructed as experiencing troubles *because* they live in single-parent homes and not because of something else.

The Characters in Social Problems Formula Stories. Every story must have characters and, as with all stories, the characters in social problems formula stories are constructed in ways making the story compelling. The central character in the social problems formula story typically is the victim. While this character can be of any age, race, gender, or social class, victims in social problems formula stories more often are children or elderly people rather than adults, more often women than men, more often white than nonwhite, more often middle-class than poor. This story character suffers great harm, is not responsible for the harm, and is morally pure. The social problems formula story dramatizes the goodness of victims— they are good people suffering unjustly.

Just as the plot of social problems formula stories is narrow, the character of victim also is narrowly constructed. The "disabled person" in the social problems formula story of "disability" is known only as a "disabled person," the "abused child" is known in the "child abuse" formula story only as an "abused child." While in real life people are multidimensional and much more than a victim of a particular sort, the social problems formula story constructs one-dimensional people who are victims and only victims.

Social problems formula stories also must contain a villain character but, because this a hard character to construct, it often is undeveloped and does not have a central role in the story. When villains do become central characters, they typically are constructed as purely evil. As with victims, villains are constructed very narrowly: there is nothing good about the "drunk driver" the "rapist," the "terrorist." In brief, while victims are characters who do no harm, villains are characters who only do harm.

The Point of Social Problems Formula Stories. A good story has a point— a reason why it is told. Social problems formula stories are *moral* tales. They are about how cultural themes are violated, about how injustices are happening to good people. The social problems formula story is about how something is wrong, why it is wrong, and why it cannot be tolerated.

Typically, social problems formula stories contain two versions of the *future*. In one version, that of the status quo, nothing is done to eliminate the condition. This is a bleak future indeed: We hear that global warming will melt the ice caps and end all life, we hear how child abuse all but ensures a next generation of abusers, we hear how budget deficits will lead elderly people in the future to have no medical care and no income. The second version of the future in social problems formula stories is upbeat: If audience members support claims-makers and something is done to resolve the condition, the future is bright, the problem will disappear, all will be well. The moral is clear: something must be done.[19]

Social Problems Formula Stories as Melodrama.[20] Narratives can take many forms. The social problems formula story is a particular type of tragedy called *melodrama*. True, claims-makers can offer statistics and scientific evidence as support for their claims and these are very definitely not melodramatic. Yet the package of claims yields a type of story similar to those presented on television soap operas or talk shows. It is a type of story form dramatizing the persecution of the good; it is characterized by inflated and extravagant expression, strong emotionalism, heroic confrontation between good and evil, and the need to choose sides.

Consider the melodrama of the social problem of "multicultural education." Activists promoting multicultural education portray cultural minorities as victims who do poorly in school and think poorly of themselves because the curriculum and the organization of schools are set up in ways that do not respect them. These children are pure victims whose talents and selves are smashed. The villains in this drama are structural: the "school system" is set up to benefit majority students at the expense of minority students. The curriculum is wrong, teachers are biased, no one cares or understands the needs of minority students trapped in these schools, which are designed to ensure their failure. This is a story of good (minority children, minority culture) and evil (majority culture, the "system"). There is great harm that must be stopped. This story encourages us to think that multiple problems experienced by minorities will be resolved by multicultural education. To be against such education is immoral. Indeed, in this story created by multicultural activists, to be against multicultural education is to threaten the very future of the United States, whose citizens increasingly are in these minority groups.[21]

Evaluating Social Problems Formula Stories

While we can look at how claims-makers can use specific strategies in answering audience questions about social problems conditions, audience members see, hear, and evaluate claims as a package. Social problems formula stories such as crime, poverty, terrorism, or obesity rarely are told by any one claims-maker. Rather, they often are pieced together by activists, scientists, researchers; they often are told through the mass media. These are *cultural stories* because audience members evaluate their believability and importance through practical experience, cultural themes, and feeling rules. Of course, this means that audience members in other times and in other places could judge believability and importance in very different ways, and thus a very successful formula story in one time or place is not necessarily so believable or important in other times and places. And given the incredible diversity among Americans in this postmodern world, we cannot expect that any one story will be evaluated as believable and important by all potential audience members.[22]

Yet still there is a measure of agreement: the overwhelming majority of people calling themselves Americans felt anger, outrage, and confusion about the terrorist attacks, few failed to feel sympathy for its immediate victims; the great majority of Americans believe children should be protected from harm; "frail elderly people" are offered sympathy and help far more often than are "sex offenders"; the more a condition might affect us personally, the more we tend to worry about it; the more harm created by a condition, the more we take it seriously, and so on. An effective social problems formula story—be it the particular story of terrorism, crime, inferior medical care, or environmental ruin—packages multiple claims about characteristics of conditions and people in ways encouraging audience members to be motivated to evaluate the condition as immoral as this is evaluated through popular wisdom, cultural themes, and feeling rules.

The Importance of Social Problems Formula Stories

We all tell stories about ourselves and others but the stories told through claims about social problems are more important than our individual stories.

First, experiences and people in real life are complex and we could (and often do) argue endlessly about which conditions should be labeled intolerable and which are acceptable, about which people in real life really are victims and which are responsible for their experiences. Social problems formula stories put those disagreements to rest. Audience members who see or hear these stories are left with few questions about whether or not the condition really is troublesome, about whether or not the people experiencing harm really are victims who should be offered sympathy and help. While the stories we tell about ourselves and our friends often are complex and lead to no clear evaluation of their meaning, social problems formula stories motivate audience members to agree with claims-makers that the condition is immoral. Social problems formula stories are more compelling than the stories we tell about ourselves in daily life.

Second, social problems formula stories are the types of stories favored by the mass media. A good social problems formula story is compelling and entertaining (in a ghoulish way). These stories have disturbing plots (extreme harm) and compelling characters (victims) who evoke sympathy. Because successful stories tend to reflect cultural themes supported by powerful people (white, middle-class), they might disturb people in these powerful groups but they do not radically challenge the ways these people think about the world.

Third, these stories are important because they are *public narratives.* They are public, of course, because claims-makers tell these stories to audiences of strangers rather than to audiences of friends—stories told in the mass media potentially are seen or heard by millions of people. More important, these stories are public because successful stories can become a part of the popular wisdom—what "we all know" about the world. As such, successful social problems formula stories can become a resource used by audience members to evaluate the believability and importance of other claims about social problems.

THE SOCIAL PROBLEMS WORK OF
CONSTRUCTING PEOPLE

Social problems work is complex and multidimensional. In order to persuade audience members, claims-makers construct typifications of conditions and people, they appeal to audience members' understandings of cultural themes and feeling rules. When claims-making is successful we can say that claims-makers have won the social problems game. Of course, in the process much has been swept under the carpet. Claims dramatize how extreme conditions lead morally pure and innocent people to experience extreme harm. Left in the background is objective reality: Most conditions are more or less severe, more or less consequential; there are many quite logical and competing ways to think about the causes of any particular condition; there are few perfect victims because there are few perfect people. The complexity of the real world cannot easily be typified and this leads to claims and counterclaims and disagreements, and this certainly will not help persuade audience members. Successful social problems claims and the social problems formula stories they construct are effective precisely because *they deny the complexity of the real world.*

If the package of claims I am calling social problems formula stories were merely stories told for amusement then it would not matter that they are effective precisely because they deny the complexity of practical experience. But the outcomes of the social problems game are very real. If successful, social problems claims lead to political, social, and cultural change. The topic of the next chapter is how claims-makers construct *prognostic* frames, which are claims about what should be done to change the condition and stop the harm. Then we will continue by looking at how these stories influence our daily lives as well as the ways we think about ourselves and others.

NOTES

1.   See Waddell (1990) for an examination of rhetorics of rationality and emotionality in scientific policies surrounding DNA research; see McCarthy (1989) and Denzin (1990) for reflections on the importance of emotions in daily life.

2.   Hochschild (1979:563) uses the term *feeling rules* to describe "the social guidelines that direct how we want to try to feel . . . a set of socially shared, albeit often latent (not thought about unless probed at), rules. See also Loseke (1993, 2000) for further reflections on relationships between social problems and motivational frames appealing to emotions rather than to logic.

3.   Most successful social problems feature people, rather than animals or the environment, as victims. Kunkel (1995, excerpted in *Social Problems: Constructionist Readings*) argues that the animal rights movement expanded its claims to include people as victims of "factory farming."

4.   Here I will draw from the work of Candace Clark (1997), who looks at the social character of sympathy. Clark argues that sympathy, like other emotions, has social roots. We learn the social rules, so to speak, for when to feel sympathy, for how to appropriately express sympathy toward others, for when and how to ask for sympathy from others.

5.   Categories of people are produced but that does not mean these categories will remain on the social scene or that their social evaluation will remain high (or low). See Loseke (1995, excerpted in *Social Problems: Constructionist Readings*) for how the "homeless mentally ill" changed from a type of person who should be "helped" to a type of person who must be "controlled." Elder and Cobb (1984) for an examination of changing evaluations of the social category of the "elderly." Malone, Boyd, and Bero (2000) examine how the social category of "smoker" has become increasingly condemned in the United States; Hufker and Cavender (1990) demonstrate how the evaluation of immigrants from Cuba in 1980 changed from positive (political refugees) to negative (criminals and other "undesirables"). In comparison, see Loseke and Fawcett (1995) for their argument that the social evaluation of the "deserving poor" did *not* change throughout the twentieth century.

6.   Roser and Thompson (1995) examine how fearful messages tend to transform low-involvement audiences into active publics wanting to do something about conditions they fear. See also Glassner (1999) and Altheide (2002) for claims that media promote such fear.

7.   Best (1999, excerpted in *Social Problems: Constructionist Readings*) discusses the rhetorical attractiveness of constructing violence as random.

8.   Public opinion polls show that while about 80 percent of the general public

expresses "a lot" or "some" sympathy for people with AIDS; that figure drops to 39 percent when the disease is said to have been acquired from homosexual activity, and it drops to 30 percent when said to be acquired from sharing needles while using illegal drugs (Rogers, Singer, and Imperio, 1993). See Albert (1989) for the argument about public concern with AIDS in relation to constructions of AIDS victims.

9.   See Jenness (1993, excerpted in *Social Problems: Constructionist Readings*) for how prostitutes' rights organizations construct prostitutes as victims. Loseke and Cavendish (2001, excerpted in *Social Problems: Constructionist Readings*) examine how another social change group constructs "homosexual Catholics" as people deserving of sympathy and support because they are morally pure.

10.   Jenkins (1994) argues that "serial murderers" have been constructed as such dangerous outsiders. Petonito (1992) argues that "Japanese Americans" were constructed as such dangerous outsiders during World War II and this construction justified placing them in internment camps. Berger (2002, excerpted in *Social Problems: Constructionist Readings*) illustrates how the "Jew" was constructed as a dangerous outsider in Nazi Germany.

11.   The classic statement on the medicalization of deviance was written by Conrad and Schneider (1980). While medical personnel themselves have not always been in the forefront of this claims-making (Appleton, 1995), the medical metaphor remains popular. Observers have examined the medicalization of a range of childhood troubles and fears (Pawluch, 1996, excerpted in *Social Problems: Constructionist Readings*), premenstrual syndrome (Figert, 1996 excerpted in *Social Problems: Constructionist Readings*), compulsive gambling (Rosencrance, 1985; Rossol 2001), deviant drinking (Schneider, 1978), Attention Deficit Hyperactivity Disorder (Levine, 1997, Conrad and Potter, 2000), crime control (Johnson and Waletzko, 1992), childbirth (Armstrong, 2000), and ethnicity (Santiago-Irizarry, 2001).

12.   A continuing theme in this text is how the actual practice of science is a social process. In this instance, feminists in the American Psychological Association offered successful counterclaims and "propensity to rape" was dropped as a possible psychiatric category.

13.   Figert (1996, excerpted in *Social Problems: Constructionist Readings*) examines the medicalization of PMS. See also Rittenhouse (1991).

14.   This tendency to deflect blame from individuals also is promoted by social scientists. As noted by Best (1997), because social science is concerned with examining social structures and social forces, the concept of individual blame is foreign to it.

15.   For an empirical example of frame disputes among members of the Austin, Texas, Peace Movement, see Benford (1993). Also, see Benford (2002) for a description of how social movement activists do very consciously train new activists in how to use the preferred set of claims when they talk about the social problem to people outside the social movement.

16.   I am assuming here that claims-makers and their audiences share a culture. This becomes a major claims-making obstacle when claims originating in one culture are interpreted by members of another culture. This is a particular problem when audiences are Americans who tend to lack knowledge of other cultures and who are prone to assume that the "American way" is the "right way."

17.   See Stone (1997: especially Chapter 7) for the multiple uses of numbers in claims offered to social policymakers.

18.   For general treatments of narratives, see Berger (1997), Bruner (1987), Linde (1993), Gergen (1994), Polkinghorne (1988), Richardson (1990), and Maines (1992). For the importance of narratives in social problems claims see Loseke (2000) and Nichols (1997). For the importance of narratives in social movements see Davis (2002), Fine (2002), and Benford (2002).

19.   Benford (2002) discusses these versions of the future contained in social problems formula stories.

20.   I will draw from work of Brooks (1976) to discuss the melodramatic narrative form.

21.   Nelson-Rowe (1995, excerpted in *Social Problems: Constructionist Readings*) examines claims about multicultural education as melodrama. Johnson (1995, excerpted in *Social Problems: Constructionist Readings*) explores the child abuse melodrama.

22.   For example, a type of person called *kyoiku mama* (education mother, a type of woman dedicating herself solely to the education of her children) was prized in the late 1900s in Japan (Yamazaki, 1994), but this type of person makes little sense to American college student women. See Maines (1999) for an argument that the evaluation of the believability of some narratives in the United States is influenced by race.

5

Constructing Solutions

My day started with a meeting about the future of higher education. The speaker said, "Welfare had to change, health care had to change, corporations had to change. Now it's higher education's turn. Government has many priorities, like health care and prisons. We can't afford to keep giving colleges more money." I wondered about a world where prisons compete with education and health care as I walked to my class on families, where we had a discussion about what we should do about the problem of "poor single mothers." A student said, "We need more daycare. Single moms can't work because there's not enough day care." Another said, "What we need are better paying jobs. Lots of women work, but they still don't make enough money." Another said, "Sure, but what about the fathers of these children? We need to make them pay child support like they're supposed to." As I leave class I talk with a secretary who tells me she's looking for a second job so she can earn enough money to pay her daughter's college tuition. She's angry: "I don't make enough to pay her tuition, but I make too much for her to get it from the government. I'm poor but I'm not poor enough."

The previous two chapters focused on the social problems work of persuading audience members to evaluate a condition as a social problem. I argued that typical social problems formula stories (all the claims about grounds, diagnostic frames, and motivational frames combined) encourage such an evaluation. Motivating audience members to evaluate a condition as intolerable is necessary to achieve the final goal in the social problems game: *changing the world* in order to eliminate the intolerable condition, to help victims, to punish or rehabilitate villains.[1]

CONSTRUCTING PROGNOSTIC FRAMES

Because social problems, by definition, are conditions we believe can and should be *changed*, it follows that the work of claims-makers is not finished until the intolerable condition is eliminated. What should be done about the problem of obesity? Teens who drink alcohol? Elderly people who cannot afford their medicines? Audience members in general can be motivated to take a condition seriously only when they are persuaded that something can be done to change it, policymakers will not take a problem seriously unless there is a proposed course of action, social activists cannot persuade others to become claims-makers themselves unless these potential recruits are convinced that social problems work can make the condition better. Claims-makers must construct images of preferred courses of action to eliminate the condition and the suffering it creates.

Prognostic frames are claims answering audience members' questions about what should be done. This frame constructs a general line of action (what should be done) and it constructs the responsibility for that action (who should do it). These claims are important because they legitimize some solutions (and not others), they construct some indicators of success (and not others), they assign some people (and not others) the responsibility for changing the condition.[2]

The social problems game always is about competition, and social problems work always is about persuading audience members that one set of constructions is more believable and important than others. I will start with the major types of competitions facing claims-makers constructing prognostic frames.

Claims-Competitions in Prognostic Frames

One form of competition in prognostic frames centers on *diagnostic frames*.[3] For example, what should be done about the condition of the "lack of transportation for disabled people"? The logical solution depends on the problem's diagnostic frame. If the diagnostic frame constructed this as a "transportation" problem, the solution reasonably could be special buses to transport disabled people. But if the problem was framed as one of the "civil rights" of disabled people, the solution would require modifying the public transportation system to make it accessible to *all* citizens. Within a civil rights frame, special transportation for disabled people would be unacceptable because it is unequal. As another example, some years ago there were many competitions about the prognostic frame constructing "shelters for battered women" as a (partial) solution for women experiencing wife abuse. In one public policy hearing, a state senator refused to support a bill giving public money to shelters because, according to him, these places were "homes for runaway wives" who simply were tired of being married. He had framed wife abuse as a problem of "unhappy marriages." But claims promoting the necessity of shelters eventually won by constructing the behavior of wife abuse as extreme and devastating, and by constructing the battered woman as trapped in an abusive relationship because she had nowhere to go. Within this framework of wife abuse as life-threatening and women as trapped, it made sense to support shelters. This became a successful frame when it was evaluated as more important than the competing frame constructing wife abuse as "unhappy marriages."

Second, there can be conflicting *cultural* themes underlying prognostic frames. The senator claiming that shelters for battered women were "homes for runaway wives," for example, constructed his concern in terms of the cultural theme of *family:* he feared shelters made it too easy for women to leave their husbands. Competing frames promoting the need for shelters were organized around a *humanitarian* theme: they were life-saving resources for the women needing them.

Other kinds of claims-competitions surrounding cultural themes construct probable *futures* and differing moralities in those futures. For example, some claims-makers argue that we should give heroin addicts free hypodermic needles because this will reduce the spread of AIDS through needle exchange. These claims construct a positive future where heroin users will not contact AIDS. But others claim that giving addicts free needles promotes an image that heroin is acceptable so the future will be one of increased drug use. Or some people claim that schools should give students free condoms because this will protect sexually active students from pregnancy and disease. The counterclaims construct giving condoms to school children as wrong because it tells children that early sexual experience is expected of them and this will increase early sexuality. Pregnancy and disease will follow when condoms are not used or when they fail.

Other proposed solutions to social problems face competitions because they raise issues of ethics contained in different cultural themes: Is it ethical to implant fetal tissue from aborted fetuses into the brains of sufferers of Parkinson's disease? Is it ethical to require women recipients of welfare to have the Norplant birth control implant?

Third, once a social problem is successful and change is implemented there can be competitions about the *consequences of solutions.* Solutions can be constructed as leading to negative consequences for some people. Think about the social problem called child abuse. Over the past few years there have been many changes: Such abuse increasingly is condemned; there are many new laws and increased watchfulness on the part of teachers and other social service providers. But claims-competitions about these solutions continue, with some parents complaining that they have been unjustly accused, and with claims that new laws have been used primarily against minority and poor parents.[4]

The case of the "War on Drugs" (primarily targeting crack cocaine use) is an obvious example of competitions about the consequences of solutions. While crack cocaine might have been constructed as a problem of public health, prognostic claims rather constructed it as a problem of crime. Years later, our prisons now are filled with people serving time for violating drug laws and there regularly are articles from a range of experts in mainstream newspapers claiming that the War on Drugs has been a massive failure that has created far more problems than it has resolved. Currently, there are an increasing number of claims that "drug use" should be constructed as a problem of public health rather than as a crime problem.[5]

Finally, there can be competitions for *time, energy,* and *money* to solve social problems. While it is possible for many claims-makers to be successful in persuading audience members that a social problem exists, only a limited number of these will be successful in actually achieving social change. We live in a world of limited resources. Bluntly stated, there is not enough sympathy, time, energy, or money to solve all social problems. There are competitions between social problems and everything else in life, and there are competitions among social problems themselves for scarce resources. *Clearly and most certainly* we could do better at resolving social problems than we do now and I certainly would not want you to interpret my comments to mean that we can just walk away from troublesome conditions. Of course not. My point is that some claims about solutions will not get our attention or resources simply because of this competition. This just takes us back to our primary focus: some claims are more effective than others in leading social change.

Claims-makers therefore must persuade audience members that their diagnostic frames are better than others, that their proposed solutions are compatible with cultural themes, and that the solution will be better than the problem. Claims about solutions also must be evaluated by audience members as more or less compatible with claims about social problems conditions and the people in them. Given this, social problems formula stories play a central role in shaping the content of prognostic claims.[6]

Social Problems Formula Stories
and Prognostic Frames

Prognostic frames are claims constructed as resolving the harm created by the conditions featured in social problems formula stories. Consider, for example, the social problem condition of homelessness, particularly the condition of "people living on the streets." What should be done to resolve this condition depends on the social problems formula story of this kind of homelessness. So, for example, if the social problems formula story is one with a moral that there is not enough affordable housing, which leads to people living on the streets, it follows that the solution is more housing. If it is a story of how people are on the streets because the city shelters are crowded and dangerous, then it follows there should be more and better shelters. If the social problems formula story is about the "mental illness" of people living on the streets then these people should be forced to leave the streets and receive care for their illness.[7] Social problems formula stories contain morals, they tell us what is wrong and why it is wrong. Prognostic frames are claims about what must be done to right this wrong.

My major final point when I discussed social problems formula stories in the previous chapter was that these stories tend to dramatize the most horrid aspects of conditions, and they tend to emphasize the purity of victims.[8] Such horror stories, of course, typically capture only a small slice of practical experience—they tend to describe few of the real people who are victims or villains. Objectively speaking, then, it does not make sense to organize prognostic claims around social problems formula stories. Yet this happens. Social problems formula stories are used by claims-makers because they are *politically* useful in mobilizing audience members—these stories encourage moral outrage. The easy-to-understand moral tales told through social problems formula stories also reduce the scope of problems and make them easier to understand. The more we focus on the incredible diversity of social life the more we will become simply confused and unwilling to make a moral evaluation that a condition is intolerable; the more we look at diversity the less likely we will be able to construct a prognostic frame.

I want to turn now to the two major ways claims-makers attempt to accomplish the social change they seek. I will begin with public policy and then move to cultural change.

THE SOCIAL CONTEXTS OF PUBLIC POLICY

Often when we think of social change we think about changes in *public policy:* solutions that use social resources to repair conditions and/or to encourage or coerce individual change.[9] There are many types of things that public policy can do. New laws can be enacted (Americans with Disability Act) or old ones struck down (contested divorces); there can be new taxes to discourage behaviors (more tax on cigarettes and alcohol, a deposit on soda cans to discourage throwing them away), or tax advantages to encourage behaviors (tax breaks to start businesses in urban enterprise zones, school vouchers for private schools). Public policy can be about starting new (or ending old) social services or educational programs. It might be a mandate to build more (or fewer) prisons or schools, to deport illegal aliens, or to give these people an easier route to becoming citizens. Public policy is about using social resources to repair conditions and/or to help or rehabilitate victims and/or to rehabilitate or punish villains.

Public policy is made in several places. Obviously, it is a matter of government at all levels—local (including school boards), state, national, and international. I am not going to wander off on a civics lecture but it is important to think of "government" as more than elected officials. Indeed, most policy decisions in our complex world are made by nonelected workers in a vast network of government departments (such as transportation, aging, and education). Only a few policy decisions go beyond this department level and reach the attention of the president or Congress. In addition, much public policy is made in legal settings: the Supreme Court has the final power to decide legal issues of national concern; various local, state, and regional courts have the final say on matters of more local interest. The United Nations can make policy for international conditions such as human rights and war.

Policy also can be made by private organizations. Corporations, for example, sometimes have policies for family leave time or flexible working hours that are in response to the problems of balancing work and family. The most obvious example is the policy of private-sector employers requiring potential (and sometimes continuing) employees to have their urine tested for evidence of drug use. This is a consequence of successful claims-making leading to concern that employees' use of drugs created danger for others as well as a loss of productivity for organizations. While these are policies of *individual* companies, this practice now is so common that it is approaching a universal status. From the perspective of people seeking work in organizations with this policy, it does not matter that the policy was formed by private organizations rather than the government. The policy exists.[10]

This vast array of government, legal, and organizational settings is what I mean when I say *public policy arena*. In many ways, people who design policy for the government or for private corporations are similar to members of general audiences seeing or hearing claims about social problems. Public policymakers (officials, bureaucrats, lawyers, corporate leaders) live in the same social order as members of more general audiences. Similar to members of general audiences, people in the policy arena more or less share belief in common cultural themes; they are most concerned when social problem conditions are constructed as immediate, terribly harmful, and close to home; they are encouraged to act when victims are evaluated as people deserving help and when villains are evaluated as people deserving punishment, as "deserving" is evaluated through cultural feeling rules, and so on.

It is important to remember, then, that policymakers share much with general audiences to social problems claims. At the same time, we cannot think of them as free agents able to evaluate social problems claims simply from their own viewpoint. People who can make public policy are *organizational actors*.

SOCIAL PROBLEMS WORK: GOVERNMENT
POLICY CONSTRUCTION

While the specific scenes for constructing social policy can be local, state, or national governments, legal settings, or corporate boardrooms, I want to narrow my focus now and continue by focusing on only one scene: *government*.

Social Problems Formula Stories
and Government Policy

At times, policy to resolve social problems can affect many, or even all, members in the general population. This happened recently, for example, when *all* Americans who paid federal income taxes last year were sent a rebate check this year to encourage spending that was to help an economy in recession. Everyone who uses airlines also was affected when these airlines were mandated to increase security precautions causing delays and added expenses for *all* passengers.

While policy can affect Americans in general, it is more common for policy to resolve social problems to have a *target population*.[11] This is policy that applies only to specific *categories* of people. Such policies can negatively affect specific categories of people by raising their taxes, constructing new laws limiting their freedom, increasing penalties for specific behaviors. Conversely, policy can positively affect categories of people by lowering their taxes, offering them greater freedom, or beneficial services.

The first important point about public policy is that when *characters* in social problems formula stories are constructed as types of people deserving help, the *actual* people in these categories will be helped; when *characters* are constructed as types of people deserving punishment, the *actual* people in these categories will be punished. My second point, however, makes this more complex: government policy outcomes also are influenced by the perceived *political power* of categories of people. What we have, then, are two ways of thinking about types of people in relation to government policy: how these types of people are socially constructed in social problems formula stories, and how powerful these types of people are in the political, economic, and social realms. This gives us four types of people. There are predictions about what kinds of prognostic frames likely will be successful for each of these types.

When cultural constructions are compatible with political power, policy decisions are straightforward.

Positive Construction, High on Political Power. When victims (positively constructed as good people) also are people who are high in political power we can predict that policy will be quick to offer them *benefits*. Elderly people are an example of this type of person who is positively constructed *and* politically powerful because of the AARP and because, as compared with younger Americans, elderly people tend to vote. Veterans are another example of a type of person who is positively constructed as well as politically organized. We can understand why there is so much attention and concern about the problems of elderly people and veterans. Offering benefits to these people is a no-lose situation for politicians: it will meet with public approval because they are evaluated as "deserving," *and* it will be politically beneficial because these groups are high in political power.

Negative Construction, Low on Political Power.   It also is easy to predict that policy will be quick to *punish* when villains (negatively constructed) are politically powerless people. People such as "drug addicts" or "sexual molesters" do not have social change groups protecting their interests; members of the general public condemn them. Here we often see "get tough" policies because this is another no-lose situation for politicians: Members of the general public believe such people should be condemned and punished; nothing will be lost politically by treating them harshly.

While it is fairly easy to predict policy outcomes when social constructions are compatible with political power, in many instances the political power / social construction dimensions are not compatible.

Positive Construction, Low on Political Power.   Some categories of people such as children (especially poor children) and migrant workers often are constructed as victims. They are socially constructed as "good" people, but they are politically powerless. There are few organized groups for such politically powerless people, these people often cannot or do not vote, they do not have money. Because there is no political payoff from showering policy benefits upon such politically powerless people, policy targeting them likely will be *symbolic* rather than offering real assistance. Politicians, for example, might call for a special task force to study the problem, they might give speeches about the importance of resolving the conditions. But relatively few social resources tend to be offered to people who are low on political power, even when these people are constructed as good people deserving sympathy and assistance.

Negative Construction, High on Political Power.   Politicians also face problems when villains are constructed as organizations or people who are high in power. What happens, for example, when "big business" (high in power) is constructed as responsible for pollution (negative construction)? In such instances the social problem construction of evil is combined with high political power, so politicians punishing the evil might pay a high political price (loss of campaign contributions, loss of support from powerful allies). Given this, policy also tends to be *symbolic:* a corporation might be forced to pay a fine that is insignificant given the company's resources; an executive responsible for decisions leading to inferior and harmful products costing lives might be sentenced to a few hours of "community service."

When social constructions and political power are not compatible, politicians are faced with the most difficult decisions and these are the decisions most influenced by the *strength of the constructions of the target population.* To receive beneficial policies, politically powerless victims must be constructed as facing hardship so extreme that politicians must help them even though there will be no political payoffs. Likewise, politically powerful groups will be punished only when there is absolute public outrage and this happens when the harm they do is constructed as simply intolerable.

This topic of relationships between social constructions and political power shows why it is an effective claims-making strategy to construct middle-class people (as opposed to poor people) as typical victims of social problems. As compared with poor people, middle-class people have more political power, so it is possible to obtain more beneficial policy outcomes by constructing them as victims.

Policy benefits and punishments therefore depend both on constructions contained in social problems formula stories as well as on the political power held by specified target populations. Neither social constructions nor political power are stable over time. Political power can change: women as a category are not as politically powerless as a few decades ago, disabled people have banded together into social change groups and now are more powerful than before. So, too, social constructions change over time. The topic for the last section of this chapter is how social activists can change public perceptions of particular types of people.

Clearly, much is at stake when claims-makers construct social problems formula stories and seek to change social policy. Not surprisingly, there are claims-making strategies associated with success in the government public policy arena.

Claims-Making Strategies

There are strategies for constructing claims encouraging audiences of government policymakers to take claims seriously. The first five strategies are the same as constructing claims for general audiences, yet the policy arena can add complexity.

Constructing Problems at the Right Time.   Recall that all audiences have limited *carrying capacities* and this certainly is true for the government policy arena. First, many prognostic frames construct the need for money to resolve the social problem condition. In years of budget deficits, policy-makers might claim they agree that the problem is important but then dismiss it by claiming there is no money to resolve it. Second, politicians at all levels of government often have particular *agendas* (called party platforms). This leads to a general *policy climate* that encourages or discourages attention to specific problems.[12] One group of politicians, for example, might be most interested in education, another in family matters, and another in crime. Claims fitting those agendas will be more successful than those that do not.

The Solution Is (Relatively) Easy and (Relatively) Inexpensive. Successful social problems formula stories tend to be vivid and easy to understand, and the same holds for effective prognostic claims. If solutions seem too complex, government officials tend to become immobilized.[13] The American public in general and public policymakers in particular are not drawn to considering complex solutions.

Effectiveness also is increased when claims construct solutions as relatively inexpensive. Cost can be in terms of money: proposed solutions that seem inexpensive are more compelling than those that will cost a great deal of money. Cost also can be in terms of required lifestyle changes. Politicians (and the public in general) will be much quicker to support policies to "recycle aluminum cans" as a solution to pollution than to "abandon our cars." Effective claims tend to construct relatively easy and relatively inexpensive solutions.

At the extreme, some solutions are merely *symbolic* and do nothing to eliminate the pain experienced by victims or to resolve the social problem condition itself. Politicians are quick to urge us to display flags, they often sign proclamations to "release political prisoners," or declare May "Obesity Awareness Month." Such solutions are appealing to politicians because they cost nothing and they make people feel good. Yet nothing tangible has been done.[14]

The Solution Is to Change Individuals. Our cultural theme of individualism (constructing individual responsibility) led to the tendency to construct diagnostic frames holding individuals responsible for causing social problems. It follows that resolution requires changing people. It is far easier to persuade politicians that we need new programs for "learning-disabled" children than to persuade them that the structure, organization, and curriculum of schools must be changed. It is easier to gain support for programs of "sensitivity training" to resolve problems of racism or sexism than to promote policies leading to a restructuring of the current racist and sexist organization of our social order.

The Solution Must Solve the Emergency. Typical social problems formula stories dramatize the extremely devastating nature of social problem conditions. Because these stories encourage public moral outrage about such conditions, as well as sympathy for its victims, it follows that proposing interventions to deal with emergencies tends to be effective in persuading government officials to support claims. Prognostic frames constructing shelters (for battered women, homeless people, abused children), emergency relief for victims of natural disasters, and so on find it easier to gain support than do policies that might stop these problems from happening in the first place. I think about the "med-fly" problem in my community. This is a fly that eats citrus, and because citrus is a major product of Florida, an infestation of med-flies is very serious. Although there are environmentally safe ways to control the med-fly population, no funds are available for this. Funds *are* available for the overhead spraying of Malathion once an emergency is declared.[15]

Declaring War on the Social Problem.[16] Claims-makers often package their prognostic claims as declaring "war" on the social problem condition. Within my lifetime, I have heard talk of declaring "war" on poverty, crime, cancer, family violence, illiteracy, obesity, and, of course, terrorism. "War" is a compelling metaphor. It encourages policymakers to believe there is an identifiable enemy, it conjures up images that the cause is righteous and that there should be a unity of purpose. War also evokes the cultural theme of patriotism and makes it difficult for opposing claims-makers to criticize.

Strategies for persuading audience members in general to do something about a social problem (constructing at the right time, constructing a simple solution, promoting individual change, constructing an emergency, declaring war) remain when the target audience for claims-making is people capable of making government or legal policy. Effective claims-making in the public policy arena also is characterized by four additional considerations.[17]

Constructing in the Language of Science and Law. Depending on the audience, social problems claims can use a wide variety of languages such as pictures, drama, poetry, or rap music. In comparison, the languages of government policy are those of science, expert knowledge, and law. It is a very formal, precise, and legalistic language. This characteristic of successful claims, of course, leads to the tendency that claims-makers who are the best at speaking these languages will be at an advantage in making claims in the public policy arena. So, this is one reason why scientists are at the top of the hierarchy of credibility in the policy arena, and it is one reason why marginalized claims-makers often do not fare well.[18]

Constructing the Problem as a Matter of Government Concern. Some claims might be successful in the mass media, in public gatherings, or in textbooks, yet not become a matter of government policy. To be successful in changing policy, the condition must be constructed in ways that make the problem a proper matter of government (political or legal) concern. An obvious example took place several years ago when claims-makers were trying to convince audiences that what we now call child abuse and wife abuse were social problems requiring the government to do something (to stop these conditions, to help victims, to punish or rehabilitate villains). While policymakers as *individuals* could be persuaded that these conditions were intolerable, as *organizational actors* they were not so easily convinced that these conditions should be matters for government policy. Referencing the cultural theme of the importance of family (family privacy, the sanctity of the family), many policymakers believed the government did not have the right to intervene. Policy solutions to child abuse and wife abuse were not possible until policymakers were persuaded that these conditions were appropriate topics of government concern. This was accomplished by the social problems formula story of family violence that features extremely widespread victimization that has extremely devastating consequences for victims and for Americans in general. Policymakers eventually were persuaded that such violence is so intolerable that stopping it was more important than protecting family privacy.

Constructing conditions as matters of government concern is getting easier. Many conditions defined as family matters a few years ago (violence, children's health, children's education, sex education) now are defined as conditions of government concern. Likewise, conditions defined as individual choices a few years ago (smoking cigarettes, wearing motorcycle helmets, using seat belts for adults and car seats for children) now also are defined as matters of government concern. Yet there remain other conditions often constructed as problems by members of the public that are not fully accepted as matters of government concern. For example, child day care and care of frail elderly people remain in a contested stage where some claims-makers argue that because these are widespread conditions they require government solutions, while others argue these are properly matters of families, and still others argue that private businesses can and should offer needed services.

Obtaining Organizational Sponsors. Claims-making becomes very complicated when the audience is government officials and the goal is to seek change in government regulations or laws or to secure funding for the programs in the troubled persons industry.[19] Only in the rare cases of social problem conditions of indisputable morality, such as terrorism, do government policymaking channels move rapidly. Most of the time, making a new law or starting new programs is very time-consuming. Furthermore, this policymaking process is rule-bound and the rules are not common sense, they often cannot be understood by practical actors without specialized training. And it can be incredibly expensive to compile the documentation, attend the meetings, pay the experts to testify, and so on, that are needed to go through this process.

These characteristics of the government policy arena pose many problems for claims-makers because it is very difficult to keep the interest of audience members. New social problems are constantly constructed and these will compete with older ones that are not yet resolved. Audience members who at one time united to form a strong public opinion to "do something" often stop worrying about an old problem and focus their attention and concern on newer problems that seem more immediate.

All this leads to the importance of *organizational sponsors* for social problems claims seeking public policy change.[20] Organizational sponsors are the established sectors of the social problems industry such as the American Medical Association (AMA), the National Organization of Women (NOW), the National Association for the Advancement of Colored People (NAACP), the National Rifle Association (NRA), the American Civil Liberties Union (ACLU), and the National Committee for the Prevention of Child Abuse (NCPCA). These are formal organizations that have the money, political power, and the expertise to follow a policy through the process. The public in general might lose interest in one or another condition but formal sectors of the social problems industry can keep the issue on the policymaking agenda.

Constructing Politically Acceptable Solutions. Government policy is formed in an arena of *politics.* As such, it contains all the political intrigue associated with politics in general. Policymakers might personally believe that a condition exists and that something must be done, but that does not mean they will support policy changes. Political parties have agendas and claims must fit into those agendas. There are personal and political loyalties, favors owed, political alliances and the support of wealthy contributors that must be maintained. Some solutions might be logical and doable, yet not politically feasible.

Because there can be somewhat large shifts in political power after elections, policy climates can suddenly change. Conditions accorded the status of a social problem during one administration can suddenly disappear when a new group takes power, conditions previously ignored can gain attention when a new group arrives. The condition of "abortion clinics bombing" is a case in point. While many abortion clinics were bombed in the 1980s and early 1990s by "pro-life" claims-makers, there was little government concern. When William Clinton became president, this condition became categorized as "terrorism." We also can understand the beginnings of the War on Drugs in 1986. Despite the lack of evidence that crack cocaine was a rapidly growing problem, declaring a war on it was good politics for both Democrats and Republicans at that time. Changing images and changing policies are about politics.[21]

In brief, just as there are strategies for constructing effective claims about the characteristics of social problems conditions, victims, and villains, there are strategies associated with constructing prognostic frames that might be more effective than others in changing public policy. While some of these strategies are similar to those that are effective with general audiences, public policy is an organizational realm with specific demands that create new concerns for claims-makers.

Government Policymakers, Audiences, and Social Problems Claims-Makers

Because public policymakers are powerful in that they can mandate social change, it is important to ask questions about their relationships with general audiences as well as with claims-makers.

Government and the Public. Clearly, while the social problems game always is about power, when we enter the realm of government policy we add much political intrigue. The winning constructions in government policy arenas might not be the most logical, they simply might be the most politically feasible. Successful claims-makers might not have the most believable and important claims but rather they might be the most politically connected. Policy benefits and costs to specific target populations often reflect the perceived power or lack of power of those populations rather than their objective need.

Yet we cannot think that the social problems game is entirely different in the government arena. The social problems game *always* is political regardless of where it is played. And even though political tactics are more obvious and blatant in government, it remains that effective claims must be *more* than "politically acceptable." Policymakers cannot support a policy, or refuse to support a policy, simply because it would be politically good for them. You never will hear a politician say, "I voted for this bill because its sponsor gave me a lot of money." Money or political agendas might well lie behind politicians' decision-making but it remains that politicians must *justify* their decisions in other terms.

This takes me to an important point: While a large part of government policymaking happens behind closed doors, there remains some measure of accountability because elected politicians need votes if they are to remain in office. If we want to understand why specific policies are enacted we must look at *public opinion* because policymakers follow this in making their decisions.[22] Public opinion is just another name for the audience of Americans who tend to vote. The more Americans who tend to vote support a social problem, the more policymakers *must* be attentive. This happened when former president Clinton ended up supporting welfare reform that was identified strongly with opposition Republicans. He was forced to do so because public opinion polls repeatedly indicated that Americans in general supported this reform. And, earlier in his term as president, he dropped plans for national health insurance because polls consistently indicated that Americans in general believed claims that the plan was too complicated and would lead to more problems than it solved. So, the strategy of constructing politically acceptable solutions does not necessarily mean these solutions must meet preexisting political agendas. Something *becomes* politically acceptable when it reflects public opinion.

The reverse also holds true: policymakers are responsive to publics who *do not care*. Indeed, while public opinion can encourage policymakers to take a condition seriously, it is more common for the *lack* of public interest to allow policymakers to ignore conditions. This leaves a vast range of troublesome conditions unattended to: Americans in general tend to not know much about or seem to care about the intricacies of health care management or industry deregulation; the complexity of ecological problems leaves us confused rather than concerned. Highly technical and complex social problem conditions tend to be outside public concern and, because of this lack of concern, politicians can ignore them if they choose or attend to them if these conditions fit within their political agenda.

Government and the Media. Claims encouraging emotional responses so effective in convincing general audiences that a social problem is at hand are not a big part of policy constructions. True, social problem victims can offer very emotional testimony for what a condition has done to them, and this testimony might be important in convincing policymakers that something must be done so that others are not so horribly harmed. Yet these claims encouraging emotional reaction can be only a backdrop because emotional appeal is not enough to form public policy. What this also means is that public policy typically is not covered by the mass media (except on PBS and some Sunday morning news programs). It is not entertaining. Because Americans receive most of our information from the mass media this means we tend to know little about policy. We rarely see it in the media, we do not see it because we are not interested in it, we are not interested in it because claims are made in scientific or legal language that is not understandable so we evaluate talk about public policy as boring.

Government and Social Activists. While it is most common for people interested in social problems to look at how social activists and other claims-makers affect public policy, it remains that social movements often fail to achieve policy changes. True, the civil rights movement achieved many changes in laws that had segregated and denied African-Americans equal opportunity. Yet other social movements have had far less success. For example, the antinuclear movement and the environmental movement in the 1980s regularly held rallies and marches attracting tens of thousands of supporters. These social change groups had public opinion on their side but they did little to change policy. Likewise, the relatively large and powerful women's movement threw its entire weight behind the Equal Rights Amendment but this amendment did not pass.[23]

At times, claims-makers might not influence public policy in the immediate moment, but they gain long-term benefits by becoming a part of the policymaking process. The Equal Opportunity Commission and the Environmental Protection Agency once were mere symbolic gestures to social movement activists. Now they are important players in the policymaking process. Such success is critical because it means these claims-makers will be much higher on the hierarchy of credibility in the next rounds of the social problems game.

SOCIAL PROBLEMS WORK AND CULTURAL CHANGE

Not all groups of social activists seek changes in public policy. First, there are some activists who believe they would need to give up too much in order to be successful in obtaining policy changes. Successful social problems formula stories reference commonly accepted cultural themes, and while successful claims can challenge these themes, they will not be successful if they seem to deny the importance of these themes. So, for example, claims that workers should be paid more might be successful, but claims that all workers should be paid the same wage go against the cultural theme of capitalism. Claims that women and men should be more equal within marriage can be successful but claims promoting the end to marriage probably will not be successful. Because successful claims tend to be those audience members evaluate as more or less compatible with cultural themes, social change through social policy tends to move at a snail's pace. If claims-makers seeking radical social change believe they have little chance of obtaining policy change, they might decide they will not even try.

Second, the possibilities of affecting social policy are influenced by the policy climate. The 1960s and 1970s, for example, saw a climate very conducive to policy changes promoting individual rights. Policies giving more rights to people in prisons were privileged in the 1970s but by the 1990s it was the rights of victims that faced a favorable policy climate and there was concern that prisoners had too many rights. Likewise, there was much concern about poverty in the 1960s and 1970s, but the current policy climate is more concerned with the problem of welfare than with poverty. Federal, state, and local administrations come and go and with them some groups of claims-makers find themselves on the "inside" and others on the "outside." Claims-makers finding themselves on the outside might decide to forgo the policy process because, like claims-makers promoting radical prognostic frames, this is very difficult and tiring social problems work when the chances of success are so slim.[24]

In brief, claims-makers might decide to not try to win the social problems game through policy changes because they evaluate such changes as requiring too much social problems work with too little chance of success. In some cases, these claims-makers would seek changes in policy if this were evaluated as more possible. Yet other claims-makers are not concerned with changing social policy. They want to win the social problems game through *cultural change.*

While changes in public policy can coerce changes in individual behavior (laws can force us to do things), public policy does not necessarily change the ways we *think.* Consider the ill-fated temperance movement in the United States. These claims-makers were successful at a policy level: the U.S. government outlawed alcohol production, sale, and consumption. Yet the movement was distinctly unsuccessful because it did not convince Americans to condemn the use of alcohol. In the end, the policy failed because it was not supported by cultural changes in how Americans evaluate alcohol.

Some groups of claims-makers argue that real social change cannot and should not be measured in terms such as the numbers of officials elected or the number of laws passed. They claim that real change will come only with changes in *culture*—the ways people think about the world.[25] Rather than seeking to pass laws against drunk driving, child abuse, or smoking, for example, claims-makers might focus on encouraging Americans to condemn these behaviors. Such prognostic claims seek cultural changes in attitudes with the belief that if we change our attitudes we will change our behaviors. So, for example, there is no specific law prohibiting "cannibalism" in the United States because it is not needed; it is not needed because the very idea of "cannibalism" is unthinkable. Claims-makers therefore can ignore the social problems work of changing social policy and focus rather on the work of changing culture. They ignore the work of changing policy because they believe this is not as important as changing culture.

This cultural change can focus on how people evaluate *behaviors.* In recent years, for example, the behavior of "smoking cigarettes" has changed from being generally evaluated as acceptable (even romantic) to unacceptable (and distinctly unromantic); "safe sex" is more commonly practiced and evaluated as necessary than in previous eras; "spanking," once considered a simple parental right, is being criticized by an increasing number of Americans; "drunk driving" has gone from something often laughed about to something now distinctly not funny.

While social change can come through changing evaluations of behaviors, other change comes from changing evaluations of *types of people*. We live in a world where specific types of people are generally valued and respected, while other types of people are generally devalued and disrespected. Social activists can focus on changing our evaluations of types of people.

These social change groups are called *new social movements*. This is a term to distinguish many of the current social movements from their historical predecessors. Traditionally, social movements focused on changing public policy because their concern was with changing the characteristics of the objective world. For example, movements for working people wanted better pay and better working conditions; the civil rights movement started with demands to end segregation and make it easier for black people to vote. In comparison, new social movements focus considerable claims-making activity on changing the subjective evaluations of people. The gay and lesbian movement, the black pride movement, and the current-day women's movement are as much—or more—about changing cultural evaluations of gays, lesbians, blacks, and women as types of people as they are about changing public policy toward these types of people.

The "size acceptance" movement is a case in point. Because we live in a culture prizing thinness, people who are not thin—particularly those who define themselves as "fat"—experience the consequences of considerable prejudice and discrimination. While social activists might seek changes in social policy such as laws against discrimination and changes in the physical environment—larger seats on airplanes and in movie theatres—these will not change the cultural climate that does not highly evaluate people who are other than thin. Therefore, it makes sense that the movement is called size *acceptance*: it primarily seeks to change cultural evaluations of people whose bodies do not conform to the cultural theme prizing thinness.[26]

Claims and Collective Identity Construction

When claims-makers construct images of victims and villains they construct *collective identities* that are images of *types of people*. Think about how our world is populated by types of people such as the "rape victim," the "prostitute," the "drunk driver," the "crime victim," the "learning disabled," the "drug dealer," and the "single mother". These images of types of people are the characters in social problems formula stories.

Critically, types of people *do not exist* until they are constructed by claims-makers. Before the twentieth century, for example, there were acts or behaviors known (and often condemned) as homosexual but there was no notion of a homosexual as a distinct type of person; types of people such as the "abusive parent" and the "abused child" did not exist in the United States until the late 1960s. Experiences can exist, behaviors can exist, but it is not until claims-makers construct images of victims and villains that particular types of people exist.

Social problems formula stories construct types of people and in doing so, they simultaneously construct images of these people as socially *valued* or as socially *devalued*.[27] Cultural transformation is achieved by increasing or decreasing the social esteem and worth accorded to types of people. So, for example, gay and lesbian activists attempt to change the image of homosexuals from the formerly discredited identity as deviant to a positive identity (gay is good). There also are groups of Catholic feminists in the United States who work to reinterpret the traditional story of the Catholic Church and women, which relegated women to a peripheral place. These activists are attempting to increase the social esteem accorded to women in the Catholic Church. Much of the women's movement in recent years has focused on increasing the cultural evaluation of women. It is not surprising that many claims competitions surround constructing images of types of people. "Progay" and "antigay" claims-makers, for example, both construct images of the "gay" person and these images promote either higher or lower cultural evaluation of this type of person.[28]

Cultural change happens when the social value and worth accorded to particular types of people change. Claims that construct typifications of people construct these as images of people who are more or less socially valued, as more or less socially worthy as these are evaluated through popular wisdom, cultural themes, and cultural feeling rules. At stake is an image of a collective identity, the typification of types of people. Cultural change for "progay" claims-makers for example, will happen when the "gay" type of person is accorded higher cultural value; cultural change for the "antigay" claims-makers will happen when this type of person is more socially devalued. In the next chapter we will turn to what this means to practical actors in daily life.

THE SOCIAL PROBLEMS WORK OF
CONSTRUCTING SOLUTIONS

Claims construct social problems formula stories and these stories set the stage for prognostic frames, which are claims about what should be done to resolve the condition. While some claims-makers focus on changing how our world is organized (laws, services, and so on), others focus on changing culture (the ways audience members think). While focusing on

policy change and focusing on cultural change are different routes to social change and require different types of social problems work, what all
claims-makers share is the desire to reach the final goal of the social problems game of constructing social problems: change in the social world. *The
power to lead social change is the very real prize for winning the social problems
game.*

While the social problems game does not end because it always is ongoing and responds to social change, effective claims at any one time have
the ability to change the world in which we live. Successful claims can
change the cultural climate of our world, they can change the objective
characteristics of our world, they can change the ways we make sense of
our selves and those around us. That is our next topic.

NOTES

1.   There are many studies of the specific activities of claims-makers seeking social change. They include Nelson (1984), child abuse laws; Rose (1977) and Tierney
(1982), wife abuse; Hillyard and Dombrink (2001), the death with dignity movement; Jenness and Grattet (2001), legislation against hate crimes; Jenness (1993),
prostitutes' rights; Stallings (1995), earthquakes; Welch (2000), flag burning; Sutton
(1988), stubborn children; Figert (1996), PMS; Kirk and Kutchins (1992), psychiatrists constructing the *Diagnostic and Statistical Manual.*

2.   Snow and Benford (1988) use the term *prognostic frames* for claims constructing proposed solutions to social problems. Alternatively, Stephen Toulmin (1958)
calls these "conclusion arguments." Within his framework, which is concerned
with the logic of arguments, given that a problem is at hand (condition) and given
that it is wrong (warrant), then we must do something (conclusion). See also Weiss
(1989) and Stone (1989) for the importance of these claims in the public policy arena.

3.   Here I am arguing that images of problems lead to images of solutions. Other
observers reverse this and claim that the availability of solutions leads to constructing problems that require those solutions (Edelman, 1988). Stone (1997), for
example, demonstrates with the example of "mass transit." In the 1950s, mass transit was proposed as the solution to the problem of "urban congestion"; in the late
1960s it was proposed as a way to reduce "automobile pollution"; in 1972, during
the OPEC oil embargo, it was proposed as an "energy-saving" alternative to private cars.

4.   See Wagner (1997) for his analysis of the negative consequences of the "get
tough" policy toward drug users, and Wexler (1990) for how increased attention to
"child abuse" has had unintended consequences.

5.   Reinarman and Levine (1995, excerpted in *Social Problems: Constructionist
Readings*) question the framing of crack cocaine as a law enforcement, rather than
a public health, problem.

6.   In studies of public policy, this is called the "problem definition" perspective. For further discussion see Weiss (1989), Stone (1997), Edelman (1977, 1988).

7.   Loseke (1995, excerpted in *Social Problems: Constructionist Readings*), examines the controversies surrounding the policy of involuntary commitment in mental hospitals for a type of person constructed as the "homeless mentally ill."

8.   I will draw from the work of Stone (1997), whose book is about relationships between narratives (social problems formula stories) and public policy.

9.   According to policy analysts Schneider and Ingram (1990:510), "Public policy almost always attempts to get people to do things they otherwise would not have done, or it enables them to do things they might not have done otherwise."

10.   Staudenmeier (1989, excerpted in *Social Problems: Constructionist Readings*) argues that in this case private industry did what government could not do: subject a large segment of the general population to intrusive tests.

11.   I will draw from the work of Schneider and Ingram (1993), who argue that policies are attentive to both social constructions *and* to the political power of constructed groups. Although they were concerned with general cultural evaluations of types of people, I am modifying their argument by using constructions generated through social problems formula stories. These stories, of course, reflect more general cultural evaluations.

12.   Elder and Cobb (1984) examine this policy climate in relation to "aging"; Almeida and Stearns (1998) examine the political climate surrounding toxic wastes in Minamata, Japan; Thayer (1997) explores this climate for the lesbian movement in Central America; Nardi (1998) for the gay and lesbian movement in Europe.

13.   Stone (1997) and Rochefort and Cobb (1993) argue that an effective strategy to *block* the interest of social policymakers is to construct the problem as complex. Claims about simple solutions, though, can quite quickly break down in the policymaking process. For example, Griset (1995) examined how a policy of "determinant sentencing" lost its widespread appeal in New York City when it came time to translate vague concepts into a concrete proposal.

14.   Such solutions are examples of what Edelman (1988:24–25) criticizes as "mere gestures." They are good for their symbolic value, not for what they actually do to change the social world. Rochefort and Cobb (1994) discuss the "instrumental" versus "expressive" forms of social policy. Instrumental policy is designed to do something; expressive policy is designed to make people feel good even though nothing tangible has been done.

15.   Lipsky and Smith (1989) illustrate how common constructions of social problem conditions as emergencies tend to lead to services responding to those emergencies. They complain that such responses are incredibly expensive. And, while expensive, they are mere bandages that do nothing to resolve the conditions leading to such emergencies.

16.   See Best (1999) and Stone (1997) for further discussion of the use of the war metaphor.

17.   This is my sorting of the characteristic of claims that tend to be effective in the social policy arena. Kingdon (1984) argues that the survival of proposals depends on their technical feasibility, value acceptability, and public acceptance.

18.   Elder and Cobb (1984) explore another consequence of this policy language. According to them, policy professionals tend to encourage debate to become specialized and esoteric and this creates barriers to popular participation and makes both the process and the product of policy not understandable to practical actors.

19. In this section, I will be drawing from Rochefort and Cobb (1994), who are proponents of the problem definition perspective for analysts of social policy. See also Rochefort (1986) for an extended example of this perspective applied to United States welfare policy.

20. Jenness and Broad (1997, excerpted in *Social Problems: Constructionist Readings*) describe the organizational sponsors for "hate crimes."

21. Jenkins (1999) discusses the political climate surrounding naming "abortion clinic bombings" as "terrorism."

22. Policymakers follow public opinion with the opinions of "registered voters, most likely to vote" being the most important. Also, the higher the issue in public salience, the more officials are likely to follow public opinion. Yet within this general tendency, policymakers exhibit an inherent *bias against change* (Monroe, 1988). Kingdon (1984) argues that it is most common for policymakers to respond to a *lack* of public interest.

23. For a discussion about social movements and the policymaking process, see Rochon and Mazmanian (1993) and W. Gamson (1990, 1992). For an analysis of the women's movement and the Equal Rights Amendment see Mansbridge (1986).

24. Sawyers and Meyer (1999) discuss how the women's movement in the 1980s stepped back from the policymaking process because the political climate was too hostile to allow success.

25. See Polletta (1997) for an extended discussion of the importance of cultural change.

26. Sobal (1999, excerpted in *Social Problems: Constructionist Readings*) examines the size acceptance movement.

27. Ian Hacking (1986) calls this the process of "making up people." For this process for people now known as homosexual see Plummer (1995); for battered women see Loseke (1992) and Rothenberg (2002).

28. For the progay and antigay issue culture, see Smith and Windes (1997), Bronski (1984), and Hequembourg and Arditi (1999).

III

From Social Constructions to Social Actions

6

Social Problems and Everyday Life

I went to the airport last night to pick up my husband. There were only a few people waiting for the plane that was late. As I sat and read a book, I felt a tug on my leg. A boy, probably three or four years old, was climbing around the chairs while holding my leg. I saw a woman sitting four chairs from me watching him and I smiled at her to let her know it was O.K. that her young charge was grabbing me. She smiled back. Then I looked at the boy, smiled, and said, "Hi, it looks like you're having a good time!" He looked at me and his previously happy expression changed. He screamed "MOMMY! MOMMY! STRANGER DANGER! STRANGER DANGER!" Crying hysterically, he scampered back through the chairs, onto the woman's lap and hid his face from me. She smiled at me while consoling him and reminding him to "stay close."

In the previous chapter we saw how effective claims about social problems could lead efforts to change the world. In the terminology I am using in this book, claims-makers win the social problems game when they change the world by shaping policy or when they change the ways people evaluate conditions and people.

In this chapter I want to do two things. First, I want to demonstrate the very practical reasons why studying social problems as social constructions should not be dismissed because this perspective ignores objective conditions and rather focuses on what claims-makers say about the world. The words of claims-makers can—and often do—change our world in very real ways. So, I will describe some of these changes in recent years to encourage you to understand how successful social problems claims-making changes the objective world around us.

My second goal in this chapter is to encourage you to think about how successful social problems claims can influence the ways we understand our own lives as well as how we make sense of people around us.

SUCCESSFUL CLAIMS AND SOCIAL CHANGE

Successful claims-making can change the objective (real) world and they can change our subjective understandings of that world.

Change in the Objective World

When successful claims lead to public policy, the objective characteristics of our world can change. This is easiest to see when claims change laws. While there are many examples, consider how as recently as the early 1960s there were no laws against parents using something then called "harsh discipline" on their children. Now we have an ever-expanding array of laws prohibiting what is categorized as child abuse. We also now live in a world where we must buckle our seat belts and where children must wear helmets when bicycling; many states have laws mandating that adults on motorcycles wear helmets. Parents now are not allowed to take their newborn babies home from hospitals unless they have properly certified infant car seats. So, too, it now is a crime to smoke cigarettes in most public buildings, and an increasing number of employers are constructing laws against "hate speech," a type of speech that in the past was categorized merely as rude or vulgar. In the not so distant past, it was perfectly legal for organizations and clubs to refuse membership to anyone who was not white or not Christian. Not so long ago, the help wanted pages in newspapers were in three separate sections labeled "Help Wanted," "Help Wanted, Women," and "Help Wanted, Colored." Behaviors now legally prohibited because they are constructed as racism or sexism or anti-Semitism were perfectly legal.

While some behaviors have been criminalized, others have been more or less decriminalized. This has happened, for example, in some places where laws prohibiting homosexuality have been struck down; some places now allow legal marriages between people of the same sex; abortion once was criminal and now it is legal; laws banning cohabitation outside marriage rarely are enforced.

New laws in response to successful claims-making include a variety of administrative laws. In the not-so-distant past, single people were not allowed to adopt children, now they often are. There now are various laws mandating special services for children with learning disabilities as well as the Americans with Disabilities Act mandating appropriate accommodations in all public buildings. Although currently being challenged by some people in some states, for many years there were a variety of laws mandating affirmative action in hiring and in school admissions.

While changes in law are the most obvious changes due to successful claims-making, successful claims also can change the physical characteristics of our world. Far more so than in the past, for example, we now live in a world with parking spaces reserved for disabled people, there are more wheelchair ramps, elevators with floors coded in Braille, and city buses equipped for wheel chair users. So, too, claims about the problems of crime have led to surveillance cameras on an increasing number of city streets; traveling by airplane is far more difficult than in the past due to increased security measures after the terrorist attacks; in addition, most children now do not go trick-or treating on Halloween, parents routinely have their children fingerprinted, there are special devices for parents to prevent children from watching particular television programs, children and young teenagers legally cannot watch some movies that now are rated for their sex, violence, and language content. These changes in our physical world are consequences of successful social problems claims-making.

Finally, the topic for the next chapter is the troubled persons' industry composed of all the services for victims, potential victims, villains, and potential villains constructed in social problems formula stories. Not so long ago, a woman abused by her husband could not go to a shelter for battered women because such places *did not exist;* not so long ago a child who was blind or learning disabled could not expect special facilities and programs because these *did not exist.* There were no special programs or services for people in "dysfunctional families," nor for women suffering from anorexia or bulimia because these *did not exist.* Of course, these conditions existed, but the programs and services did not exist because the conditions were not evaluated as social problems. Successful claims-making can lead to new social services.

When successful social problem claims lead to public policy, they change our world in very real ways. Such changes make some behaviors more possible than in past times, they discourage other behaviors that had been ignored, or perhaps even encouraged, in other historical times. Changes can give special protection to some categories of people, they can target other types of people for special punishment.

The most important point here is that claims-makers construct images of *types* of people with *types* of problems and *types* of needs requiring *types* of laws, physical environments, or services. When social change happens, *real* people are affected. At times, changes are experienced primarily by the people in particular categories of people. So laws targeted against specific behaviors or special services or programs for particular categories of people can affect the real people in these categories. At other times, changes affect social members in general such as changes in the physical environment to accommodate people in wheelchairs or increased security measures at airports and other public places.

Change in Cultural Climates

Some claims-makers believe that eliminating social problem conditions requires changing the cultural climate. Here, too, there are many changes from the recent past. Consider, for example, our national obsession with health and eating "low-fat food." Low-fat food was not even a category of food when I was a child but now many Americans deeply believe that their good health depends on eating it. While there is little evidence that eating low-fat food is necessary for good health, and while it is possible to offer counterclaims that there are more important things we could do to achieve good health, it remains that the importance of eating low-fat food is achieving the status of simply taken-for-granted popular wisdom.[1] Successful claims can generate *new* cultural themes such as the importance of eating low-fat food or the importance of practicing "safe sex."

Another relatively new cultural theme surrounds pregnancy. Claims-making has resulted in a cultural belief that pregnancy can—and should—end with a "perfect" child. Furthermore if the outcome is not so "perfect," we often look at the mother and ask what she did "wrong." In brief, pregnancy no longer is evaluated as a mysterious process where the results are understood as a matter of fate or divine will; pregnant women are expected to act and even think in ways experts maintain will yield a "perfect" child.[2]

Successful claims also can change social evaluations of conditions and people. At times, behaviors that previously were evaluated as positive or neutral become negatively evaluated. Think about the condition of drunk driving. Thirty years ago people drove while intoxicated, and while this was a troublesome behavior, a crash involving an intoxicated person nonetheless often was called an "accident," implying that the person doing this was not a villain but rather suffered from bad luck. We can say that twenty years ago there was a *different cultural climate* surrounding the condition of drunk driving and the type of person called the drunk driver.

As another example, until the recent past, white Americans often considered racial segregation a moral good. While such segregation remains common in practice, no one justifies it as good. Or, twenty years ago we smoked cigarettes during lectures in college classrooms. It was acceptable and expected. Indeed, it was a mark of sophistication. Now it is not. There is a different cultural climate surrounding cigarettes and smokers.

Successful claims therefore can change social evaluations from acceptable or at least tolerable to unacceptable and not tolerable. Successful claims also can lead to a cultural climate that previously condemned but now tolerates or even praises particular behaviors. Consider the condition of "mothers who are employed." A common cultural belief in the 1950s was that mothers, especially if they had young children, should not be employed outside their homes. This condition now is much more tolerated than in the past. Indeed, some claims-makers argue it is best for children if their mothers are employed. In the same way, earlier in the last century it was grounds for divorce if a man did not economically support his wife and family. Now the cultural climate has changed and few people condemn a fully employed man who does not earn enough by himself to be the sole economic provider for his family. In popular wisdom this is merely a fact of life.

Objective Change and Change in Cultural Climates

So far, I have separated social change into types: Changes in the how the world is set up (objective change) and changes in cultural climates (subjective change). The most successful claims-makers change *both* the objective world and the cultural climate. Drunk driving, for example, now is much more condemned than in the past *and* the criminal penalties for it have greatly increased.

But because of the complexity of social life, most claims-makers are only more or less successful in changing the social world. For example, while the condition of "mothers who are employed" is much more tolerated than in the past we cannot say that social change has been complete: Employed mothers continue to be blamed for any problems experienced by their children, there is not enough adequate child daycare, few employers offer flexible working hours, women taking time from work to care for children are on a "mommy track" rather than a "fast track" to career success. At any one time, most social change probably would be evaluated by claims-makers as insufficient. Gays and lesbians, for example, are more accepted than in the past but not by all people and not in all places. While there now is condemnation for child abuse and wife abuse, many audience members condemn these behaviors only when they are incredibly extreme, so that much troublesome violence remains evaluated as morally tolerable. Likewise, although racial segregation is illegal and most often condemned, it remains common.

We should expect that social change would be uneven, and we should expect that only in rare cases would all members of a population support a particular change. For example, there are many claims and counterclaims surrounding the behavior of "spanking" children. One group of experts claims that spanking is no different from child abuse, while another group claims that expanding the domain of child abuse to include spanking is not justified (indeed, that this expansion is ridiculous). While there probably now is less public support for spanking than in the past when such behavior was a taken-for-granted method of discipline, we certainly could not claim that all (or even the great majority) of Americans have changed their evaluations of spanking.[3]

Social Change and Social Members

Throughout this book I have discussed how claims-making is a political process, so who wins the social problems game of constructing problems might reflect politics as much as—or more than—it reflects audience support. I also have discussed how social problems formula stories are not good descriptions of the complexity of experience of real people. We have seen many twists and turns, yet when we come to this topic of social change, all of these *do not matter*.

At times, a given set of claims will be successful not because they are widely supported by audience members in general but because they are supported by a small group of powerful people. At other times, a given set of claims will be popular among the general population, but that still does not mean that each and every person supports them. Read the letters to the editor in your local newspaper for a few nights and you will see how many different views exist among the general population. What all this means is that it is very rare for *all* Americans to agree with any given set of social problem claims. Yet that *does not matter* when claims change the social world.

It *does not matter* if successful claims do not match objective reality. Claims about the problems of crack cocaine were unsupported by objective indicators when this condition first received pubic concern, yet the War on Drugs started nonetheless. Likewise, parents worry a great deal about the problem of their children being poisoned by tainted Halloween candy although there is little evidence supporting a claim that this should be a widespread worry.[4]

Nor does it matter that claims leading to social change were made by people who do claims-making because of their objective interests. Our national obsession with low-fat food, for example, is a consequence of claims made by companies who sell this food. The more we evaluate claims about low-fat food as important, the more of this food we buy from these companies. But it *does not matter* why people make claims. What matters is that the importance of eating low-fat food is becoming a part of unchallenged, taken-for-granted, popular wisdom.[5]

Nor does it matter if audience members do not personally support the social change from successful claims-making. In the previous chapter, for example, I mentioned how it is increasingly common for employers to demand their employees' urine be tested for evidence of drug use.[6] While this is justified by constructing the cultural theme that such tests are necessary to ensure productive employees and a drug free workplace, I might rather evaluate these tests as violating the cultural theme of the right to privacy. But if I want a job in an increasing number of places, I do not have a choice. And, I must pass through airport security if I want to board a plane. No one asks me if I want to do this or not. Nor does it matter if a pregnant woman disagrees with the experts about how she should conduct herself during her pregnancy. Such a woman lives in a culture where others around her will continually remind her what she should—and shouldn't— eat, drink, and think. When claims change the world it *does not matter* that some people do not agree.

This is one reason why the social problems game always is ongoing. Rarely do all (or even a great majority of) audience members evaluate a particular set of claims as believable and important. Some claims will be silenced, some will be successful primarily because of power and politics. At times, one group of claims-makers is successful in obtaining social change but this change is evaluated by others as creating a new social prob- lem. Audience members who find their own notions of morality to be vio- lated by this social change can become new claims-makers for the next round of the social problems game. So, antiabortion claims-makers block access to abortion clinics and threaten the service providers in these places; men challenge being denied custody of their children; anti—Affirmative Action claims-makers have been fairly successful in challenging this pol- icy, and so on. Claims-making most often is only more or less successful; social change can start new rounds of claims-making.

SOCIAL PROBLEMS WORK IN DAILY LIFE

So far I have focused on two types of social problems work: that of claims-makers who work to persuade audience members to evaluate a condition as a social problem, and that of audience members who evalu- ate the believability and importance of claims they see or hear. I want to extend the concept of social problems work now to talk about the work done by practical actors in our daily lives.

This is the social problems work of evaluating and categorizing experi- ences, conditions, and people. Our concern here is how we do this work every time we see some thing and decide that it is—or is not—a particu- lar instance of a social problem, every time we categorize a particular per- son as a particular type of victim (or not a victim) or a villain (or not a villain).[7]

We do this social problems work in our daily lives every time we clas- sify our own family or some other family as "dysfunctional," every time we say that a particular person is a "deadbeat dad" or a "racist." We do this work when we talk with others about problems in our local schools and construct diagnostic frames for what these problems mean. We do this social problems work when we move away from strangers because we categorize them as possible "terrorists" or "criminals." The concept of social problems work can be extended so that it includes the activities of evaluating particular conditions and particular people as concrete instances of social problems. The metaphor of the *social problems game* also can be extended to talk about the power, competitions, and goals in evaluating and categorizing experiences, conditions, and people. The activities in this game are the categorizations practical actors make, the *goal* of the game is to categorize complex conditions and real people into social problem categories. The *players* are the practical actors doing the categorizing and the individual people being categorized as victims or villains. Just as the social problems game of persuading audience members to define a condition as intolerable was surrounded by *competition,* there are competitions in categorizing practical experience and individual people. At times, competition is between two or more categories that could be used to make sense of conditions and people. (Is this *particular* lake polluted because of illegal dumping of chemicals or because of naturally occurring algae? Is this *particular* prostitute a villain or a victim? Is this *particular* child lazy or learning disabled?) At other times, competition is between people doing the categorization and those being categorized: individual people do not always agree when others categorize them as victims or villains. Finally, just as there is a hierarchy of credibility for social problems claims-makers, not all players in the game of evaluating and categorizing practical experience are equally powerful in deciding which categorizations will be used (and which will not). Clearly, how professionals categorize conditions and people is more powerful than how these conditions and people are categorized by others; how children categorize themselves is not as important as how they are categorized by adults. People in some categories (such as "mentally ill" or "mentally impaired") tend to be not as believed as others.

Social Problems Work: Evaluating and Categorizing Experiences, Conditions, and People

This social problems work of practical actors is very complicated. I suggest you reread the section in Chapter 1 on how humans make sense of our experiences as well as the section in Chapter 2 on how audience members use practical experience, popular wisdom, and our understandings of cultural themes and feeling rules to evaluate the believability and importance of social problems claims. To summarize this in three sentences: our experiences are complex, people are unique, our understandings of what is and is not morally tolerable are not fixed. We create the meaning of our world through constructing *categories* of conditions and *categories* of people and our reactions to these conditions and people depend on how we categorize them. We have no choice but to do this categorization because otherwise we would be immobilized, awash in details. Social problems claims-makers therefore are people who construct categories and, if they are successful, these categories might be used by practical actors to make sense of unique conditions and people.

I want to stress the "might" in the last sentence. While successful social problems formula stories construct typifications of conditions and new collective identities of people, that does not mean these categories automatically will be used by practical actors. Just as humans are not socialized to blindly put into practice one or another particular set of beliefs, just as we do not believe everything we see and hear, we do our evaluations and categorizations in daily life on the basis of our practical experience, popular wisdom, and personal understandings of cultural themes and feeling rules. Yet successful social problems formula stories also can be a resource to make sense of daily life. At the minimum, successful social problems give us new categories of conditions and people. Successful stories can change popular wisdom and cultural themes as well as the characteristics of the world around us. But in academic terminology, social problem claims are *members' resources:* something that *might* be used by practical actors who decide it makes sense to do so based on their experiences and understandings.

That is why this is called social problems *work.* Just as audience members do the social problems work of evaluating claims, practical actors in our daily lives think about how to categorize unique conditions and unique people. True, the more successful the social problem, the more likely it is that images of it appear all around us in media, books, pamphlets, classroom discussions, and signs on bulletin boards, and this might encourage us to think in these terms. But even the most widely circulating images are not necessarily used by practical actors.[8] Indeed, there are reasons why we might even assume that it would be difficult for practical actors to categorize unique experiences and people as instances of social problem conditions, victims, and villains.

Social Problems Formula Stories and the Complexity of Daily Life

We cannot assume that practical actors will use claims from social problems formula stories, because the conditions and people we encounter in our lives rarely are clear examples of whatever images are circulating in the media, books, and so on. This is because successful social problem formula stories tend to feature plots of *extreme* conditions with characters who are *extreme* victims and *extreme* villains. While social life *does* give us far too many examples of these extremes, much of what happens is not so extreme. For example, we might all agree that it is a condition of "sexual harassment" if an employer says to his employee "have sex with me or you'll lose your job." But is it sexual harassment if the employer says, "You look very nice today in that dress?" Or, we might all agree that a victim of crime deserves sympathy, but does a woman who is robbed while selling illegal drugs to school children deserve our sympathy and help? That might inspire debate. In real life there is no end to the complexity. The more we know about particular conditions and the particular people in them, the harder it is to easily categorize a *particular* condition or person as a *type* of condition or person.[9]

While we cannot assume that practical actors will use images contained in social problems formula stories as a resource to make sense of daily life, it remains that these stories do circulate and can influence the social problems work of evaluating and categorizing conditions and people. This is most obvious when we look at the topic of personal identity.

PERSONAL IDENTITIES AND COLLECTIVE IDENTITIES

Personal identity is a sense of who we, and others, are. For two reasons, personal identity is a problem in our postmodern era. First, personal identity is the answer to the question: Who am I? That question would not have been asked in the past because people then had a sense of self, a personal identity, that tended to be securely located in religion, family, and community. The answer was taken for granted: Who am I? I am a believer in a particular religion, I am a husband/wife, mother/father, I am a member of a particular tribe, and so on. In sharp contrast, our postmodern era is one where many people do not have ready answers to this question, Who am I? A sense of personal identity in our postmodern world is not given. Our biographies often are characterized by change—we get married, divorced, remarried; we leave one job and start another; we move from one place to another; we might experiment with different religious beliefs. How we think of ourselves at one time often does not fit with our new circumstances. We can talk about how we are trying to "find ourselves." Stated in academic terminology, the postmodern world is one in which we each must *construct* our identity, we must decide how to categorize *ourselves*. What type of person am I?[10]

Second, the problem of personal identity is about how we categorize *other people*. One of my students told me that in the past two years he has lived with twenty people. He rents a house and needs four other people to pay the rent and, according to him, a fact of life is that roommates come and roommates go. Likewise, workers in colleges regularly assign strangers to live with one another in tiny dorm rooms. We most often do not know anything about the person sitting next to us on a plane or in a classroom. When we start new jobs we find ourselves working with strangers. The problem of personal identity is about how we categorize other people. How do we evaluate and categorize other people when we do not have in-depth knowledge of their lives? When we know nothing about them?

Social problems work in daily life includes the work of evaluating and categorizing ourselves and others. The problem of categorizing the self perhaps is one of the most discussed issues of daily life. Americans are drawn to reading books, to thinking about possible lives we could lead, to talking with friends and counselors in search of ways to be comfortable with who we are or with who we might become. The largest section of books in my local Barnes and Noble is entitled Self-Help. Television talk shows offer a never-ending barrage of pointers for how to change the ways we evaluate and categorize ourselves. Dr. Phil on "Oprah," of course, is in this business of helping people construct identity. Likewise, talk about the problems of categorizing other people is all around us. Popular magazines, television talk shows, and news reports often contain pointers on "how to recognize" a variety of people (such as terrorists or alcoholics or teens likely to go on shooting rampages). Often in the form of handy checklists, these claims instruct us on how to do the social problems work of evaluating and categorizing other people.

Personal Identity, Collective Identity, and Social Problems Formula Stories

In the previous chapter I argued that social problems claims-makers construct *collective identities*, which are images of types of people. The topic here is how such collective identities can be a resource for creating a sense of the personal self and for making sense of others. The characters constructed in social problems formula stories can be important for three reasons.

First, social problems formula stories can construct *new types of people*. So, for example, it was not possible to be a "codependent," or "learning disabled" or a member of a "dysfunctional family" until recent years because those types of people did not exist. These are new collective identities, new types of people. Successful claims-making can construct new types of people, which makes it possible for practical actors to categorize themselves or others in ways that previously had been *not* possible. So, for example, some people experience identity confusion because their biological sex does not conform to how they think of themselves. Such people often do not know how to categorize themselves, yet they learn about the category of "transsexual" by seeing such people on television. Once they learn that the category is available they might choose to categorize themselves (or others) in this way. Likewise women who have been assaulted by their husbands can change their understanding of the meaning of this behavior and their understanding of themselves when they hear social problems claims about wife abuse and the battered woman.[11] Successful claims can construct new types of people and this allows practical actors to categorize themselves or others as these types of people.

Second, as evaluated through popular wisdom, cultural themes, and cultural feeling rules, each collective identity encourages particular types of *social evaluations*. At times, rather than creating new types of people, social problems formula stories rather increase or decrease social evaluations associated with existing types of people. Some categories of people, such as drunk drivers and smokers, have been devalued as the result of successful claims-making. The social evaluations of other categories of people have increased. I remember when I was a child that adults talked in hushed tones about "divorcees"; people living together while not married were "living in sin." These categories no longer are so highly discredited.

When claims change social evaluations of categories of people then the real people in these categories might experience this increased or decreased social esteem. So, for example, black women have been influenced by claims made by the civil rights movement. Their autobiographies show how civil rights claims have led them to more highly evaluate themselves.[12]

Third, because our reactions to people are influenced by how we categorize them, social evaluations of collective identities are associated with *practical experiences*.[13] A topic in the previous chapter was the relationship between social evaluation and the types of social policy likely resulting from successful claims-making. People who are highly valued tend to receive social policy benefits; those who are negatively evaluated receive few benefits but pay many costs. Discrimination in its many forms is associated with low social evaluation.

This is the very practical reason why many social change groups work diligently to construct collective identities. Collective identities can be assigned to unique people and this is associated with social evaluations. Social evaluations, in turn, influence how these people evaluate themselves and how they are evaluated by others. Social evaluations by others also influence practical experiences. So, when a person is categorized as a member of a discredited collective identity, the social evaluation of that person decreases and others treat that person with less regard; when a person is categorized as a member of a valued collective identity, the social evaluation of that person increases and others tend to treat that person with more regard. Being treated with disrespect is associated with negative evaluations of the self, being treated with respect is associated with more positive evaluations of the self.

The importance of collective identity is complex because it involves how we categorize our selves, how others categorize us, and how we categorize others; it involves both social evaluations and practical experiences. Consider the example of the homosexual type of person. Traditionally, this was a discredited identity, people categorized by others as homosexual were disrespected (low social evaluation) and often experienced discrimination (negative experiences). Because others treated the actual people in this category with disrespect, many of the people in this category suffered from low self-esteem (a low evaluation of the self). Yet gay and lesbian social change groups have constructed counterclaims promoting increased social evaluation of the homosexual type of person. To the extent that these claims have been successful, actual people in this category experience less discrimination (positive experiences), receive more social regard from others (higher social evaluation), and therefore can construct a sense of the self that is positive (higher evaluation of the self).

One such social change group, Dignity, seeks to change the ways that "homosexual Catholics" are evaluated by the Catholic Church. They do this by constructing an image of the "homosexual Catholic" as a good person, with "good person" an evaluation made through cultural themes valuing family, religion, and citizenship. Such a collective identity as a good person justifies the claim that the people in this category should be treated with more respect, and that the Catholic Church should change its beliefs that homosexual practices are sinful. Such a collective identity promotes a high sense of self.[14]

Collective identities therefore are powerful. Of course, we cannot assume that people automatically decide that a social problems formula story is *their* story, nor can we assume that we easily categorize people around us as a *type* of person. First, at any one time there are multiple stories about types of people circulating in the social world. Some stories condemn categories of people while others emphasize the goodness of people in these categories.[15] So, some social activists have constructed a "gay is deviant" story, others have constructed a "glad to be gay" story; the "prostitute as victim" story competes with the "prostitute as villain" story. There often are many social problems formula stories from which to choose so the social problems work of evaluating and categorizing self and others requires choosing the story that seems to be the most sensible. Second, it is not easy to decide that the self or a particular other person is an example of a type of person because individuals are unique and often much more complex than the characters in social problems formula stories. This is why this activity of evaluating and categorizing self and others is *social problems work*.[16]

Victim as Collective Identity

There is one clear cumulative effect of many social movements in the past thirty years: we now live in a world where there are countless collective identities as victims of social problem conditions.[17] Individuals now can choose among many possible identities: there are victims of marital rape, acquaintance rape, date rape, wife abuse, husband abuse, elder abuse, sibling abuse, peer abuse, emotional abuse, clergy abuse, Satanic ritual abuse, sexual abuse, sexual harassment, sexual addiction, love addiction, internet addiction, food addiction, eating disorders, post-traumatic stress disorder, multiple-personality disorder, chronic fatigue syndrome, false memory syndrome, battered woman's syndrome, battered child's syndrome, credit-card dependency, codependency, dysfunctional families, hate crimes, stalking, drunk driving, bullying, UFO abductions, racism, sexism, homophobia, ageism, anti-Semitism, drunk driving. Each of these is a collective victim identity constructed through social problems claims-making.

There has been a proliferation of victim identities in recent years. Indeed, claims about the problem of "codependency" explicitly construct each and every American as a victim. Just as low-fat food now often is a taken-for-granted route to achieving good health, so-called recovery movements in the United States have become increasingly common. Recovery is a set of claims promoting the importance of taking care of the self, of understanding families as places producing deep emotional scars, and of belonging to a community of people all engaged in the process of recovery. This is a set of claims promoted through self-help books and through television talk shows, it is a set of claims beginning with assumptions about victims and the need for victims to change their personal identity. Because Americans in great numbers are drawn to such groups it seems that many Americans categorize themselves as victims in need of identity change.[18]

In some ways, it makes sense that many Americans evaluate the personal identity of victim as attractive. As judged through popular wisdom and cultural feeling rules, a victim is a good person (high social evaluation). When the identity of victim is assigned by others, sympathy and help can be forthcoming (positive experience). When we categorize ourselves as victims we release ourselves from responsibility for the problems we experience or cause others (high evaluation of the self).

While denying responsibility and receiving assistance and help are positive consequences of claiming the status of victim and/or having that status assigned by others, there are social costs for this collective identity. Bluntly stated, we live in a world where a primary cultural theme is individualism, a set of beliefs prizing individual accomplishment, independence, responsibility, and self-sufficiency. Within this cultural theme of individualism, the personal identity of victim is discrediting because, by definition, victims are not in control of their lives, and need help. Most certainly, we do not blame victims for their plights, yet within the cultural theme of individualism prizing self-sufficiency and individual control, victims are failures. Americans do not grow up hoping one day to become a victim; the identity of victim is claimed more often by people who are powerless than by people who are powerful. Victims become the objects of sympathy rather than people highly regarded as models for how others might profitably live their lives.

We come, then, to a problem. It is a very effective strategy in the game of constructing social problems to construct images of pure victims. It is a very effective strategy to dramatize that victims deserve sympathy and help. Yet when such a collective identity is used as a personal identity, this sympathy and help come with the cost of emphasizing weakness and the inability to manage one's own life. Given this, it is not surprising that some feminists have criticized the tendency of claims about women to emphasize their victim status. Some claims-makers now are saying that rather than talking about how women are the *victims* of wife abuse or rape we should talk about how women are *survivors* of these conditions. Proposed new constructions could emphasize women's strengths rather than women's weaknesses.[19]

SOCIAL PROBLEMS AND SOCIAL CHANGE

Social change is a consequence of successful social problems work. This can be change in the world around us, it can be change in how specific conditions and types of people are socially evaluated. Social problems claims themselves can become resources used by practical actors to make sense of our experiences, ourselves, and the people around us. Clearly, the social problems game is very real in its consequences. The words and images constructed by claims-makers affect the world in very real ways.

Our next topic remains on the general theme of the consequences of successful claims. The next chapter moves from how successful social problems can influence our daily lives to the troubled persons industry, which includes the organizations, programs, and groups designed to help or rehabilitate victims and to rehabilitate or punish villains constructed in social problems formula stories.

NOTES

1.   Austin (1999, excerpted in *Social Problems: Constructionist Readings*) examines claims-making leading to our national obsession with low-fat food.
2.   Gardner (1994, excerpted in *Social Problems: Constructionist Readings*) analyzes the advice offered in magazines for pregnant women.

3. Davis (1994, excerpted in *Social Problems: Constructionist Readings*) examines contemporary claims and counterclaims about spanking. Nelson (1984) explores how the behavior of spanking posed problems for claims-makers trying to persuade policymakers to support legislation to make child abuse a crime. Successful claims-making required them to construct the social problem of child abuse as not including spanking.

4. For differences between objective indicators and public perceptions of crack cocaine as a problem, see Reinarman and Levine (1995, excerpted in *Social Problems: Constructionist Readings*); for tainted Halloween candy see Best (1990).

5. Austin (1999, excerpted in *Social Problems: Constructionist Readings*).

6. Staudenmeier (1989, excerpted in *Social Problems: Constructionist Readings*).

7. As defined by Miller and Holstein (1989:5), this form of social problems work addresses "how social problems categories are applied to produce meaningful, seemingly concrete instances of social problems." Riessman (1989) complains that social scientists have tended to ignore this critical question of human sense-making. Emerson and Messenger (1977) examine how individuals categorize their experiences in one way or another. Cerulo (1998) explores how practical actors evaluate the moral meaning of violence. Frazier, Cochran, and Olson (1995) examine the definitions of "sexual harassment" held by practical actors.

8. The possible exception here are social problem categories that expand so much that they include everyone. For example, Furedi (2001, excerpted in *Social Problems: Constructionist Readings*) argues that the problem of "workplace bullying" in Great Britain can include any behavior; Irvine 1999) argues that the codependency movement claims that every family is "dysfunctional" and every person is "codependent."

9. While some categories of victims such as battered women and date rape victims often are categorized by professionals as people in "denial" of their victimization, I would argue that failing to classify the self in the professionally preferred category often rather reflects the complexity of lived experience. This complexity can make the condition as experienced seem dissimilar to the condition as typified in public images. See Wood and Rennie (1994) for the problems victims experience when trying to talk about "rape."

10. There now is a vast literature surrounding the problems of personal identity in the postmodern era. For an overview of these problems see Giddens (1991), Gergen (1994), and Holstein and Gubrium (2000). For specific social sources of these problems see the articles in the collection edited by Breakwell (1983).

11. For an examination of how people experiencing differences between their biological and psychological sex learn to categorize themselves see Mason-Schrock (1996), for how homosexuals actively seek out identity models see Plummer (1995), for how social problems claims change women's understandings of the experience of assault see Riessman (1989).

12. For the influence of the civil rights movement on black women's autobiographies see Brush (1999). Malone et al. (2000) examine how criticism of the *behavior* of "smoking cigarettes" gradually was transformed to criticism of *people* who smoke these cigarettes.

13. Socall and Holtgraves (1992) discuss how the same behaviors are evaluated

quite differently depending upon whether a person is categorized as "mentally ill" or "physically ill."

14.   Loseke and Cavendish (2001, excerpted in *Social Problems: Constructionist Readings*) examine the construction of the "homosexual Catholic" by the group Dignity. See also Plummer (1995) for relationships between social evaluations and personal evaluations.

15.   Richardson (1990) argues there are two types of narratives: "cultural" narratives reflect traditional values and negatively evaluate the qualities of marginalized people, while "collective" narratives are the stories that praise and promote the goodness of previously marginalized people.

16.   Pfoul (1978) calls this diagnostic work; Loseke (2001, excerpted in *Social Problems: Constructionist Readings*) calls this identity work.

17.   I am drawing from several sources in this discussion of victims. Holstein and Miller (1990) examine victimization as the social problems work of categorizing unique individuals and victims. Best (1997) focuses on why so many new categories of victims have been created since the 1960s. Fattah (1986) discusses unintended and negative consequences of movements for victims. Westervelt (1998) examines how victimization became a criminal defense. The articles in the collection edited by Lamb (1999) discuss various costs and benefits of constructing women as victims. Dunn (2001) offers an empirical example of these costs and benefits for women victims of stalking.

18.   Lowney (1999, excerpted in *Social Problems: Constructionist Readings*) examines how television talk shows produce the "religion of recovery." Irvine (1999) discusses the codependency movement.

19.   It might be more difficult for constructions emphasizing strength to be successful in persuading audiences to take conditions seriously. After all, it sounds much more immediate to assist women victims than to assist women survivors. The category of "survivor" might lead audience members to praise women for their strengths but that does not necessarily lead to evaluations that such women need assistance.

7

Social Problems and Troubled People

I open my Tampa phone book to a heading called Social Services. There are three pages of listings including Addictions Anonymous, Center for Persons with Disabilities, Big Brothers / Big Sisters, Consumer Credit Counseling, Divine Providence Food Bank, Florida American Indian Movement, Narcotics Anonymous, Hispanic Needs and Services, Humane Society, Mary & Martha Transitional Housing, Missing Children Center, The Spring for Battered Women, Survivors of Stalking. Under a heading called Government are listings including DOPELINE, Neighborhood Watch, Elder Helpline, Equal Opportunity Commission; there are two entire columns of listings for jails and juvenile reformatories. In the front of the book are emergency numbers: AIDS, drug abuse, sexual assault, child abuse, latchkey phone friend program, and air pollution control. My local newspaper lists support groups meeting this week: Alcoholics Anonymous, Parents of Murdered Children, Rape Survivors, Parents Without Partners, Lesbian Mothers, Adult Victims of Child Abuse. I wonder, Is everyone in our world troubled?

The topic of the previous chapter was how successful claims can change both the objective characteristics and the cultural climate of our world. In doing this, they can change our experiences and they can give us new ways to evaluate and categorize our experiences, ourselves, and others. In this chapter I want to continue that topic by focusing on relationships between successful claims and services designed to do something about the victims, potential victims, villains, or potential villains of social problems conditions.

This is the topic of the *troubled persons industry*, a term for all the organizations and groups designed to do something to help or rehabilitate or punish the people in social problems formula stories. These organizations or groups range from prisons and mental hospitals to support groups and education programs of all types; they include shelters for homeless people and abused children, programs for pregnant teens and for children at risk, and Meals On Wheels.

Clearly, the term *troubled persons industry* is very general and disguises many differences among places that are sponsored by governments, charities, churches, and private individuals. Some of these places are very formally organized, some are informal. Some are about helping victims or potential victims, others are about the social control, rehabilitation, or punishment of villains or potential villains. Yet despite these differences, all such organizations and groups share two characteristics. Most important, they are each the consequence of successful social problems claims-making. After all, we would not have rape crisis hotlines without the social problem of rape; we would not have child sex abuse education without concern about the sexual abuse of children; we keep building prisons because claims framing crime as a problem resolved by prisons have been successful in convincing politicians and taxpayers that this is what we need. Second, such organizations and groups share the characteristic that each is in the same kind of industry: the "raw material" for each is people, the services of each attempt to do something with these people, and if these places are successful their products are changed people.

Think of this chapter as building from the previous in two ways. First, in the previous chapter we looked at how a changed world was a consequence of successful claims-making. The organizations and groups encompassing the troubled persons industry are other concrete examples of this change due to successful claims-making. Second, I ended the previous chapter on the social problems work of evaluating and categorizing individual people as types of people. This is what workers in the troubled persons industry do. I will start with relationships between successful claims and the troubled persons industry, then move to looking at the people in this industry and the work they do.[1]

SOCIAL PROBLEMS FORMULA STORIES AND THE TROUBLED PERSONS INDUSTRY

Each of the organizations and groups in the troubled persons industry is a consequence of successful social problems work: Audience members have been convinced that a condition is intolerable and that something needs to be done. The places and groups in the troubled persons industry are the consequence of prognostic claims focused on individual-level needs (help, rehabilitation, punishment). True, it is fairly common for programs and organizations in practice to be not exactly what claims-makers originally envisioned. For example, it is common for programs to receive inadequate funding so they cannot do all claims-makers wanted them to do. In addition, controversial aspects of programs (such as sex education) sometimes are deleted in order to gain the support of policymakers. Yet the major story remains: programs or groups designed to do something about social problem victims, potential victims, villains, or potential villains will more or less reflect images of the social problem claims that led to it.

Successful claims will be reflected in what *services* are offered. For example, claims about the lack of criminal justice response to the problems of wife abuse led to programs of victim advocacy to help women obtain restraining orders; claims about a new form of personal trouble called "codependency" led to thousands of support groups for people who categorized themselves as having such troubles.[2]

These organizations and groups also are organized for particular types of *people* who can be categorized as individual instances of collective identities such as out-of-control teen, teenage mom, alcoholic, rape victim, and disabled child. Places in the troubled persons industry will offer these *types* of people the *types* of services that seem necessary given the various grounds and diagnostic frames used to construct the typification of the social problem. For example, one recently successful social problem formula story constructed a type of character, the welfare mother, as economically dependent because she believed receiving welfare was easier than being employed. Given this image, it logically follows that gaining economic independence (defined as good through the cultural theme of individualism) requires such a woman to find employment. Programs organized from this image focus on encouraging women to obtain job skills and offering various incentives for finding work and disincentives for not finding work.

Social problems claims can produce new collective identities of people needing assistance and the troubled persons industry then offers such assistance. Consider, for example, a problem faced by pediatricians (doctors for children) in the recent past. They literally were running out of clients who needed specialized medical care: most childhood diseases had been eliminated, health was generally better than in the past. Pediatricians resolved this problem in two ways. First, they expanded the domain of "children" to include adolescents and young adults. Second, they constructed a vast range of behaviors such as temper tantrums, sibling rivalry, shyness, and fears and phobias as medical troubles they could resolve. By expanding the domain of child and by medicalizing behaviors, pediatricians greatly expanded the kinds of people (adolescents and young adults) and the kinds the troubles (shyness, fears, and so on) requiring their services.[3]

Consequences of Problems Formula Stories

Successful social problems can yield new services or programs that are evaluated as very necessary, helpful, and even lifesaving by people receiving services. Yet there can be unintended negative consequences of using social problems formula stories to inform organizations.

Social Problem Formula Stories and Service Fragmentation.   Social problems formula stories often are very narrow in their focus, and there is a tendency for actual places in the troubled persons industry to reflect this narrowness. For example, people living in rat-infested homes often will not be allowed into shelters for homeless people because claims about the problem of homelessness constructed this as a problem of not having a home at all. Likewise, although parents might want their children to participate in various after-school programs, many of these programs are for children "at risk." Parents sometimes find their children are ineligible, even if the programs would be beneficial. Of course, workers in these places will tell you that they simply do not have enough resources to offer services to *all* potential clients, and that often is true. But the end result is important: we live in a world with countless organizations, programs, and groups, yet many people experiencing troubles are unable to find an appropriate service. If the experienced trouble is not a successful social problem, there will not be services. And, because services are fragmented, people might find themselves trapped in a social service maze: a woman who is a "poor Hispanic disabled single mother" might find some services for "poor" people, others for "Hispanics," others for "disabled," and others for "single mothers." Each of these services likely will attend to only some of her needs while ignoring others. Such a woman might find it takes her many phone calls and trips to several places to obtain what she needs.

Social Problems Formula Stories and the Complexity of Experience.   Successful social problems formula stories contain specific kinds of plots featuring particular types of characters. Conditions and people in daily life are not so easily typified. Yet when social problems formula stories lead social intervention, real people can find themselves evaluated on the extent to which they seem to be instances of expectable story characters in expectable story plots.

For example, shelters for battered women seek clients who are instances of the battered-woman type of story character. Such a woman in the formula story has experienced extreme violence, so real women experiencing violence evaluated as not-so-extreme can be denied entry because they are evaluated as "not battered." Likewise, a battered-woman story character is a pure victim, so real women who are evaluated by workers as being involved in the production of violence might be classified as engaged in "mutual combat," which is not the same as "wife abuse."[4] Although social problems formula stories featuring plots of extreme harm and particular types of story characters are effective in encouraging audience members to evaluate the condition as intolerable, these same stories enter popular wisdom, what "everyone knows." These stories can become yardsticks used to evaluate the real people requesting and receiving services in the troubled persons industry.

WORKERS AND CLIENTS IN THE TROUBLED PERSONS INDUSTRY

With the exception of some support groups that do not have formal leaders, most organizations, programs, and groups in the troubled persons industry have two types of social actors: workers and clients.

Workers in the Troubled Persons Industry

The troubled persons industry generates a considerable amount of paid and unpaid work. People whose work involves doing something with victims, potential victims, villains, and potential villains include teachers, police officers, judges, prison guards, probation officers, psychiatrists, psychologists, counselors, social workers, workers in shelters (for homeless people, battered women, abused children), victim advocates, child advocates, child protective service workers, and support group leaders. Some of these workers are very highly paid, many others are poorly paid and still others are volunteers who receive no pay at all. Workers range from highly educated professionals to those who are uneducated but well trained by the organization, to those who are both uneducated and untrained. Some of these people do this kind of work because they care deeply about the social problem; others do it because it is a job and they would leave it in a moment if a better job became available.

Despite this diversity, these workers often have power over their clients and this stems from four sources. First, although we can all do the social problems work of assigning collective identities to individuals in our daily lives, workers in the troubled persons industry sometimes have the power to *enforce their categorizations.* Hence, if a judge rules a person is a criminal, that person *is* a criminal. If a psychiatrist rules a person is mentally incompetent and cannot live alone, that person *cannot* live alone. I might believe a neighbor should be categorized as a "child abuser" but it takes a worker from child protective services to make the formal categorization, and it is the formal categorization that determines what happens to my neighbor and her child.

Second, workers' categorizations can be *practically powerful* in obtaining resources individuals need and/or want. A mother might believe her child is "learning disabled," for example, but the child must be *formally* classified in that way before services are received. If a worker in a shelter for homeless people prohibiting drunkenness categorizes a person requesting service as "drunk," that person will not be granted entry. Workers in the troubled persons industry can have resources people want.

Third, workers in the troubled persons industry can administer *punishments*. Such workers, for example, can eliminate a woman's welfare benefits if she fails to do what workers tell her to do, they can send people to mental hospitals, they can make a child enroll in a special school if the child does not behave or learn as desired by the workers. Clearly, workers in law enforcement, courts, prisons, reformatories, and jails have the power to punish their clients in multiple ways.

Fourth, workers can have *interactional power* over their clients. This is due to the tendency of clients to evaluate workers' interpretations as believable and important. This is most obvious when workers claim professional knowledge and therefore are evaluated as high on the hierarchy of credibility. I will return to this in the next section because the interactional power of workers in no small part is due to the interactional powerlessness of clients.

In brief, when we talk about the social problems work in the troubled persons industry the topic necessarily includes the power of workers, and much can be at stake. It is not, of course, that all workers are all powerful but, in general, workers are more or less powerful, at least in comparison to their clients.

Clients in the Troubled Persons Industry

Just as workers in the troubled persons industry are incredibly diverse, so, too, are people using services. Some of these people are categorized by themselves or others as victims and others as potential victims. Within cultural feeling rules, such people require help and perhaps rehabilitation to counter the negative effects of their victimization. Other people receive services because they are categorized by themselves or others as villains or potential villains who, within cultural feeling rules, require punishment or perhaps rehabilitation to encourage them to stop their troublesome behavior. People receiving services include frail elderly people, wealthy businessmen who gamble too much, teens who carry knives to school, abused children, pregnant teens, divorcing people, prostitutes attempting to leave that work, poor single mothers, marginalized people who feel outcast, people who lost a loved one during the terrorist attacks. Some of these people voluntarily seek the service, others have been forced into it by courts or other authorities such as child protective services.

I will use the term "client" here to refer to these people who receive the services of the troubled persons industry. Depending on the particular organization or service, there are other terms for these service recipients. For example, people in prison or jail often are called inmates, people in schools are students, people in hospitals are patients, people are members of support groups. Yet with few exceptions, *client* is an appropriate term. In the dictionary definition, as in real life, a client is a person who is dependent and under the protection of another.[5]

Again with few exceptions, clients in the troubled persons industry have less power than workers and this lack of power stems from images of clients as *types of people*. First, people can lose power simply by being clients. After all, to appear at the door of an organization or group is to announce that there is a problem. While there might be good reasons for needing assistance, it remains that within our culture prizing individualism, it is better to be self-sufficient and to not have problems. Workers gain power over clients simply because clients are people who need assistance and workers are people who offer that assistance.

Second, some categories of people are constructed as the types of people who should not have power, so the real people in these categories tend to be powerless. Clients constructed as villains, for example, do not have power because the cultural feeling rules lead to villains being condemned. In the same way, clients constructed as "ignorant" do not have the power to decide what they should learn: teachers typically decide what students need to know. Other types of people, such as the "mentally ill" or the "mentally challenged" are constructed as incapable of making decisions.

Finally, images of victims as people deserving sympathy reduce the power of these clients. While this sounds cold and heartless in a world where giving and getting sympathy should be more encouraged, it remains that cultural feeling rules surrounding sympathy establish power relationships: The person giving sympathy gains power over the person receiving sympathy. The person getting sympathy "owes" something to the person giving sympathy. At a minimum, people receiving sympathy owe a "thank you" and respect to people offering this.[6]

Here I have painted an extreme picture of workers in the troubled persons industry having power over their clients. Think of this always as more or less power. The actual power of individual workers depends on many circumstances. For example, workers who are professionals have more power than those who are not because of the hierarchy of credibility, workers who control resources clients want have more power than those who do not control such resources, some organizations give workers more formal power over clients than others. So, too, the actual powerlessness of individual clients will depend. Clients who pay a fee for services have more power than those who do not, the power of individual clients follows social class lines in that clients who are middle-class have more of a tendency to question workers than those who are poor. After we explore some of the dimensions of social problems work in the troubled persons industry I will return to this topic and look specifically at how clients resist workers.

SOCIAL PROBLEMS WORK: CATEGORIZING
POTENTIAL CLIENTS

Workers in the troubled persons industry do two kinds of social problems work. The topic for this section is the work of categorizing people. There are very few places in the troubled persons industry where anyone requesting services automatically receives them. Workers most often categorize individual people requesting services as the types of people who are—or are not—eligible for organizational services. For example, school psychologists decide whether *individual* children are "learning disabled," "mentally retarded," or "lazy;" workers decide whether *particular* people are "disabled," and therefore qualify for special parking permits; welfare workers decide whether or not a *particular* person qualifies for "welfare;" workers in many kinds of agencies must decide to categorize a *particular* person as "insane" or merely "odd." So, too, workers in prisons decide whether or not it is safe to let *particular* villains out on parole, child protective service workers decide whether or not *particular* children should be taken out of their home because their parents are guilty of child abuse or neglect.

Just as practical actors in daily life assign collective identities to ourselves and others, many workers in the troubled persons industry must categorize people as either the types of people eligible for services or the types of people not eligible for services.

Workers' Resources for Categorizing People

Rarely in daily life do we ask questions about how workers determine the eligibility of people for services. There seems to be an image that workers in the troubled persons industry are professionals who have been highly trained to do such categorization. Of course, some workers are highly trained and they can use this knowledge as a resource. Psychiatrists, for example, have techniques for recognizing particular forms of mental illness, police officers are trained in how to categorize unique events as instances of particular types of crime. Yet professional knowledge is not enough to do the work of categorization. All workers in the troubled persons industry, be they highly trained professionals or untrained volunteers, are practical actors. As such, they draw from their practical experiences, as well as their understandings of cultural themes and feeling rules to categorize their clients.[7]

Practical Experience as Resource. Our practical experience is a primary resource we use when making sense of our daily lives. Workers' practical experiences can be much more extensive than that of others not working in the troubled persons industry. Over time, workers create their own images of typical kinds of people based on their practical experience working with these kinds of people. For example, prosecuting and defense lawyers make sense of new potential crimes and new potential criminals by comparing the perceived characteristics of the new crime/criminal to other crimes and criminals they have dealt with in the past. Their practical experience in this case leads them to develop notions of what is an expectable, "normal" crime. Particular instances and particular people are evaluated by using their understandings of a "normal" crime as a yardstick. Likewise, detectives and prosecutors use their prior experiences with women victims of rape to predict which women likely will drop charges, and therefore which cases they will not pursue. And, workers shelters for battered women compare the perceived characteristics of women requesting services to the characteristics of present and former shelter residents and decide whether the particular woman is "typical" of other women using shelter services.

Popular Wisdom as Resource.   Popular wisdom, "what we all know," can be used by workers doing categorization. Police officers, for example, are highly trained in what to look at to judge crime seriousness, so it is not surprising that police make decisions about whether or not to arrest a suspect based on how they evaluate the seriousness of the crime. Yet at times, even more important than the evaluation of crime seriousness can be popular wisdom such as beliefs among police officers that people can be categorized as type of people by the way they walk, by the style of their hair, by their clothing. Likewise, highly trained child protective services workers nonetheless rely on popular (middle-class) wisdom about what types of people are likely to abuse their children. So, these workers judge the suitability of the child's home not by some formal criteria but rather by assessing the amount of "dirt and disorder" in it.

Cultural Themes and Feeling Rules as Resource.   As practical actors, workers can draw upon their understandings of cultural themes and feeling rules. For example, psychologists and other professionals who work with alcoholic men in inner cities are specifically trained in how to diagnose the psychological problems of these men, yet they can use distinctly unprofessional language when they describe such men as "foul," "dirty," "not normal." These providers typically claim a professional status and therefore remain distant from their clients, yet they can feel compassion toward a few such clients, whom they evaluate as "worthy." This evaluation is forthcoming when a man is evaluated as not responsible for his current destitution, as trying to better himself, as exhibiting an attitude of deference toward the worker.[8] Workers, including those with extensive training, can rely on cultural feeling rules to categorize individual clients as worthy—or not worthy—of sympathy and services.

Local Culture as Resource. Organizations or groups have local cultures that are particular sets of understandings about what the organization or group wishes to accomplish, who their clients are and should be, the preferred methods of service provision, and so on. The troubled persons industry has uncountable such local cultures. Places offering food to poor people that are sponsored by Catholic Workers, for example, understand their clients as people needing social justice while places offering food to poor people sponsored by the Salvation Army see their clients as people needing to change in order to become independent. Some places offering family therapy believe troubles are created when the traditional lines of authority between men, women, and children are disturbed, while other places believe it is precisely these lines of authority that prohibit the good communication necessary for happy families. How workers categorize the trouble experienced by clients and how they evaluate clients are influenced by local culture.[9]

Consider the example of courts that do involuntary commitment of people to mental hospitals. This is a very serious decision because it overrides our cultural preference for individual freedom: involuntary commitment is when people who do not want to go to a mental hospital nonetheless are sent to one. Yet court workers can evaluate their work as helping people even when those people themselves object. This particular local culture includes beliefs that *all* people coming to the court are gravely mentally ill and that committing them to mental hospitals is for their own good. From the perspective of patients or outsiders, this process might appear to be an incredible violation of patient rights; within this local culture the process is evaluated as humane and respectful.[10]

In summary, potential clients in the troubled persons industry often will not be clear instances of the types of people constructed in the social problems formula stories leading to particular organizations or groups. Workers must do the social problems work of categorizing clients as the particular types of people who are—or are not—eligible for services. For this work they sometimes draw from their specialized training. They always will be practical actors using their experiences, popular wisdom, understanding of cultural themes and feeling rules, and local culture as resources to evaluate and categorize potential clients.

The Identity Work of Clients

While it is workers' jobs to categorize clients as types of people, clients can be very much involved in this process in that they can knowingly appear or act in particular ways encouraging workers to categorize them as one or another type of person. For example, there is an expectation in courts that women victims of stalking should be fearful and appear weak. Actual women going through this process talk about how they anticipated this expectation and *knowingly* worked to appear frightened and weak. In this instance, women categorize themselves as "stalking victims," and they give a performance in order to be categorized as a "stalking victim" by people in court. Likewise, advocates for women trying to obtain restraining orders prohibiting domestic violence *teach* women how they should tell their stories in order to conform to expectations about such victims. Such performances are associated with being successful in obtaining the desired court orders. Also, men attempting to obtain services from agencies for homeless men work to present themselves as good and deserving clients who therefore are worthy of attention and the services they desire.[11]

That clients can knowingly act or appear to be a particular type of person should not be surprising. While practical actors can misjudge or not know the *technical* requirements for being accepted as a client in a particular organization, we all know the general rules, which are the cultural themes and feeling rules circulating in our culture. Individuals might choose not to appear or act as expected, but it remains that most of us have the practical knowledge. Potential clients therefore are not passive; they can be active in encouraging workers to evaluate them as specific kinds of people.

SOCIAL PROBLEMS WORK: ENCOURAGING IDENTITY CHANGE

Some places in the troubled persons industry seek only to supply basic needs. There are emergency shelters, for example, that open only at night and offer only a place to sleep, there are food pantries that offer only food. Our interest now is in a more common form of organization or group in the troubled persons industry: those attempting to *change* people. These are the places offering services that might be called counseling, support, training, or education.[12]

Changing Personal Identities

The first type of social problems work in the troubled persons industry is the work of categorizing individual people as eligible or not eligible for services. The second type is the work of attempting to change clients' personal identities. Personal identities, the ways people define themselves, include several components. Some clients are evaluated by themselves or others as needing to change their understandings of cultural themes. Child abusers, for example, sometimes are constructed as people who believe in a cultural theme that children need to be beaten. In such cases workers might attempt to change clients' understandings of the cultural theme surrounding the acceptability of violence. Other clients are evaluated by themselves or others as needing to change their evaluations of themselves: many victims, as well as some villains, for example, are constructed as suffering from "low self-esteem." Workers in these cases seek to increase clients' self-evaluations. Other clients are evaluated by themselves or others as deficient in their knowledge. This ranges from knowledge about parenting to knowledge about the effects of drugs or alcohol. Still other clients are evaluated by themselves or others as needing change in how they understand their collective identifications. For example, young boys who identify themselves as members of gangs might be encouraged to eliminate this identity, young girls evaluated as at risk for early pregnancy might be encouraged to identify themselves as potential college students rather than as mothers. Identity work in the troubled persons industry is all but endless. In its many varieties it is the work of changing clients' personal identities.

It seems hard to underestimate the numbers of people who participate either willingly or unwillingly in programs or groups promoting identity change. Women receiving welfare, for example, must attend various programs teaching them how to think about money; there are many pregnancy counseling programs teaching new mothers how to think of themselves as good mothers; courts mandate counseling for a wide variety of wrongdoers (drunk drivers, abusers, delinquents). There are an incredible number of formal and informal support groups for people with problems such as alcoholism, gambling, sexual addiction, internet addiction, and too much debt. There are groups for people experiencing identity problems such as transgendered people, gays, lesbians, gay and lesbian Christians. There are groups for disabled people, cancer sufferers, cancer survivors, family and friends of cancer sufferers. I am sure you can add to my list but the point should be clear: we live in a time when many people evaluate themselves, or are evaluated by others, as troubled and therefore in need of change.[13]

The social problems work of changing personal identities is accomplished through *talk*. Whether this is talk between one professional worker and one client, or talk among support group members, it is about changing the personal stories clients tell about their experiences and themselves in ways that more or less shape these stories to conform to expectations in the local culture.

The expectations for the kinds of stories people should tell about themselves can be far different depending upon the particular organization or group. I will return to the example of people who are homosexual in their sexual orientation and devoutly Catholic. These are incompatible identities given that the Catholic church hierarchy constructs a homosexual orientation as "intrinsically disordered" and homosexual behavior as a sin. Such a person might turn to support groups but these groups are not all the same. A group called Exodus promotes the story that homosexuals can—and should—change and become heterosexuals. Another group called Courage promotes the story that homosexuals should remain celibate. Finally, a group called Dignity promotes a story that a person simultaneously can be a practicing homosexual and a devout Catholic.[14]

In brief, because our social world contains countless services, it is possible to find groups or services that promote very different kinds of resolutions to troubles. Yet what they all share is that they seek to transform the ways people make sense of themselves, and they do this through attempting to change the stories clients tell about their experiences and themselves.

These groups will be far different because the local culture is informed by particular social problems formula stories. Support groups for battered women, for example, are organized around the social problems formula story of wife abuse. In this story, wife abuse is extreme and frequent violence that will only get worse over time, so there is no hope that "couples counseling" will end it. The battered-woman story character is a pure victim and the abusive man is a pure villain. Yet not surprisingly, individual women drawn to these groups because they are experiencing violence might not evaluate their personal experiences, themselves, or their male partners in these ways. For example, some women might tell stories containing violence but they might evaluate the violence as troublesome yet not intolerable. Other women might tell stories in which they construct their own behavior as leading to the violence. Some women might believe their partners are not evil brutes but rather good people with problems.

The actual experience of wife abuse is complex and confusing and this is reflected in the stories women tell about it. Yet the work of support groups is to change women's stories in ways encouraging them to evaluate their experiences as intolerable, themselves as pure victims, their partners as evil offenders who will not change. And this is as it should be because within the local culture of support groups for battered women the belief is that the only way women can free themselves from violence is to identify as a member of the collective identity of battered woman and leave their abusers. Individual complex and confusing stories, in other words, must be transformed into the social problem story of "wife abuse."[15] This is social problems work.

Client Resistance

It would be misleading to claim that the social problems work of changing personal identities is always or even usually successful. Clients, for example, can refuse to talk, they can figure out the system and use it to their advantage, they can break rules. Clients in voluntary support groups can simply not return to the group.[16] But one generality is clear: the social problems work of changing personal identity will be successful to the extent that clients find the types of stories promoted in the organizations or groups to be helpful in understanding their lives. The more the social problems formula story can be evaluated by an individual client as "my story," the more likely the client will categorize the self and experiences in that way.

At times, the social problems formula story informing an organization or group actually *discourages* clients from identifying as the particular type of person for whom the organization or group is organized. For example, when collective identities are discredited, people can refuse to accept the identity as their own. Individuals who are without homes nonetheless can refuse to identify themselves as "homeless" by arguing they are different or not typical of the type of person called the "homeless." People who eat free food because they do not have the money to buy their own nonetheless can distance themselves from the collective identity of the "poor" by arguing that their characteristics or experiences are not similar to those of the type of person called the poor. Women receiving welfare payments nonetheless can say they are *not* a "welfare mother." And elderly residents of nursing homes can refuse interaction with other residents because to interact with others would be to admit that they belong there and it is better to argue that placement in the home is the result of a "mistake."[17]

THE TROUBLED PERSONS INDUSTRY AND
REPRODUCING SOCIAL PROBLEMS

In the previous chapter I argued that successful social problem claims can lead to changes in objective reality. Here I will extend that argument and make the same claim about consequences of work in the troubled persons industry: The workings of these places tends to create objective realities that reflect—and perpetuate—the social problems claims leading to these places. What I just said was complicated so I will say it in another way: Social problems claims inform the troubled persons industry and at the same time, the troubled persons industry can produce the evidence that the social problems claims are correct.

Objective Reality and the Reproduction of Social Problems

Claims-makers doing the social problems work of persuading audience members to evaluate a condition as intolerable often are asked to offer evidence that these claims are true, and they often offer personal stories that are very powerful in this task of persuasion. While this evidence and personal stories can come from many places, often claims-makers do research on, or tell stories about, clients receiving services in the troubled persons industry. The evidence gathered from the troubled persons industry tends to nicely fit the needs of claims-makers.

An obvious example involves efforts to crack down on drugs.[18] Some of the claims informing social policy focused on constructing profiles (typifications) of drug dealers so that police could be on the lookout for particular types of people. One such profile is "black man driving an expensive car." While this has led to many complaints about racial profiling, it remains common for police to routinely stop people in this category. Of course, few "black men driving nice cars" are drug dealers. Police doing this racial profiling will stop many such men for no reason other than that they fit the profile. Using the profile also means that while police *are* on the lookout for black men in nice cars, they are *not* on the lookout for other types of people in other kinds of cars. Because police make far fewer routine stops of these other kinds of people, fewer of these folks who *are* drug dealers will be caught.

Now, consider police record-keeping. Because police do *not* keep records of stops that do *not* yield an arrest, there is no way to know how many innocent black men are stopped and released. Because we do not know this, we cannot prove that using this typification is a waste of time. But police *do* keep records when they arrest a drug dealer, including when that drug dealer is a "black man driving a nice car." So, if you go down to your local police department and search through their records you will *not* find records of "black men driving nice cars" who are *not* "drug dealers;" you *will* find records of those who are. The formal records therefore confirm that the typification is correct.

This seems a clear example of how the work of the troubled persons industry can create an objective reality that seemingly confirms the rightness of the social problem formula story. In this case, we start with a typification (a typical drug dealer is a black man in a nice car), we put this image into practice (we look only for such men, we look at a great many such men in order to find the few who do fit the profile), and we end up confirming our predictions: a typical drug dealer is a black man driving a nice car.

Also consider the example of the social problems formula story of "child sexual abusers." This story typically features a male villain and claims-makers argue that *men* are the overwhelming majority of such villains. Their evidence is based on statistics gathered from police departments in charge of investigating and prosecuting crimes, where the only records kept are for incidents where criminal charges have been filed. Yet these statistics reflect the practices of police officers who often ignore or trivialize cases with a *female* villain. Because such cases tend to be not prosecuted, they leave no records. While I am certainly not arguing that women in great numbers are guilty of child sexual abuse, I am claiming that when police ignore or trivialize cases involving women as villains the resulting statistics will confirm the typification that it is only men who sexually abuse children. While the evidence for claims most certainly reflects police practice, it is not possible to know the extent to which these records reflect the objective reality.[19]

When claims-makers go to the troubled persons industry to collect their data we might predict they will find instances of people who more or less share claims-makers' constructions of the problem. This is so because only certain people are allowed into the troubled persons industry (the consequences of client selection), because voluntary clients who do not agree with workers will resist by simply leaving. When we put this together it means that clients in the troubled persons industry are not a representative sample of people experiencing trouble. Yet these are the people who most likely will become a part of research studies and the findings of these studies will become the "scientific facts" upon which further claims are made.

This is a *social process* that produces an objective reality, a reality that can be seen and counted. As another example, consider programs for "children at risk." This is an incredibly nonobjective category because "at risk" means the children have not done anything wrong. This collective identity of "at risk" is defined *retrospectively:* as they grow older, children with specific characteristics (poor children, minority children, children in a home with a single parent) *do* get into more trouble and *do* have more trouble than children with other identities. Yet *at the time a child is categorized* as "at risk," this is only a prediction, a prediction that this is a type of child likely to get into trouble in the future and therefore who needs services now. This brings us to a question: How much of the trouble seen in the future of these children is due to their preexisting individual characteristics at the time of their categorization and how much is due to characteristics created by interventions of the troubled persons industry itself?[20]

Personal Identity and the Reproduction of Social Problems

Recall that a task of the troubled persons industry is to change the personal identities of clients. The category of "children at risk" is a child constructed as headed for trouble and the troubled persons industry attempts to change that. So, too, education programs for pregnant teens attempt to encourage such women to develop a collective identity as a "good mother" so that they will become "good mothers," all programs for juvenile offenders seek to encourage these youngsters to become "respectable members of society," and so on. Although it is certain that some programs for some types of people actually manage this identity transformation in their clients, many observers of the troubled persons industry rather have focused on the ways that social interventions often *encourage* precisely what they want to *discourage*.

The concept here is *secondary deviation:* characteristics and behaviors due to the intervention itself. This is contrasted to *primary deviation:* characteristics and behaviors leading people to be categorized in a particular way. While I want to stress once again that clients often actively resist workers' attempts to change their identities, and while it would be wrong to believe the problems of secondary deviation are a part of all interventions, it certainly is important to consider the ways in which social interventions can end up producing precisely what they are organized to discourage.

I can demonstrate the problems of secondary deviation quite simply, using the well-known examples of prisons and mental hospitals. It is barely an overstatement to claim that prisons produce criminals and mental hospitals produce mental illness. Of course, people do things to become inmates of these places: that is primary deviation. But these places tend to produce secondary deviance—they often encourage their clients to become the particular types of people the places are supposed to discourage. People in prisons, for example, are not allowed contact with people outside prisons so their friends and reference groups become other prisoners. People in prisons can learn the skills necessary to survive in prisons and these certainly are not skills associated with living productively in the world outside prisons. Indeed, just having a record of being in prison will make it difficult for ex-prisoners to obtain good employment outside prison, folk wisdom about prisoners as dangerous outsiders will lead many "good working folk" to refrain from having ex-prisoners as friends. My point is that regardless of the primary deviance leading people to become inmates in prison, the experience of prison might encourage them to become dangerous outsiders.

Likewise, since the 1950s there has been general agreement in the United States that the last thing people experiencing psychological troubles need is to be put into mental hospitals where they will live their completely regimented days around others even more ill, where they will be ignored by workers who are too busy to treat them as individuals. A social movement called Community Mental Health was very successful and now we have far fewer mental hospitals than in the past.[21]

The process of the *reproduction* of social problems is obvious in the cases of prisons and mental hospitals. While it takes an evaluation of primary deviance to be mandated to such places, the places themselves encourage identity transformation, which is secondary deviance. The places can change aspects of their clients' personal identities in ways reproducing images of social problems: criminals *are* dangerous outsiders, mental patients *are* people who cannot be trusted to display good judgment.

Consider a more subtle example of the experiences of a type of student, the "black boy."[22] Successful social problems claims-making about a variety of conditions (crack cocaine, crime, violence, teen pregnancy) has constructed the "black boy" as a particular type of character who is destructive, is out of control, does poorly in school, and is highly susceptible to learning the cultural themes associated with criminals. The "black boy" character, in brief, is constructed as headed for trouble. This image now rarely is challenged, it is simply taken-for-granted popular wisdom.

As members of the common culture, teachers might begin their work with individual children who are black and boys with these beliefs about the "black boy" type of person. These expectations can lead teachers to treat their black and white boy students differently. Teachers are prone to notice the troublesome behavior of boys who are black (primary deviation) more than they notice the *same* troublesome behavior of boys who are white. Once noticed, teachers are prone to view destructive behavior of boys who are white as instances of the not particularly troublesome category of "boys will be boys," they are prone to view destructive behavior of boys who are black as evidence that such boys have a disregard for property. Because their behavior is both more noticed as well as more likely to be categorized as troublesome, boys who are black are more prone than boys who are white to be categorized as "at risk." Once so categorized, boys who are black are more likely than boys who are white to be singled out for rule breaking, more likely to get a reputation for being a troublemaker, more likely to be punished.

A constructionist belief is that we react to the world in terms of the meanings we attach to conditions and people. When workers in the troubled persons industry begin their work with a particular set of understandings they will be prone to see conditions and people in certain ways. In this case, we have the social problems formula story featuring the "black boy" character as a child headed for trouble. This becomes a filter as teachers of individual boys who are black see the behavior of these children in this way. This leads to the question about secondary deviance. We know from statistics that boys who are black, as compared to boys who are white, are more likely to experience trouble in their lives and more likely to become troublemakers. But how much of that trouble and troublemaking is secondary deviance, which is created by the experiences of being singled out and punished? It is not possible to know but it is possible to claim that boys singled out and punished will get a reputation for being troublemakers and this will reduce their chances for success.

It is possible to ask the same question about secondary deviance of a much different type of person: "gifted children," who are children categorized as superior to others in their learning abilities. Because this is a positive deviance—these children are deviant because they are evaluated as having *higher* learning abilities than others—we typically do not think of it as deviance. Yet claims-making has constructed these children as troubled because schools do not give them what they need. According to these claims, the superior intelligence of these students requires them to have superior learning experiences. Hence, there is "gifted child education." That sounds wonderful until we realize that these children have opportunities to learn that are not available to other children. This brings us to a question: Gifted children often do grow up to become talented adults, but how much of their talent in adulthood is due to their innate intelligence and how much is due to the special treatment they receive?[23]

SOCIAL PROBLEMS AND SOCIAL INTERVENTIONS

It is not possible to offer a global evaluation of the success and value of the work of the troubled persons industry. At times, particular organizations, programs, and groups are very successful: they manage to help or rehabilitate, their services are evaluated by their clients as beneficial—perhaps even lifesaving, clients feel they are treated with respect. These are successes: the troubled persons industry works as envisioned by claims-makers who constructed prognostic claims focused on individual-level assistance and change.

Yet at other times, the organizations, programs, and groups in this industry receive less glowing reviews: They make matters worse for their clients, they do not offer the services clients need, clients complain of being treated without respect. Of course, the sources of some of the negative evaluations are predictable: we would not expect a person in prison to give a glowing report of this experience; we would not expect parents being monitored by child protective services to be happy that workers are watching their every move. Also, the money these places have to do their work often is not sufficient to offer necessary services, and workers can do too little for individual clients because there are too many clients and too few workers.

But there are other, perhaps less obvious, reasons why the places in the troubled persons industry can be less than successful. These relate to the local cultures of such places, which are informed by social problems formula stories. First, recall that successful claims reflect power and this is associated with race and social class. Claims made by powerless people tend to be silenced. At times, programs organized around the cultural themes supported by the white middle class serve clients who are not members of that group. So, for example, there are programs teaching young girls how to become "good mothers" as "good mother" is understood by members of the dominant culture. Clients in these programs find their own understandings and needs ignored; service providers can assume their clients have access to resources (such as cars and husbands) that real clients do not have.[24] Programs can be unsuccessful in their work and clients might give less than favorable evaluations of programs due to cultural biases implicit in social problems formula stories.

Second, the experiences and characteristics of real people who use these services are most often only more or less similar to the images in social problems formula stories informing local cultures. The more real people evaluate their experiences and themselves as similar to those in the story, the more successful the services will be; the less real people evaluate their experiences and themselves as similar to those in the story, the less successful the services will be. Support groups, for example, can be successful when they promote a story that their clients find useful. When some women who experience assault, for example, hear the social problems story of wife abuse they experience a sense of sanity—they are not, after all, alone in their experiences. This story in some instances can given women new—and better—ways to make sense of their experiences and themselves. But because clients come into the places promoting identity change with very different kinds of experiences, it also is the case that the stories promoted by support groups might be evaluated by an individual as "This is not my story, I do not want this to be my story." When the experiences and characteristics of actual clients differ too much from the social problems formula story informing local culture, services are not beneficial and clients might evaluate workers as people who are coercing them to change in ways that simply do not make sense. Clients can actively resist changing their personal identity, and the more workers pressure them to do so, the more clients resist.

While it is therefore not possible to offer one evaluation of the success or value of work in the troubled persons industry, it is clear that the services of these organizations and the understandings of workers (local culture) in these places are informed by social problems formula stories. For better or for worse, the social problems formula stories constructed by claims-makers become very real in their consequences.

I want to finish this book by going back to where we started and look a bit further at the general issues in social constructionists' perspectives on social problems. Bluntly stated, we live in an objective world of want and pain and oppression and suffering, and through all these chapters I have focused on how humans construct meaning. In the final chapter I want to summarize what we can learn about our world when we use social constructionist perspectives on social problems.

NOTES

1.   An excellent introduction to work in the troubled persons industry is by Lipsky (1980), who looks at the complexities and the routines of offering services in what he terms "street level bureaucracies." I will draw from his insights throughout this chapter.

2.   For empirical examinations of relationships between social problems claims and the organizational philosophy of programs or groups see G. Miller (1991), the philosophy of a work incentive program; Loseke (1992) and Baker (1996), the battered woman social problem and the organization of shelters; Emerson (1994), claims about wife abuse and the work of advocates helping women obtain domestic violence restraining orders; Gubrium (1992), work in two family therapy organizations; Irvine (1999), the codependency movement and support groups for people who categorize themselves as codependent.

3.   Pawluch (1996, excerpted in *Social Problems: Constructionist Readings*) examines how this crisis faced by pediatricians led them to expand the domain of their services and how this led to medicalizing a vast range of behaviors and troubles.

4.   Loseke's (1992) study of a shelter for battered women examines how workers evaluated and categorized women requesting services; Dunn (2001) explores the demands placed on women victims of stalking to appear fearful and weak in order to have their court cases treated seriously.

5.   Some organizations and services seek to empower people who use their services so they refrain from using the term *client*. Support groups use the term *member* and when these groups are led by members themselves power primarily will be interactional: people with the greatest verbal skills will be more powerful than those who have fewer such skills. In the case of Alcoholics Anonymous, interactional power is based on experience (Pollner and Stein, 1996).

6.   See Clark (1997) for her discussion of how cultural feeling rules surrounding sympathy lead to a power imbalance in that people offering sympathy gain in social prestige while people requiring sympathy lose social prestige.

7.   There is a considerable literature on how service providers make sense of their work and clients using practical experience, cultural themes, cultural feeling rules, and understandings of local culture. See Holstein (1993, excerpted in *Social Problems: Constructionist Readings*) for court workers' construction of "insanity"; Sudnow (1965) for attorney's understandings of "normal crimes"; LaFree (1989) and Sanders (1980) for police and prosecutor decisions to pursue cases of rape; Pfoul (1978) for how psychiatrists evaluate and categorize "dangerousness;" Loseke (1992) for work in a shelter for battered women; Joffe (1978) for the understandings of family planning workers; Werthman and Piliavin (1967) for police perspectives on juvenile delinquency; Giovannoni and Becerra (1979), O'Toole,

Turbett, and Naepka (1983), and Swift (1995) for how professional service providers diagnose child abuse; Hartnett (1997) for how male and female workers
tend to differentially evaluate their clients; Martin (1995) for how police construct
hate crimes; Wiseman (1979) for how police decide to arrest people for public
drunkenness.

8.   See Wiseman (1979) for how the attitudes of professionals working on "skid
row" reflect cultural themes denouncing dependent alcoholics and the feeling rules
surrounding sympathy. See also Snow and Anderson (1993) for similar beliefs
among people working with clients who are homeless.

9.   Holstein and Gubrium (2000) elaborate on what they term local culture, what
Fine (1979) terms idioculture. For empirical examples see Daniels (1970) for the philosophy of combat psychiatry during World War II; Scott (1969) for the theories of
workers for the blind; Jeffrey (1979) for theories of "good patients" and "rubbish"
among personnel in a British emergency hospital; Allahyari (2000) for differences
in local culture in two soup kitchens; Gubrium (1992) for differences in the local
cultures of two counseling services for troubled families; G. Miller (1997) for how
one counseling group changed its treatment philosophy over time; Rice (1992), for
"rules of true statements" in codependency discourse; Nolan (2002), for the meaning and importance of "drug court"; Weinburg (2001) for local culture in drug
treatment.

10.   Holstein (1993, excerpted in *Social Problems: Constructionist Readings*) examined how court workers making decisions for involuntary commitment to mental
hospitals made sense of their work.

11.   For women victims in court see Dunn (2001); for the work of victim advocates see Emerson (1994); for the presentations of homeless men see Spencer (1994).

12.   Snow and Anderson (1993) talk of the "accommodative" response of sup-
plying basic needs versus the "restorative" response of attending to actual or perceived physiological, psychological, and spiritual problems.

13.   For examples of the work of support groups for identity change see Denzin
(1986, 1987a, 1987b) for alcoholics; Ponticelli (1999) for gay and lesbian Christians
who wish to become heterosexual; Wolkomir (2001) for gay and ex-gay Christians;
Rossol (2001) for gamblers; Mason-Schrock (1996) for transgendered people;
McKendy (1992) for abusive men; Irvine (1999) and Rice (2002) for codependents;
Maines (1991) for diabetics; Francis (1997) for divorce and bereavement groups.

14.   Loseke and Cavendish (2001, excerpted in *Social Problems: Constructionist
Readings*), Ponticelli (1999), Wolkomir (2001).

15.   Loseke (2001, excerpted in *Social Problems: Constructionist Readings*) examines how support group leaders and other members of support groups attempt to
change women's stories so that they conform to images of the social problem formula story of wife abuse.

16.   For examples of client resistance techniques, see Trethewey (1997) for
clients in a women's group; McKendy (1992) for clients categorized as wife abusers
in court-mandated counseling; Kivett and Warren (2002) for boys living in a home
for "juvenile delinquents"; Fox (1999, 2001) for violent men in prison; Paterniti
(2000) for residents in a chronic care clinic.

17.   For examples of how people can refuse to embrace a discredited collective

identity, see Cohen (1997) for poverty, Snow and Anderson (1993) for homelessness, Seccombe, James, and Walters (1998) for welfare mothers, Fontana (1977) for elderly in nursing homes, Jarvinen (2001) for alcoholics in Copenhagen.

18.   When I wrote the first edition of this text in 1998, "racial profiling" had not yet achieved the status of a social problem. By 2000 it had achieved this status and police departments all over the country were criticized and mandated to stop the practice of targeting "black men" as automatic suspects for a range of crimes. At the time I am writing this second edition in early 2002, there is another type of profiling that is pervasive: targeting "Arab-looking men" as potential "terrorists." This profile is a part of airline security checks, it is promoted by the U.S. Attorney General's Office, it has been used in federally mandated surveys where colleges must report on the status of their "Arab students." While the racial profiling of African-Americans became an accepted social problem, profiling of "Arab-looking men" has not achieved this status.

19.   Nelson (1994) examined the work of police officers investigating reports of child sexual abuse. According to her, when assailants are women and victims are young boys, officers could dismiss the incident as one of the boy's "good luck" in gaining knowledge about sex from an experienced woman.

20.   See Lemert (1951) and Goffman (1961) for classic statements on primary and secondary deviation.

21.   The classic statements about mental hospitals were written by Goffman. These include the "Moral Career of a Mental Patient" (1959), *Asylums* (1961), and "The Insanity of Place" (1969). See also Estroff (1981) for the experiences of psychiatric clients in community settings.

22.   For my discussion of "black boys" I draw from the work of Ferguson (2000), who spent two years observing and participating in a middle school on the West Coast. Her data include these observations as well as interviews with parents, teachers, social workers, and the students themselves. Other examples of how workers in the troubled persons industry can create secondary deviance include Nelson-Rowe (1995, excerpted in *Social Problems: Constructionist Readings*), who examined claims that the educational system encourages ethnic minorities to fail and to have a low self-evaluation; Chambliss (1973), who studied how police treated members of two groups of juveniles very differently; Rist (1970), who observed how kindergarten teachers categorized students in ways having nothing to do with measures of academic potential.

23.   Margolin (1994, excerpted in *Social Problems: Constructionist Readings*) examines the claims and programs surrounding "gifted children."

24.   Armstrong's (2000) study of a program of prenatal education for poor women demonstrates both how such programs implicitly and explicitly teach values associated with the white middle class, as well as how the concerns of these poor women are ignored by service providers.

8

Evaluating Constructionist Perspectives on Social Problems

Today in my social problems class we talked about poverty and changes in welfare programs. Women with children now can receive welfare benefits for only a short time. Then, there's no choice: It's work or no money. Students were most interested in debating the morality of this policy: Was it good or bad? "I think it's good," offered one student. "Shouldn't those women have to work like the rest of us? It's not fair—they're paid to do nothing, I have to work for my money." Another student disagreed: "I don't think the new policy is good at all," she said, "it's going to hurt their children; it's not fair; the kids didn't do anything wrong." "Don't worry about the kids," said another student, "they didn't do anything wrong; private charity will take care of them." "Stop blaming women," another student said, "the problem is sexism. This new policy is only going to make it worse." Students stopped their conversation and looked to me to tell them who was right. I glanced at my watch and was thankful that there wasn't enough time to respond. Who was right? Well, that depends. It depends on who "those women" are that my students were talking about; it depends on what visions of morality are the most important. But, anyway, who's right doesn't matter. The policy is in place. It would take a new social problems game and a lot of social problems work to change it.

We are coming to the end of my introduction to social constructionist approaches to social problems. I will finish by first comparing the two general perspectives on social problems, and then summarize what the constructionist framework tells us about social problems in particular and social life in general.

OBJECTIVIST AND CONSTRUCTIONIST PERSPECTIVES ON SOCIAL PROBLEMS

I started Chapter 1 by briefly describing the theoretical approach to social problems that examines problems as objective conditions in the social

163

environment. I will look more closely at this objectivist approach in order to highlight differences between it and social constructionist perspectives.

Social Problems as Objective Conditions

There are many different *objectivist* perspectives on social problems. In this current historical time, approaches called conflict theory (and the variant of feminism) and deviance seem to be the most popular; an approach called functionalism also often is included in social problems textbooks but this perspective was far more important in the past than in the present. While each of these frameworks is different, what is important here are the ways in which they are similar to each other and how they differ from social constructionist approaches.

First and foremost, conflict theory, feminism, deviance, and functionalism all approach social problems as *objective conditions.* These objectivist perspectives begin by assuming there *are* conditions in the social environment that *do* cause harm; their concern is with examining these conditions. Most often, objectivist approaches are *not* concerned with how problems are defined by practical actors. When they do ask questions about how practical actors understand social problems, their concern primarily is with understanding why people fail to understand that a problem is at hand and that something must be done.

Second, each objectivist approach to social problems begins with its own vision of what conditions cannot be tolerated and its own theory about what causes social problems. *Conflict* perspectives, for example, begin with the beliefs that the social order is held together by power and coercion and that the primary cause of social problems is the oppression of groups of people such as racial and ethnic minorities, poor people, and women. Conflict perspectives emphasize the importance of the cultural theme of equality so intolerable conditions are those violating this theme. A version of conflict theory is *feminism,* which also emphasizes the cultural theme of equality but reduces this to the importance of gender inequality. Intolerable conditions are those promoting men's superiority and the oppression of women.

Not surprisingly, given the tendency of Americans to focus on individual behavior as troublesome, the *deviance* perspective also is a popular objectivist approach to social problems. A deviance perspective promotes the cultural theme of individualism with its mandate for individuals to act responsibly. This perspective focuses on the troublesome behaviors of individuals (crime, alcoholism, and so on) and examines what leads people to do these behaviors.

Finally, although increasingly out of favor among academics, and in sharp contrast to conflict perspectives, *functionalist* approaches begin with the conviction that the social order is held together by widely shared beliefs in cultural themes and by social institutions (such as family, the economy, religion) that pattern behavior in acceptable ways. Within this approach, social problems are a consequence of social disorganization, which happens when institutions fail (conditions such as a high rate of divorce, falling religious belief, and schools that do not teach) and when social members no longer share beliefs in cultural themes.

While these are clearly different frameworks, they are similar because it is the *theoretical framework* that determines what is and what is not an acceptable way for the world to be organized. A condition is a problem because it violates a belief contained in the theoretical framework.

Third and finally, people approaching social problems as objective conditions present themselves as experts who can and should tell audience members how the world *should* work. So, for example, conflict perspectives are organized around a belief that inequality is bad, so chapters in textbooks tell readers that we must eliminate inequality. Deviance perspectives begin with the belief that some individual behavior is troublesome so prognostic frames focus on how to change these behaviors. Functionalist perspectives lead to prognostic frames centered on how to make families, the economy, education, and so on work better.

Differences between Objectivist and Constructionist Perspectives on Social Problems

Even with such a brief definition of what is shared by objectivist approaches to social problems, it is clear that they differ from social constructionist perspectives in several ways.

(1) Objectivist approaches assume that social problem conditions exist in the real world and that claims-makers (activists, researchers, scientists) merely bring these to the attention of the public. People, in other words, "find" social problem conditions. Constructionist approaches assume that conditions are not social problems until they are constructed as such. Within constructionist approaches, troublesome conditions might well exist but they do not become social problems until claims are made and audience members evaluate the conditions as intolerable.[1]

(2) Objectivist approaches to social problems are concerned with how the world *is*. Constructionist approaches focus on what humans *believe* the world is and how our understandings of the world are a consequence of humans who construct this meaning.

(3) Objectivist approaches to social problems categorize a condition as a problem because it violates a *theoretical* belief about how the world should work. Constructionist perspectives focus on how people come to hold one or another set of beliefs about how the world should work.

(4) Proponents of objectivist approaches to social problems often make claims about how the world should be set up. Proponents of constructionist approaches focus on how claims-makers construct these claims about the characteristics of a better world.

(5) Objectivist approaches lead to a series of questions such as: What causes social problems? What should be done to eliminate these conditions? Constructionist approaches lead to questions such as: Why do we worry about some things and not about others that are, objectively speaking, just as harmful? How do claims-makers construct typifications of social problems in ways that persuade audience members to evaluate claims as believable and important? How do successful constructions change the objective world around us? How do successful constructions influence the ways we evaluate and categorize experiences, ourselves, and those around us?

Criticisms of Constructionist Perspectives

From the perspective of practical actors, understanding social problems as objective conditions is very sensible. Granted, you or I might not personally agree with the particular cultural theme promoted by one or another of the specific theories, but it makes sense, in a commonsense type of a way, to want to understand and change social problems conditions. After all, social problem conditions are very real in the harm they create so it makes sense to be concerned with what causes the harm and what can be done to resolve it. In the first chapter I offered a series of criticisms about objectivist approaches to social problems. Because I wanted to encourage you to read this book, I did not offer criticisms of constructionist perspectives. But criticisms do exist. From the perspective of practical actors interested in making the world a better place to live, there are three primary questions about the usefulness of social constructionist perspectives.

First, does social constructionism divert our attention from more important questions about social problems? While we live in a world that creates endless amounts of want and pain, constructionists study how humans *define* this want and pain. Are social constructionist perspectives a waste of time? Is it really important to understand why and how social problems are created? Would it make more sense to spend our time and energy trying to understand the condition itself? For example, as long as there are some people who believe the Holocaust did not happen, does it make sense to study how the Nazis constructed the "Jew" as a type of person? Would it not make more sense to concentrate on persuading people that the Holocaust was hideously real? Or, does it make sense to study how U.S. government officials constructed the "Japanese-American" as a particular type of person in a way that would justify placing them in internment camps during World War II? Would it not be better to focus our energies on condemning this policy rather than understanding how it was justified?[2] Questions associated with constructionism might not seem as real or immediate as those associated with examining social problems as objective conditions.

Second, constructionist perspectives can be criticized for their apparent lack of explicit value judgments. That is, objectivist frameworks contain clear statements of values: Conflict theories contain explicit statements that inequality is intolerable, functionalism contains clear statements about the importance of well-functioning social institutions, deviance perspectives are about the intolerability of troublesome individual behaviors. Social constructionist perspectives do not contain such value statements. Critics can argue that constructionist perspectives therefore are morally suspect because they do not concern themselves with the critical questions of what is right and what is wrong.

Third, because constructionists' interest is in understanding the extent to which audience members *evaluate* claims as truthful, these studies rarely concern themselves with examining the actual truthfulness of claims. So, a constructionist study might examine characteristics of claims about the vast number of "Satanists" in the United States but critics might wonder why constructionists do not pay more attention to criticizing the actual truthfulness of these claims.[3]

So, social constructionism is not without its critics who believe that we should examine social problems as troublesome conditions in the environment. While I am *not* offering constructionism as a substitute for objectivist perspectives on social problems, and while I am *not* saying that objectivist perspectives are wrong or not useful, I do believe constructionism is important. Studies from this perspective offer us important insights about the characteristics of social problems in particular, of social life in general. I would claim that we cannot understand social problems if we confine ourselves to thinking of them as objective conditions in the social environment. What might we might learn from examining social problems as social constructions?

LESSONS LEARNED FROM CONSTRUCTIONIST PERSPECTIVES ON SOCIAL PROBLEMS

While the questions associated with constructionist perspectives might seem esoteric and not as important as questions raised by objectivist perspectives, constructionist studies nonetheless can give us very important information about the world around us. I will focus on how constructionist perspectives can answer some very practical questions.

Why Do We Worry About Some Conditions
and Not Others That Create Harm?

Americans can worry about conditions that do not objectively exist, we can fail to worry about other conditions that are, objectively speaking, more harmful than those we worry about. Of course, we can note that people worry when conditions affect them or their loved ones. Also, people using conflict theories to examine social problems often note that public worry can be misdirected because of power and politics, and likewise constructionists examine the importance of the hierarchy of credibility and the hierarchy of audience significance. Constructionist analysis can go beyond these relatively simple explanations of why we worry about some conditions and not others.

First, we can understand our worries only by placing them within larger historical, political, and cultural contexts. What conditions are evaluated as troublesome in one time and place are not evaluated as troublesome in other times and in other places. The example of smoking cigarettes is a case in point. That behavior is not evaluated as a major social problem in Japan and the reasons are political (the demand of the U.S. government on Japan to import more cigarettes), economic (the Japanese government's need for the tax money on cigarettes), and cultural (the Japanese cultural theme stressing harmony and the resulting hesitancy of Japanese people to complain about cigarette smoking). The behavior of cigarette smoking in the United States is evaluated as a problem because we live in a different political, economic, and cultural environment.[4] As this environment changes so, too, will the social problems we hear about.

Second, claims about social problem conditions often are about far more than they appear to be on the surface. Specific conditions can be *symbolic* of larger problems. So, Americans worry a great deal about "street crime," which reflects a larger middle-class worry about race and class. We worry about "threatened children" because this reflects more diffuse worries about the future of our country. At times, we worry about conditions because the condition is constructed as part of a larger problem.

Consider, for example, the perplexing problem of "pedophile priests." Why is this of such public concern? Because this is yet another instance of fears about the well-being of children, we would expect audience members to be receptive to claims. Indeed, because Americans are particularly prone to worry when children are *sexually* endangered, we can understand the outrage. In addition, we could note that public attention is related to changes in the mass media: in the past, media had exercised considerable constraint in reporting scandals in mainstream churches. This has changed and, if anything, media now are prone to emphasize scandals because they are compelling stories. Yet there remains a question: Because it is not possible to know the objective extent of this problem, it is not possible to argue that, if compared with rabbis and ministers, a greater percentage of *priests* are pedophiles. Nor is it possible to argue that there is a greater percentage of pedophile priests than, say, pedophile school teachers, pedophile police officers, or pedophile coaches. It does not diminish the importance of the problem to ask: Why have "pedophile *priests*" been targeted for special attention?

The "pedophile priest" problem can be understood as symbolic of a range of problems associated with the Catholic church by claims-makers in the United States. In particular, the church has remained steadfast in resisting change in matters like divorce, abortion, and contraception. In addition, lay Catholics have wanted a larger role in the church and have complained about the power of the entrenched church hierarchy; feminists have criticized the Church for its refusals to ordain women. In brief, the Catholic church has become a prominent and primary opponent of social change in the United States. Yet while claims promoting change have been unsuccessful—the church hierarchy has refused to change—the abuse issue cannot be ignored. No one can argue that "pedophile priests" can be accepted, no one can argue that the church should "protect" such immorality. The problem leads to a solution: the church must change! Furthermore, it must change in the ways claims-makers long have advocated: The church must be modernized.[5]

Constructionist analysis of who makes claims and what claims mean can lead to questions such as, Why is it that priests—and not ministers or schoolteachers or coaches—have been singled out? What is going on in the social environment that leads us to look in one place for problems and not in other places?

Why Does It Matter What Terms We Use to Categorize Conditions and People?

Every social problems formula story involves notions of morality, cause, and possible solution; each victim and villain in these stories is constructed as being worthy of sympathy or condemnation. Therefore, the social problems categories we use to evaluate and categorize conditions and people in daily life cannot be understood as merely reflecting common sense and therefore not very interesting. Granted, some words that are the result of successful claims-making eventually become so commonly used that practical actors rarely ask where the words came from and what they mean. Practical actors often do not know about the claims-competitions leading to the success of one set of claims, and the silencing of other claims. So, terms such as "PMS" or "moron" or "gifted children" are used by practical actors to categorize unique conditions and people. Yet behind this taken-for-granted status lies a more complex reality: words often subtly convey entire *systems of meaning*. Categorizing a particular family as "dys-functional" is very different from evaluating that family as "odd"; cate-gorizing an event as "child abuse" is different from categorizing it as "punishment"; categorizing a child as "learning disabled" is different from categorizing that child as "mentally challenged". Words matter: successful claims can give us new categories of conditions and people, they can change the ways we evaluate and react to these conditions and people.[6]

Why Does Social Policy Often Fail to Eliminate Social Problems?

Constructionist perspectives do not answer audience members' ques-tions about what should be done to resolve social problems. Yet construc-tionist studies can tell us something about the unintended consequences of using social problems claims to direct public policy.

First, when social problem images of conditions and people lead public policy they encourage us to focus on doing something about the conditions experienced by the *types* of victims featured in claims. So, for example, Americans spend a great deal of money fingerprinting children. This makes sense given claims about the problems of children abducted by strangers. But we have not done much about resolving the far larger prob-lem, that of child custody contests leading parents not receiving custody to feel they have no choice but to kidnap their own children. Or, given the image of AIDS as an equal opportunity disease, it makes sense that con-siderable money has been spent on programs to educate Americans in gen-eral. Yet we might have had more success in stopping the spread of AIDS if money had been concentrated in geographic areas and on people most likely to become its victims.

Second, and related, when social problem images lead to organizations and groups in the troubled persons industry, these places tend to be for victims, potential victims, villains, and potential villains who experience problems similar to those in social problems formula stories. Again, this makes sense: social problem claims will inform policymakers who want to be responsive to the social problem. Yet successful social problems formula stories tend to contain plots of the most horrid of conditions with charac-ters who are the purest of victims and the most evil of villains. But real peo-ple, not types of people, enter the troubled persons industry. These places often have clients who do not evaluate their own experiences or selves as similar to the characters in the social problems formula story informing the place. This gives us a social world with many different kinds of services, but a world where it can be very difficult for people wanting help to find what they want and need.

So, an unintended consequence of using social problems claims to direct public policy is that these claims can lead us to direct our resources in particular ways. I must be clear about this: I am definitely *not* claiming that we should not put resources toward resolving the problem of children abducted by strangers, nor am I saying that we should not educate all Americans about the problem of AIDS. But what I *am* claiming is that there always are trade-offs in that audience and public arena carrying capacities mean there is only so much worry, time, and money. Public policy should try to achieve the *greatest good* for the *greatest number* of people, but successful social problem constructions are tilted toward extreme conditions and particular kinds of victims and villains. Social constructionist examinations can alert us to the problems that likely come from using social problem typifications of people and conditions to inform social policy.

How Do Social Problems Reflect and Perpetuate Inequality?

Although constructionism does not begin by emphasizing the importance of the cultural theme of equality, this perspective can show how inequalities of every type matter in shaping public consciousness of social problems and how these inequalities are maintained. For example, constructionist examinations of diagnostic frames can show how these frames reflect—and perpetuate—*racial/ethnic inequality.* The case of "crack mothers" is a good example. This has been constructed as a problem of poor and black women who use illegal drugs during pregnancy and therefore produce children who—according to claims—are doomed to failure. The most popular diagnostic frame constructs an individual-level cause of this problem: Such women are simply evil, they do not act responsibly during pregnancy. Left out of this most common frame are social structural constraints—poor black women lack medical care, they have limited economic opportunities; women who do have problems with drugs cannot find help because there are far too few drug treatment programs. The individual-level diagnostic frame blaming women was successful, at least in part, because it reflected biases of the dominant classes, who do not perceive black women as "good mothers" as this is measured through dominant-class cultural themes. This individual-level diagnostic frame also perpetuates inequality: it leads to blaming and punishing women and ignores all that could be done to assist them.[7]

The collective identity of "welfare mother" is another example of how racial/ethnic inequality shapes public perceptions of social problems. Objectively speaking, in sheer numbers, there are more white women who rely on welfare than there are black women. Objectively speaking, most women who rely on welfare have one or two children. But the public image of the "welfare mother" leading the 1996 welfare reform was of a black woman with many children. Claims leading to an image that the category of "welfare mother" contained first, foremost, and primarily black women were effective at least in part because they reflected racial biases of the dominant class.[8]

Or, consider again the case of "gifted children," a type of child who often receives more resources and assistance than children not categorized as "gifted." Objectively speaking, very few children categorized as "gifted" are other than white. Yet certainly we cannot use this to claim that minority children simply are not as intelligent. On the contrary, constructionist examinations of claims made by people constructing the "gifted child" collective identity show that this type of person was constructed in ways making it very difficult for other than white children to fit the requirements for the category. The racism here is not obvious, it is covert and contained within the claims constructing the category. Objectivist examinations would show only that minority children rarely are categorized as "gifted," but a constructionist examination can show how this happens.[9]

We can see further reflections of racial inequality when we look at the common types of constructions of villains in social problem conditions. Susan Smith, for example, was a white woman in North Carolina who drowned her two young children. She constructed a story to account for their disappearance: a black man kidnapped them. Why did she specify a *black* villain? Charles Stuart, as another example, was a wealthy white man in Boston who killed his pregnant wife. He, too, told a story to account for her death—he said his wife was killed by a *black* attacker. Why did he specify a *black* villain? Is it merely coincidence that villains often are constructed as members of minority groups?

When we study the construction of social problems we also can see how claims reflect and perpetuate *social class inequality*. Remember that one characteristic of effective claims is that they tend to emphasize middle-class people as victims of social problems. Although we know, objectively speaking, that it is much more likely that poor people will be victims of social problems of all kinds, powerful middle-class audiences are more concerned when victims are middle-class. Claims reflect inequality. At the same time, claims constructing middle-class people as social problems victims perpetuate inequality: We spend a great deal of time worrying about, and offering services to, middle-class victims. This is worry and services not received by poor people, who, objectively speaking, need more consideration and services.

What we have here is complicated. Successful claims-makers often are white, middle-class, and well-educated. They might begin their work with biases privileging others of their kind. Even if they do not, they can learn that claims featuring certain types of people as villains (minority, poor) and certain types of people as victims (not minority, not poor) are more associated with success than are claims featuring other types of victims or other types of villains. The claims are successful in part because they reflect inequality.

Such claims also perpetuate this inequality because *real* people who are perceived as members of particular collective identities (racial / ethic / social class) are singled out for special punishment or special assistance because they are types of people. Disadvantaged people therefore tend to face further disadvantages and advantaged people tend to be granted further advantages so inequality is perpetuated.

In brief, although social constructionist frameworks do not begin with the statement that "inequality is bad," this approach can show us a great deal about how inequality matters in the ways we make sense of the world around us. Within constructionism, racism or classism become much more than vague social forces. Within constructionism we can examine racism or classism or other types of inequalities, as behaviors—the behaviors of claims-makers who choose their examples, the behaviors of audience members who evaluate particular kinds of claims as believable and important, the behaviors of practical actors and workers in the troubled persons industry who use the images of collective identity to evaluate and categorize individual people.

What Do Social Problems Tell Us About Our Cultural Worries?

Social problem conditions are things we worry about. Examining commonalities among claims about many kinds of conditions can tell us something about the structure of worry among Americans.

What Kinds of Conditions Do Americans Worry About?   First, Americans have a tendency to worry only about the *most troublesome* conditions producing the *most extremely harmed* victims. This first of all reflects our tendency to think of social problems as entertainment: Transplanting a baboon heart into a child is much more interesting than doing something about the hundreds of thousands of Americans who have chronic diseases such as multiple sclerosis, diabetes, or hypertension. This tendency to worry only about very extreme conditions also reflects a characteristic of the postmodern world: daily we are bombarded with claims about social problems, each one seemingly more devastating than the others. Our sympathy is stretched so we require increasingly dire images of harm before we are moved.[10]

Our tendency to focus on extreme harm also might tell us something about our current *cultural climate.* While constructing grounds featuring extreme harm can be effective because they encourage audience members to feel sympathy, such extreme grounds also are effective because they can eliminate possible counterclaims constructing the condition as tolerable and therefore not a problem. Our postmodern world is one of moral fragmentation: Americans tend to unite in our understandings of what is right or wrong only at the extreme, at those places that are clearly and most certainly and without a doubt intolerable. So, you and I might *not* agree that "spanking" a child is intolerable, but my hunch is that we *do* agree that "putting out a cigarette on a child's arm" is intolerable. We might not agree that a pregnant nineteen-year-old married woman should be closely monitored because she is too young to be a mother, but we likely will agree that an unmarried fourteen-year-old pregnant woman should be so monitored. We unite at the extreme so this is where claims likely will be effective.

Second, and closely related, Americans worry far more about harm that already has happened than we worry about how to *prevent* harm. Successful claims often construct images of social problem conditions as emergencies and this leads to the tendency for public policy to focus on emergencies rather than on conditions that are not so dire. Most of the cost of health care in this country is for heroic medicine for the most devastating illnesses; we put far less into disease prevention. While this makes sense—we must care for people in emergencies—this means we do not have the money or the time to think about preventing the devastating conditions, we are not putting our time or money into efforts to resolve conditions *before* they produce victims.[11] So we tend to ignore claims about the potential devastation of environmental ruin or earthquakes. We worry, it seems, only when we have dead birds or falling buildings, we worry after damage has been done. This is unfortunate because it is far easier, and far less expensive, to prevent problems than it is to cure them.

While troublesome, this tendency to do little in the way of prevention makes sense given the logic of social problems. First, claims focused on possible harm in the future will compete with claims about devastating harm in the present. Our carrying capacity for social problems is exhausted by attending to already dire conditions. Second, many people are drawn to doing the social problems work of constructing problems or working in the troubled persons' industry because the work seems exciting and noble: It is about rescuing victims and righting the scales of justice. Prevention work is not so glamorous. Prevention is successful to the extent that something does *not* happen and there is no way to know for sure that it was the prevention work, and not something else, that led to successful outcomes.

Third and finally, American worry can be motivated through appeals to *emotion* in addition to—or rather than—appeals to logic. Our worries, in other words, are not always grounded in our logical reflections. We can feel about social problems when we have no grounds for thinking about them.

This, too, might tell us something about our postmodern culture. We live in a time when an increasing number of Americans believe there is no clear right or wrong. This also is a time characterized by a lack of trust in people who formerly were in positions of authority, such as parents, teachers, politicians, and, increasingly, even scientists. Many Americans no longer believe that the truth is out there waiting to be found. The more we lose the belief that there is truth, the more we must trust our emotions.

So, it is not surprising that successful claims often are emotionally compelling. Claims about "child abuse" are a case in point. Often, these claims do not attempt to explain how child abuse could happen—they are not constructed in ways giving audience members information so that claims can be evaluated for their logic. No, claims about child abuse typically go to great lengths to emphasize the extreme brutality and the extreme harm. Such claims are emotionally compelling.[12]

While emotions are very much a part of the human experience and while we certainly should not diminish their importance, this characteristic of American worry should give us pause because it means we are open to being emotionally manipulated by claims-makers. We might worry when claims are logically indefensible but emotionally compelling. In addition, emotions often are transitory. As such, emotional appeal might not be sufficient to convince audience members to have the long-term commitment necessary to resolve social problems.

Social construction analysis can tell us that social problem claims reflect cultural worries. Successful claims tend to be those reflecting the general kinds of things that Americans already are worried about. Social problems claims also serve to perpetuate that worry. We tend to worry about extreme conditions, for example, and social problems claims give us all sorts of examples of such conditions. As long as we have a constant supply of extreme conditions to worry about, it is unlikely we will turn our attention to less extreme conditions. In the same way, as long as we have a constant supply of social problem claims about devastation that already has happened, it is unlikely we will be very interested in how to stop devastation from happening in the first place. In brief, constructionist analysis can tell us about the characteristics of cultural worry; they can show us how social problem claims both reflect that worry as well as perpetuate it.

Why Do We Live in a Culture Characterized by Fear and Pessimism?   Americans worry and we worry a lot. We are increasingly fearful of others and often pessimistic about the country's future. If we took all social problems claims seriously we might well believe there is nowhere to run, nowhere to hide, and that we are all destined to be victimized by multiple problems.

Our fear of others can lead us to react in particular ways. A student in one of my classes, for example, is a worker in a child day care center. According to her, these workers never hold young children on their laps anymore because such close physical contact between an adult and child can be misevaluated as "child molestation." Also, college faculty members now often are cautioned to leave our office doors open when we meet with students. There are so many allegations of harassment that it is wise to avoid any interaction with students that is not in a public place. And, people now talk about how they sit in airports and look at others around them trying to gauge if any "terrorists" will be aboard the plane. And, of course, there is the often noted problem of *black* men. A *black* man walking along a street will see others cross to the other side of the street rather than walking past him. We live in a culture of fear and distrust.

Despite the objective reality that we have less to fear than in times past (people live longer and healthier lives, standards of living are better), fear and pessimism are pervasive in the United States. Our fear and distrust of others and our pessimism that things are getting worse rather than better are consequences of the process of constructing social problems in ways emphasizing random and common victimization featuring good victims and evil offenders. Social problems claims-makers of all types perpetuate a culture of distrust and fear. Commercial media promote this by giving massive attention to social problems because audience members evaluate claims about drama, evil, and suffering as good entertainment. Audience members who are fearful and who distrust others are fairly easy to convince that yet another social problem involving yet another type of villain exists and must be eliminated.[13]

In summary, I would argue that social constructionism tells us a great deal about social problems in particular, about social life in general. Granted, its questions about how humans construct meaning and about the meanings we construct do not seem as immediate as questions about the causes, consequences, and solutions to social problems. But it nonetheless makes sense to remember that humans live in two worlds. We live in a physical world and in this world there are polluted rivers, teens having babies, people with AIDS, rat-infested housing, crime, hazardous work, planes falling from the sky, and children who cannot read. But this physical world has no meaning apart from what is constructed. In our daily lives it is important to ask how we know what we know; it is important to know why we worry about some things and why we do not worry about others; it is important to understand relationships among our emotions, our knowledge, and our behaviors.

The social construction perspective allows us to see some aspects of our lives that are not visible when social problems are examined only as objective conditions in the environment. So, I will return to some questions I raised earlier in this chapter: When so many Americans need to be educated about the objective characteristics of social problems, why should we take our energy to look at how humans create meaning? For example, it is clear that a few people still refuse to believe that the Holocaust happened, so claims about the reality of the Holocaust are needed. Nonetheless, it is important to know how a type of person, the "Jew," was constructed in Nazi Germany. In this case, the "Jew" was constructed as a type of person whose killing was not morally troublesome. If we understand how this construction of a type of person was one reason, however small, why the Holocaust could happen, we might be more hesitant to accept constructions of other types of people as such dangerous outsiders whose deaths are morally tolerable. In the same way, many Americans need to hear claims about the policy of the U.S. government during World War II to place Japanese Americans in internment camps. While such internment camps certainly were not similar to the concentration camps used by the Nazis, this policy nonetheless was an extreme violation of the cultural theme of freedom. While in historical retrospect that policy now is hotly criticized, at the time it was generally supported. Perhaps if we understood how the American government justified this policy by constructing "Japanese Americans" as dangerous outsiders, we will be more hesitant to offer our support for that type of program again.

This takes me to my final comments about how important you are in the process of constructing social problems.

PRACTICAL ACTORS AND SOCIAL PROBLEMS

Throughout this book I have focused on various types of social problems work such as the work of persuading audience members to evaluate a condition as a social problem, the work of audience members evaluating claims, and the work done by practical actors both in daily life and in the troubled persons industry to evaluate and categorize unique experiences, conditions, and people. I want to conclude by talking about your importance in the social problems game.

First, we are all members of audiences for social problems claims trying to persuade us to evaluate conditions as intolerable. We are audience members when we watch the television news or read a paper, sit in college classrooms, attend lectures or rallies, or merely listen to friends making claims about social problem conditions and the people in them. Although the "vote" of one individual most often means little to the outcome of the game of constructing social problems, it remains that, as a collective, audience members are the judges and juries for evaluating the believability and importance of claims. Audiences matter even in the world of politics, where much goes on behind closed doors and where policy can be made by a small number of people striking political deals. Politicians must be responsive to public opinion, and public opinion is just another name for an audience of "Americans who tend to vote."

Second, as practical actors, we each do the social problems work of evaluating and categorizing unique conditions, experiences, ourselves, and others around us. This is what we do every day of our lives as we decide to cross a street to avoid walking past a group of teens, when we ponder our troubles to decide what particular type of problem we have, when we talk with a neighbor about another neighbor who is "alcoholic," when we try to convince a friend that she is "depressed" and should go to a doctor.

My point is that practical actors control the outcome of social problems games. Claims are effective when audience members evaluate them as believable and important. If successful claims have particular kinds of characteristics it is because *audience members* are drawn to these images. If images from social problems formula stories are used as a resource to make sense of practical experience it is because practical actors decide to use these images to make sense of their selves and others.

What I am doing here is complaining about the tendency to blame claims-makers—politicians, media personalities, social movement activists, and so on—for selling us, the American public, the wrong images. I think it is a mistake to do this because all that effective claims-makers do is package claims in ways that are attractive to members of targeted audiences. We (Americans in general) are prone to worry only about extremely horrid conditions, we are prone to see only some kinds of people as victims and only some kinds of people as villains, we are drawn to notions of individual causes and therefore individual solutions to social problems, we do not like complex problems, we like simple solutions. Successful claims-makers, in other words, give us what we want.

Furthermore, while there can be huge differences between the characteristics and experiences of unique people and the simple, if not simplistic images contained in social problems formula stories, we often seem quite willing to use whatever social problem images currently are in style to make sense of our selves and those around us. New social problems, such as "codependency," are constructed and literally millions of people begin using these categories to make sense of themselves and others around them. The federal government reduces the weight it takes to be categorized as "obese" and declares war on obesity and millions of people begin to define themselves and others around them as "obese" and in need of change. Parents flock in droves to professionals who will categorize their children as "learning disabled" and therefore eligible for special services. Students talk of how they cannot be expected to excel because they are members of "dysfunctional families" so their fate is doomed. We look at a man sitting next to us on a plane and suspect that because he looks "Arabic" he is a terrorist.

Because practical actors are so critical in constructing public worry, I would suggest that it is important for each of us become more knowledgeable *consumers* of social problems claims. Just as we are taught by a variety of experts how to buy automobiles or mutual funds or computers, we should be taught how to be thoughtful audience members for social problems claims we hear in our daily lives and thoughtful in how we use these claims. I will end by offering some suggestions for how we all can train ourselves to become good consumers of social problems claims and good users of social problem images in our daily lives.[14]

1.   Become an active member of audiences for social problems claims. Rather than being an audience member who does not care, become an active participant. If you do not care, if you do not actively participate, you are allowing others to direct social change.

2.   When you hear social problems claims, be open to the possibility that you can be convinced. Audience members who do not listen simply because they do not agree with the claims will be stuck in their own world and cannot learn anything new. But just as clearly, when you hear claims, do not be automatically convinced. Do the social problems work of evaluating claims for their believability and their importance.

3.   Just as we read labels on packages of food when we go to the grocery store, ask questions about social problems claims. Ask, for example, about the specific meaning of words being used, ask how terms are defined, ask how the research underlying claims about the facts of the condition was conducted. Do not allow claims-makers to use words without defining their precise meanings, and be careful of thinking that one extreme example is typical of a huge category. Thoughtful claims-makers will be able to answer your questions. If they refuse to answer, or offer only glib responses to your questions, then be extra careful in accepting the believability of their claims.

4.   Remember the hierarchy of credibility: Many audience members are prone to believe claims made by some types of people (such as scientists) and to disbelieve claims made by others (such as children, members of disadvantaged minority groups, poor people). When you evaluate the believability and importance of claims think about how your response might be influenced by the characteristics of the person making the claim. Ask the same questions of claims made by scientists and others high on the hierarchy of credibility as you do of claims made by others with less prestige. Try to evaluate the believability and importance of *claims* rather than the assumed prestige of *claims-makers*.

5.   In every social problem seek the underlying moral problem defined through the diagnostic frame. Always ask yourself *why* is the condition a problem? What cultural theme is being violated? Will resolving a condition involve violating another cultural theme? Is the tradeoff justified?

6.   Think of disagreements among claims-makers as claims-competitions. Ask yourself, What are the disagreements really about? Do not focus on the details (they can be endless), but rather concentrate on identifying the general issues leading to disagreements. Do not be satisfied if claims-makers attempt to persuade you that people making counterclaims are simply evil or ignorant.

7.   Remember that social problems claims are as much about how we feel as about how we think. If we ignore this and examine claims only for their logical content, our emotions can be manipulated. When you see or hear social problems claims ask: What are these claims encouraging me to *think*? What are they encouraging me to *feel*? Clearly, there is nothing wrong in feeling about social problems. Feeling sympathy for victims is a good human quality and our world would be better if we felt more sympathy for more people. Yet it is important for us to know the extent to which we are reacting (positively or negatively) because of how we are thinking and because of how we are feeling. If you are reacting because of your feelings, think about your feelings (Why do I feel this way about these claims?) If you are reacting because of your thinking, try to feel about your thinking (How do I feel about the way I think about these claims?)

8.   The troubled persons industry arising from successful social problems claims-making sometimes includes too many choices for people needing assistance. Before you voluntarily enter a program for counseling, education, or other assistance, talk with workers about the program's or group's philosophy. How do they describe their typical clients? What types of problems do they believe their clients experience? What do they offer clients? What is their vision of success?

9.   Think about the collective identities you use to make sense of your own life and the lives of those around you and do not be too quick to categorize yourself or others into one or another of these identities. Be always aware that when you categorize yourself or others into specific collective identities you are referencing whole systems of meaning. Some collective identities can be liberating, but some can be oppressive so think through the complex of meaning before categorizing unique people as types of people.

We live in a very odd time. While we talk proudly about how we are a democracy and about how we value individual freedom, Americans in general increasingly do not participate in politics, increasingly we look to a variety of experts to tell us how we should think, how we should feel, and how we should live our lives. Social problems claims-makers are one such type of expert and I have spent my time here examining the social problems work they do. Clearly and most certainly and without a doubt, this social problems game is political. Who wins and who loses is a matter of inequalities, power, and politics. It is wise to not forget that. But I do not want to stress that here because the more we talk about the power of politics, the politics of power, the more it seems as if you and I as individuals are powerless. As individuals it is true, we have little power. But we can band together into social change groups, we can become claims-makers in the next rounds of a social problems game. Perhaps more important because it is a routine part of our daily lives, we can become good members of social problems audiences. We can become active audience members with our understandings of how the social problems game is played. We can examine the form of claims and the process of claims-making. We can think more about the meaning of the words we use. We can be more thoughtful in using images of social problems to categorize ourselves and others. This is the promise of a social construction approach to social problems, an approach encouraging us to think about the world around us, a world whose meanings are created by humans.

NOTES

1. According to Gusfield (1981:3): "Human problems do not spring up, full-blown and announced, into the consciousness of bystanders. Even to recognize a situation as painful requires a system for categorizing and defining events. All situations that are experienced by people as painful do not become matters of public activity and targets for public action. Neither are they given the same meaning at all times and by all peoples. 'Objective' conditions are seldom so compelling and so clear in their form that they spontaneously generate a 'true' consciousness."

2. R. Berger (2002, excerpted in *Social Problems: Constructionist Readings*) explores the construction of "Jew" in Nazi Germany, Petonito (1992) examines the construction of "Japanese Americans" as dangerous outsiders in the United States during World War II.

3. Lowney (1994) explores how "Satanism" is constructed on television talk shows.

4. Ayukawa (2001, excerpted in *Social Problems: Constructionist Readings*) places the behavior of cigarette smoking in Japan within these larger contexts; Linders (1998) studies the contexts of the abortion controversy in Sweden and the United States.

5. Jenkins (1995, excerpted in *Social Problems: Constructionist Readings*) examines "pedophile priests" as a symbolic problem.

6. For claims-competitions about PMS and the importance of this category see Pawluch (1996, excerpted in *Social Problems: Constructionist Readings*); for the technical meaning and the social meaning of "moron" see Spector and Kitsuse ([1977] 1987).

7. Litt and McNeil (1994, excerpted in *Social Problems: Constructionist Readings*) discuss the American tendency to construct poor, minority women as individual failures as mothers.

8. For this argument about the "color" of welfare, see Quadagno (1994) and

Neubeck and Cazenave (2001). Also, Clawson and Trice (2000) examine race as portrayed in media images of poverty.

9.   Margolin (1994) examined the covert racism in gifted child rhetoric.

10.   For this tendency of audience members to require ever greater images of harm to be emotionally moved, see Loseke (1993), Best (1990), Denzin (1990).

11.   As Best (1990:188) argues in his discussion of resources used for the problems of children: "A society which is mobilized to keep child molesters, kidnappers, and Satanists away from innocent children is not necessarily prepared to protect children from ignorance, poverty, and ill health." See Lipsky and Smith (1989) for the analysis of problems from responding to social problems as emergencies.

12.   Johnson (1995, excerpted in *Social Problems: Constructionist Readings*) examines the typical format of claims about child abuse.

13.   Best (1999, excerpted in *Social Problems: Constructionist Readings*) argues that constructions of "random violence" lead to this culture of fear, Best (2001b) discusses how social progress can lead to perceptions that "things are getting worse." Altheide (2002) and Glassner (1999) illustrate how mass media presentations lead to a culture of fear and mistrust.

14.   Best (2001a, excerpted in *Social Problems: Constructionist Readings*) also offers advice about how to ask questions about claims made with statistics.

APPENDIX

Social Construction Theories and Issues

My intent in writing this book was to offer readers an introduction to social constructionist perspectives on social problems. I thought this was an important project for two reasons. First, while in daily life we most often seek knowledge about things that bother us, we also should ask how we know what we know and this is the topic of social constructionist perspectives. Second, although social constructionism has been called the most influential development in social problems theory in the past twenty-five years, its audience has remained somewhat confined to academics, and I believe this is at least partially due to a lack of general introductory statements to the perspective. While there are many books and countless journal articles describing and using this perspective, this literature tends to be not very good as a general introduction. The *empirical* literature, for example, is characterized by case studies. While these can be very informative and incredibly interesting, it is not always obvious how case studies are parts of a larger constructionist project. Also, although there is a constantly expanding *theoretical* literature, readers must already know a great deal about the perspective in order to understand these works. My goal in this book was to interpret theory and synthesize empirical literature. But doing this led me to all but ignore important theoretical understandings leading the empirical studies as well as theoretical debates among people working within constructionist perspectives. In this chapter I want to offer a slightly more elaborate theoretical framework than I used in the rest of this book. I offer this as a road map of sorts for people who want to do a further exploration of constructionist perspectives. In this chapter I will focus on two major questions: What are the justifications for social constructionist perspectives on social problems? What are the current theoretical debates?

I will confine myself in three ways. First, although constructionist approaches to social problems are found in sociology, communication studies, and public policy, I will remain true to my training as a sociologist and focus on theoretical statements written by people identifying themselves as sociologists.[1] Second, I will organize my comments around one book,

Constructing Social Problems, originally published in 1977, by Malcolm Spector and John Kitsuse. While other reference points would lead to different perspectives on theories and debates, this book is the commonly cited beginning of social construction perspectives on social problems among sociologists. For example, the back cover of the present edition contains quotes from well-respected sociologists claiming that *Constructing Social Problems* is "the major and originating statement of the social constructionist perspective on social problems," a "seminal contribution to the study of social problems," a book that "must be consulted by anyone who wants to understand the social constructionist approach." Sociologists working in this perspective must agree with such praise because this book is all but invariably cited whenever social constructionist perspectives are used. The third way in which I will confine myself here is that I will not discuss the empirical research informing theory. I have offered many examples of empirical' findings in notes at the end of every chapter in this book.

JUSTIFICATIONS FOR SOCIAL CONSTRUCTION PERSPECTIVES ON SOCIAL PROBLEMS

Any theoretical or intellectual perspective is similar to a lens on a camera. A "zoom" lens, for example, allows us to see fine details but we can look at very little; a wide-angle lens shows a larger picture, but the details are lost. In this camera metaphor, social constructionism is a lens allowing us to see how what we call social problems are constructed by people who say things and do things in order to persuade audience members that a troublesome condition exists and cannot be tolerated. But in encouraging us to look at questions about the meaning of social problems, this social constructionist lens does not make visible the characteristics of an objective world. Yet it is the characteristics of the objective world that are of concern to practical actors who most often want to know the characteristics of social problem conditions, what causes them, what can be done to resolve them. Because the questions asked by constructionists about human meaning are not questions arising in daily life we need to examine why a constructionist approach is justified. I will begin with the justifications for this perspective offered by Spector and Kitsuse in *Constructing Social Problems.*

Social Constructionism as a Corrective

The first sentence in *Constructing Social Problems* sets the tone for the book: "There is no adequate definition of social problems within sociology, and there is not and never has been a sociology of social problems."[2] A constructionist approach is justified by emphasizing how there are problems with objectivist perspectives on social problems. Indeed, a large part of the book details the multiple problems in examining social problems as objective conditions.

First, what is the topic matter when we talk about social problems as objective conditions? People studying social life must use precise and unambiguous definitions, but what, precisely, is a "social problem"? Spector and Kitsuse present and then criticize one objectivist definition of social problems that appeared in a then-popular textbook: "A social problem exists when organized society's ability to order relationships among people seems to be failing; when its institutions are faltering, its laws are being flouted, the transmission of its values from one generation to the next is breaking down, the framework of social expectations is being shaken." Spector and Kitsuse ask questions about this definition: "What constitutes 'collective society,' or a 'public recognition'; which 'practices,' and how do they constitute 'threats'; which 'relationships,' and how do you know when they 'fail'; when are institutions 'faltering,' laws being 'flouted,' and so on?" In asking these questions, they support their argument that definitions of social problems as objective conditions often contain "ambiguous, and often outright sloppy, definitional statements." This is not acceptable for science.

Spector and Kitsuse also argue that when social problems are conceptualized as objective conditions there is no justification for a concept of "social problems." They ask: "Is anything added to the study of deviant behavior by calling it a social problem? Do we increase our understanding of crime or poverty by pointing out that it is a social problem?" Spector and Kitsuse ask: How can scientists study something that is not even defined?

Next, Spector and Kitsuse ask how it is possible to study social problems as objective conditions when there is no necessary relationship between what people believe are social problems and objective measures of those conditions. To demonstrate, they use an example of a lack of attention to the condition of "organized crime." They argue that organized crime, objectively speaking, *is* a harmful condition, but it often is *not* categorized as a social problem. They also use the example of changes in laws and attitudes surrounding marijuana smoking. It is not possible to say that changes in laws reflect changing physiological characteristics of that drug because physiological characteristics do not change. We can have no worry when a troublesome condition objectively exists, we can have new worry although an objective condition is unchanged. Given this, it is not possible to say that people worry when conditions exist and they do not worry when conditions do not exist. There is something important about how people define social problems regardless of the characteristics of the objective world.

Next, Spector and Kitsuse note that when social problems are studied as objective conditions, it is up to the expert to decide when a condition is harmful, to decide when social standards are being violated. Yet by what criteria do experts decide that a given condition is harmful? By what criteria do experts decide that social standards are being violated? It is not possible to argue that these evaluations are made on *technical* criteria, because evaluations of harm require moral, rather than scientific, criteria. This leads to a problem for sociologists who often present themselves as value-neutral scientists. According to Spector and Kitsuse, when experts assume the responsibility of deciding what is—and what is not—a social problem, the "values of the sociologist are still the guiding force behind the definitions, now disguised behind a facade of science." They argue that as members of the social order, sociologists can have their personal views about social problems. But "this practice must be clearly separated from a *theoretical* mandate to do so."

In summary, Spector and Kitsuse describe multiple theoretical problems of examining social problems as objective conditions.[3] Constructionist perspectives therefore are justified as a corrective. Their goal is to construct a theory "amenable to empirical elaboration in which the process of definition and not 'objective conditions' is the central concern"; one that would "define the phenomenon, the subject matter for analysis, in a clear and unambiguous manner that is amenable to empirical investigation"; one that would justify "the addition of the new conceptual category, 'social problems,' by distinguishing its content from that of other previously defined or related categories."

Their proposal in *Constructing Social Problems* is to *completely abandon* the notion of social problems as a kind of condition. They propose that social problems rather should be understood as a kind of *activity:* "Social problems [are] the activities of individuals or groups making assertions of grievances and claims with respect to some putative conditions." Within this perspective, constructionists are to examine claims-making, which is defined in *behavioral* terms as "demanding services, filing out forms, lodging complaints, filing lawsuits, calling press conferences, writing letters of protest, passing resolutions, publishing exposes, placing ads in newspapers, supporting or opposing some governmental practice or policy, setting up picket lines or boycotts." Notice that this activity has nothing to do with social problem conditions. All attention is on the activity of people who say things and do things to persuade audience members to evaluate a condition as a social problem. Conditions assumed to be problems in other perspectives become merely "putative" conditions, conditions *alleged* to exist. Within this perspective, the "term putative conditions is used to indicate the focus of our interest in the members' claims without regard to their validity." So, Spector and Kitsuse "are not concerned with whether or not the alleged condition exists. If the alleged condition were a complex hoax—a fabrication—we would maintain a noncommittal stance toward it."

Spector and Kitsuse propose a framework for studying social problems that resolves the many problems they describe with approaches examining social problems as objective conditions. For example, the topic matter is clearly defined: "to account for the emergence, nature, and maintenance of claims-making and responding activities." Their proposal also offers a justification for a conceptual category called social problems: social problems are claims-making activities. This, in turn, allows sociologists to be true experts. While it is *not* possible for any person—no matter how intelligent or educated—to be an expert on the countless and ever changing conditions called social problems, it *is* possible to be an expert on what all social problems share: claims-making activity. A constructionist perspective on social problems resolves the many problems associated with approaches focusing on social problems as objective conditions. It is justified as a corrective to these other approaches.

Constructing Social Problems is an important book often credited with starting a new tradition of empirical research on social problems. The perspective formally arrived in mainstream sociology in 1985 when Joseph Schneider published "Social Problems Theory: The Constructionist View" in the *Annual Review of Sociology,* which is one of the most highly respected publication sites for sociologists in general. Schneider argued that constructionists' interest in subjective definitions is preferable to the more common interest in social problems as objective conditions. Simply stated, "research based ostensibly on a condition-focused approach, or even on a subjective/objective elements approach to social problems has given us few distinct insights."

In summary, Spector and Kitsuse in 1977, and Schneider in 1985, justify constructionist perspectives on social problems through emphasizing the failures of objectivist approaches. This justification for constructionist perspectives was successful in encouraging a flurry of empirical research.[4] At the same time, when a perspective is justified primarily as a corrective to problems in alternative perspectives, two important questions remain unanswered. The first is the question of practical actors who most often want to know how we can eliminate the pain and suffering created by social problems. Their primary question about a social construction approach is "What does it tell us that is useful?" Especially in Chapter 8, but throughout this book, I offered answers to that practical question about why constructionist examinations are important for daily life concerns. Now I will turn to a question, one asked by academics who study social problems: Regardless of problems in other approaches, what are the *theoretical* justifications for social constructionist perspectives?

Social Constructionism as
a Theoretical Perspective

Constructing Social Problems offers its readers a list of reasons why approaches to social problems as objective conditions should be abandoned. It is a forceful synthesis of many earlier critiques of objectivist approaches. But because this book focuses on promoting constructionist perspectives as a corrective, there is little attention to developing a *theoretical* mandate. But I agree with others that there is an *implicit* theoretical framework in *Constructing Social Problems*. While the social construction perspective on social problems as formed by Spector and Kitsuse was a radical break in studying social problems, it also can be understood as an application of long-established and rich intellectual traditions outside the particular area of social problems.

While there are many people who have worked over the years to fill in the implicit theory in *Constructing Social Problems*, here I will focus on the work of Gale Miller and James Holstein.[5] While my choice to focus on these authors has the unfortunate consequence of not emphasizing important contributions made by others, I made this choice for two reasons. First, I began the history of constructionist approaches to social problems with a book, *Constructing Social Problems*, and Holstein and Miller begin their own work by explicitly embracing the Spector and Kitsuse framework. This allows me to discuss the historical progression of the theory. Second, unlike many people who have developed constructionist theories for one or another subset of questions about social problems, Miller and Holstein have an interest in the social construction perspective writ large.

The first article in the first volume of their *Perspectives on Social Problems: A Research Annual* begins with Miller and Holstein applauding *Constructing Social Problems* by calling it a "watershed in the development of the contemporary sociology of social problems."[6] They then describe their interest in theoretically grounding this approach in ways that are distinctly phenomenological, ethnomethodological, and Durkheimian. While I will not attempt to offer an adequate primer for each of these broad theories on social life, I will note the most important elements in each. Then, I will move to examining how these elements theoretically ground the social constructionist approach to social problems. I will start with the basic theoretical perspective called *phenomenology* and its more empirical variant, *ethnomethodology.*

Social constructionist approaches to social problems are an application of a general social constructionist perspective on social life which has philosophical and methodological roots in phenomenology, particularly that associated with Edmund Husserl and Alfred Schutz. This theoretical perspective begins with the belief that we cannot merely transport the models and assumptions of natural science into the study of human social life because humans are different from the planets, rocks, weather, frogs, or other objects of concern to natural science. Human social life is characterized by meaning. Phenomenology stakes out for itself the task of understanding how humans create this meaning. For that reason, it is categorized as an *interpretive* approach to social life because interest is in how humans interpret, or make sense of, our lives.

A variant of phenomenology, called ethnomethodology, also is relevant although it cannot be called an historical precursor because it arose at the same time that Spector and Kitsuse were writing their book. Associated with Harold Garfinkel, ethnomethodology literally defined is the study of the practical activities (methods) of ethnos (folk). While phenomenology can be quite abstract, ethnomethodology is quite grounded. The primary question for ethnomethodology is, how do practical actors create and sustain a sense of objective reality?

The sensibilities of phenomenology and ethnomethodology obviously inform social construction perspectives of all types. First, phenomenology, social constructionism, and ethnomethodology share beliefs that we must examine the creation and maintenance of human meaning. Second, all three share belief that meaning is social and socially created. Third, these perspectives share the belief that while humans must create meaning, the social order gives us resources for doing this. Although not elaborated in *Constructing Social Problems*, Spector and Kitsuse's call to examine social problems as matters of definition is in keeping with the general phenomenological framework, the call to examine social problems as matters of human activity is in keeping with an ethnomethodological framework. What Miller and Holstein explicitly take from the phenomenological perspective is the general belief that humans create meaning, and the specific concept of "schemes of interpretation," which is the term the phenomenologist Alfred Schutz used for the social resources we can use to make sense of practical experience. What they take from ethnomethodology is the interest in understanding how making meaning is a practical activity: people do things that create meaning.

A constructionist perspective on social problems also is Durkheimian. It is risky to discuss so briefly the work of Emile Durkheim because, like most classical theorists, his interests were broad, changed over time, and can be interpreted in different ways. Yet it might seem odd to add Durkheim to phenomenology and ethnomethodology because, in contrast to interpretive approaches focusing on human meaning, Durkheim's work often is taken as an example of a social structural approach emphasizing how humans are influenced, directed, or even controlled by social forces outside us. Yet in his book, *The Elementary Forms of Religious Life*, he seems to have a different interest. This book can be interpreted as indicating that

Durkheim shared with phenomenologists an interest in how the meaning that directs individuals is both socially created and socially shared. This, too, is compatible with Spector and Kitsuse's view of social problems: Social problems claims-makers are creators of meaning; if they are successful then the meanings they create are socially shared. Miller and Holstein take from Durkheim two explicit points: First, while culture might well be experienced as constraining, humans make this culture. Second, in every culture there exist socially shared beliefs, values, and ideas, what Durkheim called "collective representations."

Miller and Holstein blend together these elements of phenomenology, ethnomethodology, and Durkheimian sociology in ways that place social constructionist perspectives on social problems within a much larger theoretical framework. They begin by arguing that they want to ground social constructionist perspectives within a Durkheimian perspective. Because Durkheim was most interested in social structures and forces existing outside individuals, this gives a new meaning to claims-making activities. Within this perspective, social problems claims-making is the "procedure for producing and extending culture."[7] Miller and Holstein argue that we might consider Durkheim's concept of "collective representation" as an alternative way of thinking about typifications or images of social problems. If we do this then social problem typifications are not merely images floating around the social world. According to Durkheim, collective representations are *social structure*.

Miller and Holstein then proceed to link Durkheim's concerns about pre-existing social ideas (typifications, collective representations, social structure) with phenomenological concerns with how humans make sense of our lives. They do this by arguing that collective representations can become schemes of interpretation—frameworks for making sense of our lives. This means that the products of successful social problems claims, whether called typifications or collective representations, are important because they can be used by practical actors as resources to make sense of our experiences and ourselves.

Yet so far this seems far too deterministic. Linking Durkheim's thinking about the importance of preexisting ideas with the concept of schemes of interpretation might encourage an image of practical actors somewhat automatically using images to make sense of experiences and selves. Miller and Holstein counter this robot image of humans by adding a distinctly ethnomethodological understanding: individual actors are not cultural robots; representations might exist in the social environment, but that does not mean practical actors automatically or necessarily use them. Collective representations are cultural resources, they are tools practical actors can use, yet their practical use depends on human sense making. This, of course, takes us back to the general phenomenological interest in how humans create meaning.

In the course of this theoretical development, Miller and Holstein advance a new concept they call "social problems work." This is most broadly defined as "any and all activity implicated in the recognition, identification, interpretation, and definition of conditions that are called 'social problems.'"[8] The concept of social problems work is a vehicle to explore "the processes of creating both social problems categories and concrete instances that are assigned membership in those categories."

This theoretical framework allows us to examine a full range of human activity (social problems work) involved in the construction of social problems. First, we can examine the activities of claims-makers, who construct typifications of conditions, victims, and villains. These claims-makers are doing social problems work when they decide what to include in the condition, how to define harm, what examples to use to typify the problem at hand, how to package claims for the media, and so on. Within a Durkheimian perspective, these claims-makers are creating *culture* as they create collective representations. Within an ethnomethodological perspective, we understand claims-makers as *practical actors:* They are using their understandings (Durkheimian collective representations) to construct new understandings. This gives us an answer to the question of why there are typical characteristics of successful claims: the characteristics of successful claims reflect the existing culture. For example, social problems claims-makers are practical actors when they construct new types of people as sympathy worthy by using cultural feeling rules, they are practical actors when they construct conditions as violating cultural themes. Good claims-makers are not a breed apart—they simply are good practical actors who, as members of a common culture, know which cultural themes, ideas, and images are compelling. In a Durkheimian framework, social problems claims-making *reflects* preexisting ideas (popular wisdom, cultural themes, cultural feeling rules) and preexisting social structure (class, race, gender, and so on). At the same time, successful claims-making creates new collective representations. Within a Durkheimian perspective, successful claims-making produces culture.

Second, social problems work includes the activities of practical actors, who use collective representations as social resources to categorize experiences, the self, and others. In a Durkheimian sense, this is the *reproduction* of culture as practical actors (either as individuals or as in the troubled persons industry workers) decide on a case-by-case basis that some (and only some) conditions are instances of a particular social problem, that some (and only some) people are instances of particular types of victims or villains. Here, too, we retain the ethnomethodological focus: social problems work is only "partly a process of 'imposing' cultural categories on objects, events, and persons" because the "process is open-ended . . . and subject to change based on a variety of practical circumstances."[9]

Holstein and Miller have grounded social construction perspectives on social problems in larger theoretical frameworks that are about much more than social problems. Within this framework, understanding the creation of social problems is a subtopic of more general questions about how humans create the meaning that then can appear to stand outside us.

While Miller and Holstein argue that they simply have made explicit what remained implicit in *Constructing Social Problems,* their elaboration repaired some of the unfortunate narrowing of social constructionist agendas created by the emphases and examples used in *Constructing Social Problems.* For example, while Spector and Kitsuse offered a very broad definition of claims-making as *all* of the "activities of individuals or groups making assertions of grievances and claims with respect to some putative conditions," this broad focus often seemed to be narrowed. To begin, Spector and Kitsuse tend to narrow interest to how social problems are *defined.* In doing this, they do not ask questions about how the products of successful claims-making can become socially shared collective representations that can be used by practical actors as schemes of interpretation to categorize practical experience.

Likewise, although Spector and Kitsuse talk about claims as including the "activities of individuals," they also write of how social constructionism would "emphasize the importance of reformers and action organizations." Such a statement tends to narrow the focus from claims-making in general to claims-making by social change groups. And, when Spector and Kitsuse write that "claims-making most readily brings to mind the demands that crusaders for various social reform and social movements made on governmental agencies and officials," attention to audiences for claims is reduced to government officials. Given this narrowing in *Constructing Social Problems,* observers have noted that early empirical studies tended to focus on the activities of social change groups attempting to change public policy. This leaves out many important claims-makers such as scientists, academic researchers, and claims made through the mass media. Also ignored is the question of how people make sense of troubles before these are formed as social problems. Miller and Holstein's broad concept of social problems work brings in all of these important topics.

When the social construction perspective on social problems is placed within larger Durkheimian, phenomenological, and ethnomethodological frameworks we have the justification for why this perspective is important *regardless* of what we might (or might not) perceive as problems with objectivist perspectives. I am arguing that it is logical to believe that social problems *can* be examined as objective conditions yet also believe that constructionist perspectives are important and valuable; they are theoretically grounded.

So far I have traced out what I have called theoretical *development* within this perspective. At the same time, there have been other proposed theoretical *changes* to the original framework. I turn now to challenges to the original Spector and Kitsuse framework and to the kinds of theoretical (and accompanying empirical) changes they suggest.

CHALLENGES TO CONSTRUCTIONIST THEORY

If they are to be viable, theoretical perspectives must constantly be examined for their internal consistency, they must be continually modified or elaborated to account for new empirical findings as well as for changes in the social and intellectual environment. While I do not know of any *empirical* studies that call the original Spector and Kitsuse framework into question, this perspective is not without *theoretical* controversy.[10] I will begin with criticisms raised by the theoretical perspectives of social criticism and postmodernism, and conclude with controversies internal to constructionism.

Challenges from Social Criticism

Social criticism is a broad label for a variety of theoretical perspectives including multiple versions of Marxism and feminism. What these theories share is a vision that the purpose of analyzing social life is to change it and that academic work should be consciously biased toward helping oppressed people. These social criticism theories also share an understanding that the causes of social problems lie in social structures such as capitalism or patriarchy. Finally, locating science within capitalism and patriarchy, proponents of social criticism theories argue that science is not an objective search for the truth but rather is merely a legitimation for the powers that be. Social criticism perspectives differ from social constructionism in three major ways.

First, constructionist perspectives bracket attention to objective conditions because, theoretically, objective conditions are not problems until they are reacted to as such. But from a social criticism perspective, objective conditions *do* exist and these conditions *are* problems even if they are not reacted to as such. For example, consider the condition of "black women's poverty." While there are countless indicators that this objective condition does exist, it will not be the topic for constructionist analysis unless or until claims are made about it. Yet claims about black women's poverty most often are silenced, they are made but rarely heard because of a lack of public concern for the problems of black women. According to proponents of social criticism, ethical issues are raised when construction-ists ignore the real conditions causing pain and suffering. Social construc-tionism is not ethical and can be made ethical only by examining objective conditions as problems in their own right.[11]

Constructionism and social criticism also are not compatible because so-cial critics believe that theory *cannot* and *should not* be value-neutral. This is the antiscience stance of social criticism, yet Spector and Kitsuse pro-moted the value of social constructionism precisely because this perspec-tive had the potential to be a value-neutral and scientific way to examine social problems.

Third, while social criticism is a theoretical perspective to promote so-cial change, social constructionism does not contain an explicit social change agenda. Indeed, Spector and Kitsuse were clear in arguing that while sociologists studying social problems are entitled to participate in social problems as practical actors, they should *not* enter the social prob-lems process as experts. Social criticism is about working to achieve social change, social constructionism is about working to achieve new know-ledge.

In brief, theoretical perspectives of social constructionism as outlined by Spector and Kitsuse in 1977 and social criticism are *necessarily* incompati-ble in three ways. In other ways, at least theoretically, social construction-ism can inform social criticism. This can be accomplished when social constructionist perspectives expand definitions of claims-making activi-ties to include talk by powerless people, even when such talk does not lead to social change. Social constructionist examinations also can be used to show how knowledge is socially constructed and how that knowledge re-flects power and politics.[12]

Challenges from Postmodernism

The basic elements of a postmodernism *theory* more or less follow from the characteristics of postmodernism as a *condition* that I discussed in Chapter 1 and alluded to throughout this book.[13] This includes the loss of faith in institutions, particularly the loss of faith that scientists produce knowledge; the concern with equality in an ever-expanding world of di-versity; and the problems of achieving a sense of self without institutional moorings. Such a condition leads to multiple practical questions: How can we trust science? How can we say there is any objective reality? Given di-versity there is no "truth," so whose story should we tell and for what pur-pose? Postmodernism as a stance for understanding and examining social life has been called a "challenge to the Enlightenment" because it reverses understandings associated with the modern era. Postmodernism is a challenge to Enlightenment beliefs that progress is good, that knowledge is created through science, that science can correctly measure the world, that reason is distinct from emotion, that democracies work the way they are supposed to work, that language objectively expresses reality. Postmodernists question disciplinary boundaries between science, social science, art, and literature; they distrust society's moral claims and traditional institutions; they reject conventional styles of academic discourse; they prefer relativism to objectivity; they prefer fragmentation to totalization; they abandon absolute standards. When all of these threads are taken to the extreme, there is no truth or reality, there are only multiple perspectives.

In some respects, social constructionist theories were precursors to postmodern trends now found throughout the social sciences and humanities. Constructionist perspectives bracket all questions about objective reality, so that the "truth" about conditions is not an issue. And, constructionist perspectives do not seek to tell people how the world "should" be organized, so there are none of the moral claims that are so troublesome in this world of fragmented morality. Some of the typical complaints of postmodernist theorists therefore do not apply to social constructionism. Yet postmodernism also is a response to perceived failures of Enlightenment beliefs in reason and science as the routes to knowledge. Because social constructionism is aligned with science, postmodernism raises a variety of questions about social constructionist theory, which, according to observers began as a "traditional social science project," a project whose value now is challenged.[14]

Postmodernist criticisms of constructionism pose the most fundamental of questions. At the most basic—and unchangeable—level, postmodernists argue that while social constructionists say they are objectively examining language, this is not possible. Language—in the claims made by others as well as the claims made by constructionists—is embedded in culture. What is and is not heard as a claim, what is and is not heard as moral, and so on, will depend on the social context. Postmodernists argue that it is not possible to examine constructions of subjective meaning without using language, and language reflects and perpetuates characteristics of the larger culture. Because the culture is not objective, it is not possible for constructionist analyses to be objective. While Spector and Kitsuse proposed social constructionism as an unbiased method of knowing about social problems, postmodernists argue there is no such thing as an unbiased way of knowing. According to postmodernists, the constructionist project is not possible because it cannot be freed from the bias of language.

In a related way, social constructionist writings can be challenged because, in practice, constructionists most often write what are called *realist* texts, writings advanced as correct and true. This is the problem that "On the one hand, [constructionism] insists that members' claims are constructed realities . . . ; on the other hand, [constructionism] grows nervous at the thought that observer's claims are no less constructed."[15] Within a postmodernist world of multiple and often contradictory truths, people doing social constructionist examinations often are guilty of portraying their texts as truthful and scientific, while these texts written by social constructionists are no more truthful or scientific than the claims analyzed within them. Postmodernism is about examining how *theorists* and *researchers* construct realities by the choices made about what to write and about how to write it. Constructionists are open to criticism when they fail to practice radical self-reflexivity, which is a method where texts written by constructionists are themselves examined as social constructions.

Finally, postmodernism rejects general theories of all types. Within postmodernism, a constructionist agenda to understand "the" claims-making process is doomed to failure because there is no process, there is no cause, there is no truth. Within postmodern sensibilities, the world is a scene of multiple competitions that are each unique. There can be no theory about *anything*, there only are competing perspectives.

Such criticisms are not easily reconciled with images of social constructionism as a scientific way of understanding social problems. If language is culturally embedded then it is not possible to study it in a value-neutral way; if science is fatally flawed, and if social constructionism is a scientific method, then social constructionism is fatally flawed. To meet challenges posed by some postmodernists, social constructionists could not advance their work as containing any truth, they could not claim expertise of any type. Rather, the job of postmodern constructionists would be to collect and retell the stories told by others. Social constructionism would be journalism.

Challenges from within Social Constructionism

While questions raised by postmodernism are relatively new, another question about social construction has not changed from the beginning: What is the status of objective conditions within this perspective? Although Spector and Kitsuse were clear in 1977 that interest in objective conditions should be *totally abandoned*, there remain to this day questions about how people advancing supposedly social constructionist examinations often make objective conditions into a topic for examination, and about the extent to which this should be allowed and to which it is justified.

The most important theoretical criticism about social construction perspectives was published in 1985 by Steven Woolgar and Dorothy Pawluch. While both are supporters of constructionist perspectives, they accused constructionists of practicing what they call "ontological gerrymandering," which they define as a practice of analytically manipulating a boundary, "making certain phenomena problematic while leaving others unproblematic."[16] According to them, there are three key moves in most constructionist arguments: "First, authors identify certain conditions or behaviors. Second, they identify various definitions (or claims) made about these conditions (or behaviors). Third, the authors stress the variability of the definitions vis-à-vis the constancy of the conditions to which they relate." Their accusation is that "the lynch pin is the assumption that the condition itself does not vary."[17] While making assumptions about the constancy of conditions, of course, violates the mandate to analytically bracket conditions, Woolgar and Pawluch note the frequency of empirical work containing statements that implicitly assume a condition exists independent of human's understanding. Constructionists making such statements violate the mandate to ignore objective conditions.[18]

While Woolgar and Pawluch speculate that these inconsistencies could merely be examples of sloppy scholarship that could be corrected by taking more care in crafting arguments, they also note that because ontological gerrymandering is so frequent it is possible that inconsistencies "are not mere technical difficulties in social problems arguments, but pervasive features of all attempts to explain social phenomenon."[19] They raise the disturbing possibility that it might not be possible to make a constructionist argument without at least vague and implicit references to the world outside our understandings of it. If so, then social constructionism is irrevocably theoretically flawed.

In 1993, Peter Ibarra and John Kitsuse attempted to respond to the Woolgar and Pawluch criticism while defending the original Spector and Kitsuse agenda. Their proposal for overcoming problems of references to objective conditions creeping into constructionist examinations is to stake out *rhetoric* as the topic matter. They also reason that Spector and Kitsuse's term of "putative condition" might have subtly allowed people doing constructionist analysis to attend to conditions. They substitute the term "condition-category" in order to remove any references to objective conditions and in order to highlight the importance of language. By locating the topic of constructionism in rhetoric rather than in the previous broader category of claims-making activity, and by substituting "condition-category" for "putative condition," they advance a method allowing constructionists to return to the original intent of Spector and Kitsuse: constructionism completely ignores objective reality.

But that neglects a critical question: *Should* objective conditions be ignored completely? True, in 1977 Spector and Kitsuse said constructionists should totally bracket objective conditions, Woolgar and Pawluch in 1985 criticized constructionists for not doing this, Ibarra and Kitsuse in 1993 again stated that constructionists must do this and offered an empirical method focusing solely on talk. Yet the question remains, does it make sense to completely ignore objective conditions?

I will focus my comments here on an article written by Joel Best that directly addresses this question of what social constructionists should do about the place of objective conditions within their examinations. Using his terminology, there are two choices. First, there is *strict constructionism*, which requires analysts to "avoid making assumptions about objective reality."[20] This requires not allowing any explicit *or* implicit references about a world outside human understanding to enter into the analysis. So, for example, when working within a stance of strict constructionism, analysts cannot assume that the Holocaust did (or did not) happen, they cannot assume that large numbers of Satanic cults practicing human sacrifice do (or do not) exist in the United States. In strict constructionism, analysts cannot point to historical records or to public records to argue about the constancy or the presence of a condition in the social world. Within strict constructionism, such records are only other constructions. They cannot be judged as better (or worse) than other constructions because evaluations of their "truth" would require objective indicators and these are not allowed.

In comparison, in a stance called *contextual constructionism* analysts remain focused on the claims-making process and the construction of meaning yet they might acknowledge making some assumptions about objective conditions.[21] Contextual constructionism allows some of the social context for claims to be brought into the analysis. For example, within contextual constructionism, analysts can look at some claims (such as historical records and government statistics) and use these claims to comment on the truth of other claims; analysts can ask questions such as what was going on in the social environment that led to claims-making about this particular problem at this particular historical time. Contextual constructionism allows analysts to make some references or illusions to the objective world *as long as it is done carefully and as long as the questions remain tightly focused on the process of creating human meaning.*

In brief, a stance of strict constructionism completely brackets references to the world beyond our understandings of it while a stance of contextual constructionism allows analysts to reference the world as if it existed apart from our understandings. The theoretical and practical usefulness of these two views should be evaluated.

Strict constructionism has much to recommend it as a theoretical stance. Remember that Spector and Kitsuse wrote an entire book in 1977 detailing the theoretical problems that come from examining social problems as objective conditions. Constructionist agendas on social problems were first proposed as a way to resolve those many problems. Furthermore, since 1977, postmodernist sensibilities have raised multiple questions about our abilities to comprehend, objectively measure, and report on the world outside our consciousness and socially created meanings. A strict constructionist agenda is in keeping with those postmodernist concerns. Perhaps more important, questions about how we create our world of meaning are theoretically important regardless of problems in other perspectives. Continuing phenomenological, Durkheimian, and ethnomethodological traditions, we need to explore how humans create and sustain a meaningful world and how what we experience as constraining and outside us is a consequence of human activity and meaning. Strict constructionism makes good theoretical sense.

It is more difficult to develop theoretical justifications for contextual constructionism. In particular, once we argue that it is acceptable for analysts to bring statements about objective conditions into their examinations, where do we draw the line? How many assumptions or statements about the existence of conditions do we allow? Also, and critically, if we allow analysts to compare claims and assess their truth value, what guidelines can be used to judge truthfulness? Will government statistics simply be accepted as the truth and not examined for their socially constructed nature? Or, conversely, will claims made by powerless people simply be accepted as the truth? While proponents of social criticism might applaud using constructionism to show how powerful people construct the world, whenever ideology masks itself as science it can be used for *any* purpose. In brief, contextual constructionism raises a host of questions that social constructionism was designed to overcome in the first place. Theoretically, contextual constructionism is incoherent and confused.

While strict constructionism is easier to defend on theoretical grounds, contextual construction is easier to defend when attention turns to how these perspectives might offer information of interest to practical actors. Clearly and most certainly, the knowledge gained through studies following strict constructionism should not be ignored or trivialized. While knowledge of how we create our world might not have an obvious practical benefit, and while postmodern theorists can deny the relevance of a modernist agenda that seeks knowledge, most practical actors want knowledge and alternative ways of making sense of our lives. Art, literature, and philosophy are important even when they do not have immediate and obvious practical benefits. In the same way, studies following a stance of strict constructionism can show us how humans create the meaningful world in which we live.

But in comparison to the fairly abstract and academic understandings possible with strict constructionism, contextual constructionism is much more likely to speak to issues of obvious practical relevance. Within strict constructionism, for example, we never could ask a question of such obvious concern as, Why was the federal government so slow in responding to

AIDS? Such a question requires us to point to an objective reality of people dying from AIDS before it was accorded the status of a social problem. The question of why government failed to act can be examined within contextual constructionism. Or, only a contextual constructionist analysis could doubt the validity of a claim such as, "Satanists sacrifice sixty thousand victims per year" and go on to ask questions about how such claims are constructed in ways encouraging audience members to evaluate them as believable and important. Only a contextual constructionist could examine claims that the "Holocaust did not happen" and ask how, in the face of massive evidence to the contrary, some people evaluate those claims as believable. In brief, while the findings from studies using a strict constructionist stance often are of interest to only a small number of academic theorists, contextual constructionist analyses offer something of value for practical actors engaged in the social problems work of understanding social life.

These, then, are the perplexing theoretical questions: Does strict constructionism sacrifice practical relevance for analytic purity? Can a theoretically compromised stance of contextual constructionism yield findings that can be evaluated as believable and true?

I have concluded this book by raising questions about the theoretical framework of social constructionist perspectives on social problems. But I certainly do not want to convey the impression that this perspective is being demolished by criticisms from postmodernists and social critics or being torn apart by debates about strict versus contextual constructionism. On the contrary, an important mark of a strong and growing theoretical perspective is that internal debate is encouraged and external criticisms are debated rather than ignored. In practice, social constructionism has not been—and will not be—a singular perspective where people advancing analysis under its umbrella are (or are expected to be) card-carrying believers in a rigid doctrine. Disagreements and debates within social constructionism and between social constructionism and other perspectives are healthy and productive. Not all people will be drawn to social constructionism. Of those who are, some will be drawn to versions of contextual constructionism and will be willing to make theoretical compromises for practical utility. Others will be drawn to versions of strict constructionism for its promise of theoretical knowledge through analytic clarity. A few others will be drawn to postmodern interests in how knowledge is created and will focus their attention on how the texts written by constructionists themselves create that knowledge. The umbrella of social constructionism is large enough to hold all these interests because each is a variation on the same question: How is our world one of human creation?

NOTES

1.   Also, I will not do an intellectual history of the general social construction perspective. For example, while not referenced by Spector and Kitsuse, *The Social Construction of Reality* written by Berger and Luckmann (1966) is an obvious precursor to their work. In emphasizing works written by sociologists I also ignore other important theorists. For example, Murray Edelman published *Political Language: Words That Succeed and Policies That Fail* the same year that *Constructing Social Problems* was published (1977). His constructionist examination of the language of social policy now often is used as a reference point for studies in public policy and communication. In the present day, *An Invitation to Social Construction* by Kenneth Gergen (1999) is an important theoretical statement.

2.   I will not cite the page numbers in *Constructing Social Problems* containing the quotes I will use. This chapter is meant to be an introduction into the theoretical writings of social constructionism. Readers who wish to pursue this approach should begin by reading all of *Constructing Social Problems*.

3.   To demonstrate problems, Spector and Kitsuse examine value conflict and labeling theory. While they draw heavily from these perspectives in proposing an agenda for social constructionism, they argue that both perspectives are contaminated with concern about objective conditions. For example, the major proponents of the value conflict perspective had written the "objective condition is necessary, but not in itself sufficient to constitute a social problem" (Fuller and Myers 1941). So, although the value conflict perspective had promoted examining social problems as issues of value judgments, attention to objective conditions nonetheless remained. Likewise, Spector and Kitsuse find problems in labeling theory when proposed models include objective characteristics such as Lemert's (1951) model of "primary and secondary deviance," or Becker's (1963) typology of "perceived as deviant/not perceived as deviant" and "rule-breaking/obedient behavior." According to Spector and Kitsuse, although both value conflict and labeling theory started to turn attention from objective conditions to subjective definitions, in practice they had not abandoned interest in objective conditions and this leads to inconsistencies and problems.

4.   Schneider's review (1985) was a testament to the wide variety of empirical studies led by this newly emerging perspective on social problems. He categorized these as (1) studies on containing trouble and avoiding problems (such as Emerson and Messinger, 1977; Goffman, 1959, 1969; Schneider, 1984; Ball and Lilly 1984); (2) studies on the creation of bureaucratic and professional categories for problematic conditions, conduct, and people (such as Gusfield, 1975, 1976, 1981; Maynard, 1984; Peyrot, 1982; Joffee, 1978); (3) studies on public regulatory bureaucracies and legal institutions (such as Becker, 1963; Troyer and Markle, 1983); (4) studies on medicalizing problems and troubles (such as Pfoul, 1977; Becker, 1963); (5) studies on social problems and the news media (such as Fishman, 1978; Gitlin, 1980; Tierney, 1982). Clearly, by 1985, constructionist perspectives were producing empirical works of many types.

5.   Miller and Holstein (1989, 1993).

6.   Miller and Holstein (1989:2).

7. Miller and Holstein (1989:9). Yet theoretical development does not happen in isolation. In this case, Miller and Holstein credit Gubrium (1988) for originally applying Durkheim's concept of collective representations in this way.

8. Miller and Holstein (1989:5).

9. Miller and Holstein (1989:13).

10. However, *Constructing Social Problems* does contains a chapter promoting the study of the "natural history" of social problems, and this never became a popular research question.

11. Collins (1989:89).

12. Malaire and Maynard (1993) make this argument that constructionism should expand in the direction of examining troubles before they are socially recognized as problems; L. Miller (1993) argues for the importance of examining claims made by powerless people; Smith (1984) examines relationships between texts and power.

13. I want to retain my goal of being accessible so I will not try to do justice to the wide varieties of theories loosely categorized as postmodernist. A good introductory reader containing original readings is Seidman (1994); Dinkens and Fontana (1994) edited a volume examining what postmodernism means for people doing social science; an excellent introduction to postmodernism is offered by Rosenau (1992:3–10). In addition, while I am drawing from G. Miller's (1993) article, he uses the category "poststructuralism" rather than the term "postmodernism" I use here. In this particular historical time, all terms beginning with "post" have no clear definition. I use the term "postmodernism" to highlight a range of theories that share a "challenge to the Enlightenment" (Seidman, 1994:7; Dinkens and Fontana, 1994:3).

14. Troyer (1993:117–18).

15. Hazelrigg (1993:497). Within a postmodern view, the story I have written about constructionist perspectives on social problems is one of many (countless) possible stories. A postmodernist reading of this book might note that I emphasized some things (and not others), that I chose some examples (and not others), that I made some interpretations of these examples (and not others), that I organized this chapter around some theorists (and not others). Postmodernists would examine how my choices reflect my place in the gender/race/class/world system, they would examine what these choices do to change or perpetuate those systems. Such an examination would be clear in arguing that this book (any book) does not contain "the" truth—or even any truth. From this postmodern perspective, this book (any book) is merely a story written by a particular person located in a particular social/geographic/historical place.

16. Woolgar and Pawluch (1985:214).

17. Woolgar and Pawluch (1985:215).

18. The criticisms of Woolgar and Pawluch were strengthened by the fact that they found such statements in the writings of the most respected social constructionists such as Howard Becker, Peter Conrad, Joseph Schneider, and Joseph Gusfield.

19. Woolgar and Pawluch (1985:224).

20. Best (1989:245–46).

21. Best (1989:246).

References

Albert, Edward (1989). "AIDS and the Press: The Creation and Transformation of a Social Problem." Pp. 39–54 in *Images of Issues: Typifying Contemporary Social Problems*, edited by Joel Best. Hawthorne, NY: Aldine de Gruyter.

Allahyari, Rebecca Anne (2000). *Visions of Charity: Volunteer Workers and Moral Community*. Berkeley: University of California Press.

Almeida, Paul and Linda Brewster Stearns (1998). "Political Opportunities and Local Grassroots Environmental Movements: The Case of Minamata." *Social Problems* 45:37–60.

Altheide, David L. (2002). *Creating Fear: News and the Construction of Crisis*. Hawthorne, NY: Aldine de Gruyter.

Appleton, Lynn M. (1995). "Rethinking Medicalization: Alcoholism and Anomalies." Pp. 59–80 in *Images of Issues: Typifying Contemporary Social Problems* (2d ed.), edited by Joel Best. Hawthorne, NY: Aldine de Gruyter.

Armstrong, Elizabeth M. (2000). "Lessons in Control: Prenatal Education in the Hospital." *Social Problems* 47:583–605.

Aronson, Naomi (1984). "Science as a Claims-Making Activity: Implications for Social Problems Research." Pp. 1–30 in *Studies in the Sociology of Social Problems*, edited by Joseph W. Schneider and John I. Kitsuse. Norwood, NJ: Ablex.

Austin, S. Bryn (1999). "Commodity Knowledge in Consumer Culture: The Role of Nutritional Health Promotion in the Making of the Diet Industry." Pp. 159–82 in *Weighty Issues: Fatness and Thinness as Social Problems*, edited by Jeffery Sobal and Donna Maurer. Hawthorne, NY: Aldine de Gruyter.

Ayukawa, Jun (1995). "The Construction of Juvenile Delinquency as a Social Problem in Post World War II Japan." Pp. 311–29 in *Perspectives on Social Problems* (Volume 3), edited by Gale Miller and James A. Holstein. Greenwich, CT: JAI.

Ayukawa, Jun (2001). "The United States and Smoking Problems in Japan." Pp. 215–42 in *How Claims Spread: Cross-National Diffusion of Social Problems*, edited by Joel Best. Hawthorne, NY: Aldine de Gruyter.

Baker, Phyllis L. (1996). "Doing What it Takes to Survive: Battered Women and the Consequence of Compliance to a Cultural Script." Pp. 73–90 in *Studies in Symbolic Interaction* (Volume 20), edited by Norman K. Denzin. Greenwich, CT: JAI.

Ball, Richard and J. Robert Lilly (1984). "When Is a 'Problem' Not a Problem? Deflection Activities in a Clandestine Motel." Pp. 114–39 in *Studies in the Sociol-*

ogy of Social Problems, edited by Joseph W. Schneider and John I. Kitsuse. Nor-wood, NJ: Ablex.

Barak, Gregg (1994). "Media, Society, and Criminology." Pp. 3–45 in *Media, Process, and the Social Construction of Crime,* edited by Gregg Barak. New York: Garland.

Baumgartner, Frank R. and Bryan D. Jones (1994). "Attention, Boundary Effects, and Large-Scale Policy Change in Air Transportation Policy." Pp. 50–66 in *The Politics of Problem Definition: Shaping the Policy Agenda,* edited by David A. Rochefort and Roger W. Cobb. Lawrence: University of Kansas Press.

Becker, Howard S. (1963). *Outsiders: Studies in the Sociology of Deviance.* New York: MacMillan.

Bellah, Robert N., Richard Madsen, William M. Sullivan, Ann Swidler, and Steven M. Tipton (1985). *Habits of the Heart: Individualism and Commitment in American Life.* Berkeley: University of California Press.

Benford, Robert D. (1993). "Frame Disputes within the Nuclear Disarmament Movement." *Social Forces* 71:677–702.

Benford, Robert D. (2002). "Controlling Narratives and Narratives as Control within Social Movements." Pp. 53–78 in *Stories of Change: Narrative and Social Movements,* edited by Joseph E. Davis. Albany: State University of New York Press.

Berger, Arthur Asa (1997). *Narratives in Popular Culture, Media and Everyday Life.* Thousand Oaks, CA: Sage.

Berger, Peter and Thomas Luckmann (1966). *The Social Construction of Reality: A Treatise in the Sociology of Knowledge.* New York: Anchor.

Berger, Ronald J. (2002). *Fathoming the Holocaust: A Social Problems Approach.* Hawthorne, NY: Aldine de Gruyter.

Best, Joel (1989). "Dark Figures and Child Victims: Statistical Claims About Missing Children." Pp. 21–25 in *Images of Issues: Typifying Contemporary Social Problems,* edited by Joel Best. Hawthorne, NY: Aldine de Gruyter.

Best, Joel (1990). *Threatened Children: Rhetoric and Concern about Child-Victims.* Chicago: University of Chicago Press.

Best, Joel (1991). "'Road Warriors' on 'Hair-Trigger Highways': Cultural Resources and the Media's Construction of the 1987 Freeway Shootings Problem." *Sociological Inquiry* 61:327–45.

Best, Joel (1995). "Typification and Social Problems Construction." Pp. 1–16 in *Images of Issues: Typifying Contemporary Social Problems* (2d ed.), edited by Joel Best. Hawthorne, NY: Aldine de Gruyter.

Best, Joel (1997). "Victimization and the Victim Industry." *Society* 34:9–17.

Best, Joel (1999). *Random Violence: How We Talk About New Crimes and New Victims.* Berkeley: University of California Press.

Best, Joel (2001a). *Damned Lies and Statistics: Untangling Numbers from the Media, Politicians, and Activists.* Berkeley: University of California Press.

Best, Joel (2001b). "Social Progress and Social Problems: Toward a Sociology of Gloom." *Sociological Quarterly* 42:1–12.

Breakwell, Glynis M. (1983). *Threatened Identities.* New York: John Wiley and Sons.

Bronski, Michael (1984). *Culture Clash: The Making of Gay Sensibility.* Boston: South End.

Brooks, Peter (1976). *The Melodramatic Imagination: Balzac, Henry James, Melodrama and the Mode of Excess.* New Haven, CT: Yale University Press.

Bruner, Jerome (1987). "Life as Narrative." *Social Research* 54:11–32.

Brush, Paula Stewart (1999). "The Influence of Social Movements on Articulation of Race and Gender in Black Women's Biographies." *Gender & Society* 13:120–37.

Campbell, Richard (1991). *60 Minutes and the News: A Mythology for Middle America.* Urbana: University of Illinois Press.

Cavender, Gray (1998). "In 'The Shadow of Shadows': Television Reality Crime Programming." Pp. 79–94 in *Entertaining Crime: Television Reality Programs,* edited by Mark Fishman and Gray Cavender. Hawthorne, NY: Aldine de Gruyter.

Cerulo, Karen A. (1998). *Deciphering Violence: The Cognitive Structure of Right and Wrong.* New York: Routledge.

Chamblis, William (1973). "The Saints and the Roughnecks." *Society* 11:24–31.

Christiansen, Adrienne E. and Jeremy J. Hanson (1996). "Comedy as Cure for Tragedy: ACT-UP and the Rhetoric of AIDS." *Quarterly Journal of Speech* 82:157–70.

Clark, Candace (1997). *Misery and Company: Sympathy in Everyday Life.* Chicago: University of Chicago Press.

Clawson, Rosalee A. and Rakuya Trice (2000). "Poverty as We Know It: Media Portrayals of the Poor." *Public Opinion Quarterly* 64:53–64.

Cohen, Jodi R. (1997). "Poverty: Talk, Identity, and Action." *Qualitative Inquiry* 3:71–92.

Coleman, James and Cressey, Donald (1996). *Social Problems* (sixth ed.). New York: HarperCollins.

Collins, Patricia Hill (1989). "The Social Construction of Invisibility: Black Women's Poverty in Social Problems Discourse." Pp. 77–94 in *Perspectives on Social Problems* (Volume 1), edited by James A. Holstein and Gale Miller. Greenwich, CT: JAI.

Commoner, Barry (2002). "Unraveling the DNA Myth: The Spurious Foundation of Genetic Engineering." *Harpers* 304 (February):39–47.

Conrad, Peter (1997). "Public Eyes and Private Genes: Historical Frames, News Constructions, and Social Problems." *Social Problems* 44:139–54.

Conrad, Peter and Deborah Potter (2000). "From Hyperactive Children to ADHD Adults: Observation on the Expansion of Medical Categories." *Social Problems* 47:559–82.

Conrad, Peter and Joseph Schneider (1980). *Deviance and Medicalization.* St. Louis: Mosby.

Converse, Philip E. (1964). "The Nature of Belief Systems in Mass Publics." Pp. 206–55 in *Ideology and Discontent,* edited by David Apter. London: Free Press of Glencoe.

Coughlin, Joseph F. (1994). "The Tragedy of the Concrete Commons: Defining Traffic Congestion as a Public Problem." Pp. 138–58 in *The Politics of Problem Definition: Shaping the Policy Agenda,* edited by David A. Rochefort and Roger W. Cobb. Lawrence: University of Kansas Press.

Daniels, Arlene K. (1970). "Normal Mental Illness and Understandable Excuses: The Philosophy of Combat Psychiatry." *American Behavioral Scientist* 14:169– 78.

Darsey, James (1991). "From 'Gay is Good' to the Scourge of AIDS: The Evolution of Gay Liberation Rhetoric, 1977–1990." *Communication Studies* 42:43–66.

Davis, Joseph E. (2002). "Narrative and Social Movements: The Power of Stories." Pp. 3–30 in *Stories of Change: Narrative and Social Movements,* edited by Joseph E. Davis. Albany: State University of New York Press.

Davis, Phillip W. (1994). "The Changing Meanings of Spanking." Pp. 133–54 in *Troubling Children: Studies of Children and Social Problems,* edited by Joel Best. Hawthorne, NY: Aldine de Gruyter.

Denzin, Norman K. (1986). *Treating Alcoholism.* Newbury Park: Sage.

Denzin, Norman K. (1987a). *The Recovering Alcoholic.* Newbury Park: Sage.

Denzin, Norman K. (1987b). *The Alcoholic Self.* Newbury Park: Sage.

Denzin, Norman K. (1990). "On Understanding Emotion: The Interpretive-Cultural Agenda." Pp. 85–116 in *Research Agendas in the Sociology of Emotions,* edited by Theodore Kemper. Albany: State University of New York Press.

Dinkens, David and Andrea Fontana (1994). *Postmodernism & Social Inquiry.* New York: Guilford.

Downs, Anthony (1972). "Up and Down with Ecology—The 'Issue Attention Cycle.'" *Public Interest* 28:38–50.

Dull, R. Thomas and Arthur Wint (1997). "Criminal Victimization and Its Effect on Fear of Crime and Justice Attitudes." *Journal of Interpersonal Violence* 12:748– 59.

Dunn, Jennifer (2001). "Innocence Lost: Accomplishing Victimization in Intimate Stalking Cases." *Symbolic Interaction* 24(3):285–313.

Durkheim, Emile (1961). *The Elementary Forms of Religious Life.* New York: Collier-MacMillan.

Edelman, Murray (1977). *Political Language: Words That Succeed and Policies That Fail.* New York: Academic.

Edelman, Murray (1988). *Constructing the Political Spectacle.* Chicago: University of Chicago Press.

Elder, Charles D. and Roger W. Cobb (1984). "Agenda-Building and the Politics of Aging." *Policy Studies Journal* 13:115–30.

Emerson, Robert (1994). "Constructing Serious Violence: Processing a Domestic Violence Restraining Order." Pp. 3–28 in *Perspectives on Social Problems* (Volume 6), edited by James A. Holstein and Gale Miller. Greenwich, CT: JAI.

Emerson, Robert and Sheldon L. Messinger (1977). "The Micro-Politics of Trouble." *Social Problems* 25:121–34.

Epstein, Steven (1996). *Impure Science: AIDS, Activism, and the Politics of Knowledge.* Berkley: University of California Press.

Estroff, Sue E. (1981). *Making It Crazy: An Ethnography of Psychiatric Clients in an American Community.* Berkeley: University of California Press.

Fattah, Ezzat (1986). "Prologue: On Some Visible and Hidden Dangers of Victim Movements." Pp. 1–14 in *From Crime Policy to Victim Policy: Reorienting the Justice System,* edited by Ezzat Fattah. New York: St. Martin's.

Ferguson, Ann Arnett (2000). *Bad Boys: Public Schools in the Making of Black Masculinity.* Ann Arbor: University of Michigan Press.

Ferrell, Jeff and Neil Websdale (1999). *Making Trouble: Cultural Constructions of Crime, Deviance, and Control.* Hawthorne, NY: Aldine de Gruyter.

Fetner, Tina (2001). "Working Anita Bryant: The Impact of Christian Anti-Gay Activism on Lesbian and Gay Movement Claims." *Social Problems* 48:411–27.

Figert, Anne E. (1996). *Women and the Ownership of PMS: The Structuring of a Psychiatric Disorder.* Hawthorne, NY: Aldine de Gruyter.

Fine, Gary Alan (1979). "Small Groups and Cultural Creation: The Idioculture of Little League Baseball Teams." *American Sociological Review* 44:733–45.

Fine, Gary Alan (2002). "The Storied Group: Social Movements as 'Bundles of Narratives.'" Pp. 229–46 in *Stories of Change: Narrative and Social Movements,* edited by Joseph E. Davis. Albany: State University of New York Press.

Fishman, Mark (1978). "Crime Waves as Ideology." *Social Problems* 25:531–43.

Fishman, Mark and Gray Cavender (1998). *Entertaining Crime: Television Reality Programs.* Hawthorne, NY: Aldine de Gruyter.

Fontana, Andrea (1977). *The Last Frontier.* Beverly Hills: Sage.

Fox, Kathryn J. (1999). "Changing Violent Minds: Discursive Correction and Resistance in the Cognitive Treatment of Violent Offenders in Prison." *Social Problems* 46:88–103.

Fox, Kathryn J. (2001). "Self-Change and Resistance in Prison." Pp. 176–92 in *Institutional Selves: Troubled Identities in a Postmodern World,* edited by Jaber F. Gubrium and James A. Holstein. New York: Oxford University Press.

Francis, Linda E. (1997). "Ideology and Interpersonal Emotion Management: Redefining Identity in Two Support Groups." *Social Psychology Quarterly* 60(2): 153–71.

Frazier, Patricia A., Caroline C. Cochran, and Andrea M. Olson (1995). "Social Science Research on Lay Definitions of Sexual Harassment." *Journal of Social Issues* 51:21–37.

Fuller, Richard and Richard Myers (1941). "Some Aspects of a Theory of Social Problems." *American Sociological Review* 6:24–32.

Funkhouser, G. Ray (1973). "The Issues of the Sixties: An Exploratory Study in the Dynamics of Public Opinion." *Public Opinion Quarterly* 37:62–75.

Furedi, Frank (2001). "Bullying: The British Contribution to the Construction of a Social Problem." Pp. 89–106 in *How Claims Spread: Cross-National Diffusion of Social Problems,* edited by Joel Best. Hawthorne, NY: Aldine de Gruyter.

Furstenberg, Frank. F. (1999). "Children and Family Change: Discourse between Social Scientists and the Media." *Contemporary Sociology* 28:10–17.

Gamson, Joshua S. (1997). "Messages of Exclusion: Gender, Movements, and Symbolic Boundaries." *Gender & Society* 11:178–99.

Gamson, Joshua S. (1998). *Freaks Talk Back: Tabloid Talk Shows and Sexual Nonconformity.* Chicago: University of Chicago Press.

Gamson, William (1988). "Political Discourse and Collective Action." Pp. 219–44 in *From Structure to Action: Comparing Social Movement Research across Cultures,* edited by Bert Klandermans, Hanspeter Kriesi, and Sidney Tarrow. Greenwich, CT: JAI.

Gamson, William (1990). *The Strategy of Social Protest* (2nd ed.). Belmont, CA: Wadsworth.

Gamson, William (1992). *Talking Politics*. New York: Cambridge University Press.

Gamson, William, David Croteau, William Hoynes, and Theodore Sasson (1992). "Media Images and the Social Construction of Reality." Pp. 373–93 in *Annual Review of Sociology*, edited by Judith Blake. Palo Alto, CA: Annual Reviews.

Gamson, William and Gadi Wolfsfeld (1993). "Movements and Media as Interacting Systems." *Annals of the American Academy of Political and Social Science* 528:114–25.

Gans, Herbert J. (1979). *Deciding What's News: A Study of CBS Evening News, NBC Nightly News, Newsweek, and Time*. New York: Vintage.

Gans, Herbert J. (1993). "Reopening the Black Box: Toward a Limited Effects Theory." *Journal of Communication* 43:29–35

Gardner, Carol Brooks (1994). "Little Strangers: Pregnancy Conduct and the Twentieth-Century Rhetoric of Endangerment." Pp. 69–92 in *Troubling Children: Studies of Children and Social Problems*, edited by Joel Best. Hawthorne, NY: Aldine de Gruyter.

Gergen, Kenneth J. (1994). *Realities and Relationships: Soundings in Social Construction*. Cambridge, MA: Harvard University Press.

Gergen, Kenneth J. (1999). *An Invitation to Social Construction*. CA: Sage.

Giddens, Anthony (1991). *Modernity and Self Identity: Self and Society in the Late Modern Age*. Stanford, CA: Stanford University Press.

Gilbert, Neil (1993). "Examining the Facts: Advocacy Research Overstates the Incidence of Date and Acquaintance Rape." Pp. 120–32 in *Current Controversies on Family Violence*, edited by Richard J. Gelles and Donileen R. Loseke. Newbury Park, CA: Sage.

Giovannoni, Jeanne and Rosina Becerra (1979). *Defining Child Abuse*. New York: Free Press.

Gitlin, Todd (1980). *The Whole World Is Watching: Mass Media in the Making and Unmaking of the New Left*. Berkeley: University of California Press.

Glassner, Barry (1999). *The Culture of Fear: Why Americans Are Afraid of the Wrong Things*. New York: Basic Books.

Goffman, Erving (1959). "The Moral Career of a Mental Patient." *Psychiatry* 22:123–42.

Goffman, Erving (1961). *Asylums: Essays on the Social Situation of Mental Patients and Other Inmates*. New York: Anchor.

Goffman, Erving (1969). "The Insanity of Place." *Psychiatry* 32:357–88.

Goffman, Erving (1974). *Frame Analysis*. Cambridge, MA: Harvard University Press.

Goode, Erich and Nachman Ben-Yehuda (1994). *Moral Panics: The Social Construction of Deviance*. Cambridge: Blackwell.

Griset, Pamela L. (1995). "Determinate Sentencing and Agenda Building: A Case Study of the Failure of a Reform." *Journal of Criminal Justice* 23:349–62.

Gubrium, Jaber F. (1992). *Out of Control: Family Therapy and Domestic Disorder*. Thousand Oaks, CA: Sage.

Gusfield, Joseph (1975). "Categories of Ownership and Responsibility in Social Issues: Alcohol Abuse and Automobile Use." *Journal of Drug Issues* 5:285–303.

Gusfield, Joseph (1976). "The Literary Rhetoric of Science: Comedy and Pathos in Drinking Driver Research." *American Sociological Review* 41:16–34.

Gusfield, Joseph (1981). *The Culture of Public Problems: Drinking-Driving and the Symbolic Order.* Chicago: University of Chicago Press

Hacking, Ian (1986). "Making Up People." Pp. 222–36 in *Reconstructing Individualism: Autonomy, Individuality, and the Self in Western Thought,* edited by Thomas C. Heller, Morton Sosna, and David E. Wellbery. Stanford, CA: Stanford University Press.

Hartnett, Paul H. (1997). "The Attitudes of Female and Male Residential Care Workers to the Perpetrators of Sexual and Physical Assault." *Child Abuse and Neglect* 21:861–69.

Hazelrigg, Lawrence E. (1993). "Constructionism and Practices of Objectivity." Pp. 485–500 in *Reconsidering Social Constructionism: Debates in Social Problems Theory,* edited by James A. Holstein and Gale Miller. Hawthorne, NY: Aldine de Gruyter.

Hequembourg, Amy and Jorge Arditi (1999). "Fractured Resistances: The Debate over Assimilationism Among Gays and Lesbians in the United States." *Sociological Quarterly* 40:663–80.

Hilgartner, Stephen (2000). *Science on Stage: Expert Advice as Public Drama.* Stanford, CA: Stanford University Press.

Hilgartner, Stephen and Charles Bosk (1988). "The Rise and Fall of Social Problems: A Public Arenas Model." *American Journal of Sociology* 94:53–78.

Hillyard, Daniel and John Dombrink (2001). *Dying Right: The Death With Dignity Movement.* New York: Routledge.

Hochschild, Arlie Russell (1979). "Emotion Work, Feeling Rules, and Social Structure." *American Journal of Sociology* 85:551–75.

Holstein, James A. (1993). *Court-Ordered Insanity: Interpretive Practice and Involuntary Commitment.* Hawthorne, NY: Aldine de Gruyter.

Holstein, James A. and Jaber F. Gubrium (2000). *The Self We Live By: Narrative Identity in a Postmodern World.* New York: Oxford University Press.

Holstein, James A. and Gale Miller (1990). "Rethinking Victimization: An Interactional Approach to Victimology." *Symbolic Interaction* 13:103–22.

Hufker, Brian and Gray Cavender (1990). "From Freedom Flotilla to America's Burden: The Social Construction of the Mariel Immigrants." *Sociological Quarterly* 31:321–35.

Hunt, Scott A. and Robert D. Benford (1994). "Identity Talk in the Peace and Justice Movement." *Journal of Contemporary Ethnography* 22:488–517.

Ibarra, Peter and John Kitsuse (1993). "Vernacular Constituents of Moral Discourse: An Interactionist Proposal for the Study of Social Problems." Pp. 25–28 in *Reconsidering Social Constructionism: Debates in Social Problems Theory,* edited by James A. Holstein and Gale Miller. Hawthorne, NY: Aldine de Gruyter.

Irvine, Leslie (1999). *Codependent Forevermore: The Invention of Self in a Twelve Step Group.* Chicago: University of Chicago Press.

Iyengar, Shanto (1987). "Television News and Citizens' Explanations of National Affairs." *American Political Science Review* 81:815–31.

Jarvinen, Margaretha (2001). "Accounting for Trouble: Identity Negotiations in Qualitative Interviews with Alcoholics." *Symbolic Interaction* 24:263–84.

Jasper, James M. (1997). *The Art of Moral Protest: Culture, Biography, and Creativity in Social Movements.* Chicago: University of Chicago Press.

Jasper, James M. and Jane D. Poulsen (1995). "Recruiting Strangers and Friends: Moral Shocks and Social Networks in Animal Rights and Anti-Nuclear Protests." *Social Problems* 42:493–512.

Jeffrey, Roger (1979). "Rubbish: Deviant Patients in Casualty Departments." *Sociology of Health and Illness* 1:90–107.

Jenkins, Philip (1992). *Intimate Enemies: Moral Panics in Contemporary Great Britain.* Hawthorne, NY: Aldine de Gruyter.

Jenkins, Philip (1994). *Using Murder: The Social Construction of Serial Homicide.* Hawthorne, NY: Aldine de Gruyter.

Jenkins, Philip (1995). "Clergy Sexual Abuse: The Symbolic Politics of a Social Problem." Pp. 105–30 in *Images of Issues: Typifying Contemporary Social Problems* (2d ed.), edited by Joel Best. Hawthorne, NY: Aldine de Gruyter.

Jenkins, Philip (1999). "Fighting Terrorism as if Women Mattered: Anti-Abortion Violence as Unconstructed Terrorism." Pp. 319–48 in *Making Trouble: Cultural Constructions of Crime, Deviance, and Control,* edited by Jeff Ferrell and Neil Websdale. Hawthorne, NY: Aldine de Gruyter.

Jenness, Valerie (1993). *Making It Work: The Prostitutes' Rights Movement in Perspective.* Hawthorne, NY: Aldine de Gruyter.

Jenness, Valerie and Kendal Broad (1997). *Hate Crimes: New Social Movements and the Politics of Violence.* Hawthorne, NY: Aldine de Gruyter.

Jenness, Valerie and Ryken Grattet (2001). *Making Hate a Crime: From Social Movement to Law Enforcement.* New York: Russell Sage Foundation.

Joffe, Carol (1978). "What Abortion Counselors Want from their Clients." *Social Problems* 26:112–21.

Johnson, John M. (1995). "Horror Stories and the Construction of Child Abuse." Pp. 17–32 in *Images of Issues: Typifying Contemporary Social Problems* (2d ed.), edited by Joel Best. Hawthorne, NY: Aldine de Gruyter.

Johnson, John M. and Linda Waletzko (1992). "Drugs and Crime: A Study in the Medicalization of Crime Control." Pp. 197–219 in *Perspectives on Social Problems* (Volume 3), edited by Gale Miller and James A. Holstein. Greenwich, CT: JAI.

Jordan, Donald (1993). "Newspaper Effects on Policy Preferences." *Public Opinion Quarterly* 57:191–204.

Katz, Jack (1987). "What Makes Crime 'News'?" *Media, Culture and Society* 9:47–75.

Kellner, Douglas (1995). *Media Culture: Cultural Studies, Identity and Politics between the Modern and the Postmodern.* New York: Routledge.

Kingdon, John (1984). *Agendas, Alternatives, and Public Policies.* Boston: Little Brown.

Kirk, Stuart A. and Herb Kutchins (1992). *The Selling of DSM: The Rhetoric of Science in Psychiatry.* Hawthorne, NY: Aldine de Gruyter.

Kivett, Douglas D. and Carol A. B. Warren (2002). "Social Control in a Group Home for Delinquent Boys." *Journal of Contemporary Ethnography* 31:3–32.

Knorr-Cetina, Karin D. (1981). *The Manufacture of Knowledge: An Essay on the Constructivist and Contextual Nature of Science.* New York: Pergamon.

Koss, Mary and Sarah Cook (1993). "Facing the Facts: Date and Acquaintance Rape are Significant Problems for Women." Pp. 104–19 in *Current Controversies on Family Violence,* edited by Richard J. Gelles and Donileen R. Loseke. Newbury Park, CA: Sage

Kubal, Timothy J. (1998). "The Presentation of Political Self: Cultural Resonance and the Construction of Collective Action Frames." *Sociological Quarterly* 39:539–54.

Kunkel, Karl R. (1995). "Down on the Farm: Rationale Expansion in the Construction of Factory Farming as a Social Problem." Pp. 239–60 in *Images of Issues: Typifying Contemporary Social Problems* (2d ed.), edited by Joel Best. Hawthorne, NY: Aldine de Gruyter.

LaFree, Gary (1989) *Rape and Criminal Justice: The Social Construction of Sexual Assault.* Belmont, CA: Wadsworth.

Lamb, Sharon (1999). *New Versions of Victims: Feminists Struggle with the Concept.* New York: New York University Press.

Lemert, Edwin M. (1951). "Primary and Secondary Deviation." Pp. 75–78 in *Social Pathology: A Systematic Approach to the Theory of Sociopathic Behavior,* edited by Edwin M. Lemert. New York: McGraw Hill.

Levine, James E. (1997). "Re-visioning Attention Deficit Hyperactivity Disorder (ADHD)." *Clinical Social Work Journal* 25:197–209.

Linberry, Robert L. (1981). *Government in America: People, Politics, and Policy.* Boston: Little Brown.

Linde, Charotte (1993). *Life Stories: The Creation of Coherence.* New York: Oxford University Press.

Linders, Annulla (1998). "Abortion as a Social Problem: The Construction of 'Opposite' Solutions in Sweden and the United States." *Social Problems* 45:486–509.

Lipsky, Michael (1980). *Street Level Bureaucracy: Dilemmas of the Individual in Public Services.* New York: Russell Sage Foundation.

Lipsky, Michael and Steven Rathgeb Smith (1989). "When Social Problems Are Treated as Emergencies." *Social Service Review* (March):5–25.

Litt, Jacquelyn and Maureen McNeil (1994). "'Crack Babies' and the Politics of Reproduction and Nurturance." Pp. 93–116 in *Troubling Children: Studies of Children and Social Problems,* edited by Joel Best. Hawthorne, NY: Aldine de Gruyter.

Loseke, Donileen R. (1992). *The Battered Woman and Shelters: The Social Construction of Wife Abuse.* Albany: State University of New York Press.

Loseke, Donileen R. (1993). "Constructing Conditions, People, Morality, and Emotion: Expanding the Agenda of Constructionism." Pp. 207–16 in *Constructionist Controversies: Issues in Social Problems Theory,* edited by Gale Miller and James A. Holstein. Hawthorne, NY: Aldine de Gruyter.

Loseke, Donileen R. (1995). "Writing Rights: The Homeless Mentally Ill and Involuntary Hospitalization." Pp. 261–86 in *Images of Issues: Typifying Contemporary Social Problems* (2d ed.), edited by Joel Best. Hawthorne, NY: Aldine De Gruyter.

Loseke, Donileen R. (1997) "The Whole Sprit of Modern Philanthropy: The Idea of Charity, 1912–1992." *Social Problems* 44:425–44.

Loseke, Donileen R. (2000). "Ethos, Pathos, and Social Problems: Reflections on Formula Narratives." Pp. 41–54 in *Perspectives on Social Problems* (Volume 12), edited by James A. Holstein and Gale Miller. Greenwich, CT: JAI.

Loseke, Donileen R. (2001). "Lived Realities and Formula Stories of 'Battered Women.'" Pp. 107–26 in *Institutional Selves: Troubled Identities in a Postmodern World*, edited by Jaber F. Gubrium and James A. Holstein. New York: Oxford University Press.

Loseke, Donileen R. and Joel Best (2002). *Social Problems: Constructionist Readings.* Hawathorne, NY: Aldine de Gruyter.

Loseke, Donileen R. and James C. Cavendish (2001). "Producing Institutional Selves: Rhetorically Constructing the Dignity of Sexually Marginalized Catholics." *Social Psychology Quarterly* 64:347–62,

Loseke, Donileen R. and Kirsten Fawcett (1995). "Appealing Appeals: Constructing Moral Worthiness, 1912–1917." *Sociological Quarterly* 36:61–78.

Lowney, Kathleen (1994). "Speak of the Devil: Talk Shows and the Social Construction of Satanism." Pp. 99–127 in *Perspectives on Social Problems* (Volume 6), edited by James A. Holstein and Gale Miller. Greenwich, CT: JAI.

Lowney, Kathleen (1999). *Baring Our Souls: TV Talk Shows and the Religion of Recovery.* Hawthorne, NY: Aldine de Gruyter.

Luker, Kristin (1984). *Abortion and the Politics of Motherhood.* Berkeley: University of California Press.

Lynch, James P. (1996). "Clarifying Divergent Estimates of Rape from Two National Surveys." *Public Opinion Quarterly* 60:410–30.

Maines, David R. (1991). "The Storied Nature of Health and Diabetic Self-Help Groups." Pp. 185–202 in *Advances in Medical Sociology* (Volume 2), edited by Gary L. Albrecht and Judith A. Levy. Greenwich, CT: JAI.

Maines, David R. (1992). "Narrative's Movement and Sociology's Phenomena: Toward a Narrative Sociology." *Sociological Quarterly* 3:17–38.

Maines, David R. (1999). "Information Pools and Racialized Narrative Structures." *Sociological Quarterly* 40:317–26.

Malaire, Courtney and Douglas Maynard (1993). "Social Problems and the Organization of Talk and Interaction." Pp. 173–98 in *Reconsidering Social Constructionism: Debates in Social Problems Theory*, edited by James A. Holstein and Gale Miller. Hawthorne, NY: Aldine de Gruyter.

Malone, Ruth E., Elizabeth Boyd, and Lisa A. Bero (2000). "Journalists' Constructions of Passive Smoking as a Social Problem." *Social Studies of Science* 30:713–35.

Mann, Coramae Richey and Marjorie S. Zatz (1998). *Images of Color, Images of Crime: Readings.* Los Angeles: Roxbury.

Mansbridge, Jane J. (1986). *Why We Lost the ERA.* Chicago: University of Chicago Press.

Margolin, Leslie (1994). *Goodness Personified: The Emergence of Gifted Children.* Hawthorne, NY: Aldine de Gruyter.

Martin, Susan (1995). "A Cross Burning Is Not Just an Arson: Police Social Construction of Hate Crimes in Baltimore County." *Criminology* 33:303–26.

Mason-Schrock, Douglas (1996). "Transsexual's Narrative Construction of the 'True Self.'" *Social Psychology Quarterly* 59:176–92.

May, Rubin Buford (2001). *Talking at Trinas.* New York: New York University Press.

Maynard, Douglas W. (1984). *Inside Plea Bargaining: The Language of Negotiation.* New York: Plenum.

McCaffrey, Dawn and Jennifer Keys (2000). "Competitive Framing Processes in the Abortion Debate: Polarization, Vilification, Frame Saving, and Frame Debunking." *Sociological Quarterly* 41:41–61.

McCarthy, E. Doyle (1989). "Emotions Are Social Things: An Essay in the Sociology of Emotions." Pp. 51–72 in *The Sociology of Emotions: Original Essays and Research Papers,* edited by David D. Franks and E. Doyle McCarthy. Greenwich, CT: JAI.

McCombs, Maxwell and Jian-Hua Zhu (1995). "Capacity, Diversity, and Volatility of the Public Agenda: Trends from 1954–1994." *Public Opinion Quarterly* 59:495–525.

McCright, Aaron M. and Riley E. Dunlap (2000). "Challenging Global Warming as a Social Problem: An Analysis of the Conservative Movement's Counter-Claims." *Social Problems* 47:499–522.

McKendy, John P. (1992). "Ideological Practices and the Management of Emotions: The Case of 'Wife Abusers.'" *Critical Sociology* 19:61–80.

Melucci, Alberto (1989). *Nomads of the Present: Social Movements and Individual Needs in Contemporary Society.* Philadelphia: Temple University Press.

Merton, Robert (1971). "Epilogue: Social Problems and Sociological Theory." Pp. 793–846 in *Contemporary Social Problems,* edited by Robert K. Mertin and Robert Nisbet. New York: Harcourt Brace Jovanovich.

Miller, Gale (1991). *Enforcing the Work Ethic: Rhetoric and Everyday Life in a Work Incentive Program.* New York: State University of New York Press.

Miller, Gale (1993). "New Challenges to Social Constructionism: Alternative Perspectives on Social Problems Theory." Pp. 253–80 in *Reconsidering Social Constructionism: Debates in Social Problems Theory,* edited by James A. Holstein and Gale Miller. Hawthorne, NY: Aldine de Gruyter.

Miller, Gale (1997). *Becoming Miracle Workers: Language and Meaning in Brief Therapy.* Hawthorne, NY: Aldine de Gruyter.

Miller, Gale and James A. Holstein (1989). "On the Sociology of Social Problems." Pp. 1–18 in *Perspectives on Social Problems* (Volume 1), edited by James A. Holstein and Gale Miller. Greenwich, CT: JAI.

Miller, Gale and James A. Holstein (1993). "Reconsidering Social Constructionism." Pp. 5–24 in *Reconsidering Social Constructionism: Debates in Social Problems Theory,* edited by James A. Holstein and Gale Miller. Hawthorne, NY: Aldine de Gruyter.

Miller, Leslie (1993). "Claims-Making from the Underside: Marginalization and Social Problems Analysis." Pp. 349–76 in *Reconsidering Social Constructionism: Debates in Social Problems Theory,* edited by James A. Holstein and Gale Miller. Hawthorne, NY: Aldine de Gruyter.

Mills, C. Wright (1959). *The Sociological Imagination.* New York: Oxford University Press.

Monroe, Alan D. (1988). "Public Opinion and Pubic Policy, 1980–1993." *Public Opinion Quarterly* 62:6–28.

Morris, Aldon D. (1984). *The Origins of the Civil Rights Movement: Black Communities Organizing for Change*. New York: Free Press.

Najafizadeh, Mehrangiz and Lewis A. Mennerick (1989). "Defining Third World Education as a Social Problem: Educational Ideologies and Education Entrepreneurship in Nicaragua and Iran." Pp. 283–315 in *Perspectives on Social Problems* (Volume 1), edited by James A. Holstein and Gale Miller. Greenwich, CT: JAI.

Nakagawa, Nobutoshi (1995). "Social Constructionism in Japan: Toward an Indigenous Empirical Inquiry." Pp. 295–310 in *Perspectives on Social Problems* (Volume 7), edited by James A. Holstein and Gale Miller. Greenwich, CT: JAI.

Nardi, Peter M. (1998). "The Globalization of the Gay and Lesbian Socio-Political Movement: Some Observations about Europe with a Focus on Italy." *Sociological Perspectives* 41:567–86.

Nelson, Barbara (1984). *Making an Issue of Child Abuse: Political Agenda Setting for Social Problems*. Chicago: University of Chicago Press.

Nelson, E. D. (1994). "Females Who Sexually Abuse Children: A Discussion of Gender Stereotypes and Symbolic Assailants." *Qualitative Sociology* 17:63–87.

Nelson-Rowe, Shan (1995). "The Moral Drama of Multicultural Education." Pp. 81–104 in *Images of Issues: Typifying Contemporary Social Problems* (2d ed.), edited by Joel Best. Hawthorne, NY: Aldine de Gruyter.

Neubeck, Kenneth J. and Noel A. Cazenave (2001). *Welfare Racism: Playing the Race Card Against America's Poor*. New York: Routledge.

Neuman, W. Russell, Marion R. Just, and Ann N. Crigler (1992). *Common Knowledge: News and the Construction of Political Meaning*. Chicago: University of Chicago.

Nichols, Lawrence T. (1997). "Social Problems as Landmark Narratives: Bank of Boston, Mass Media and 'Money Laundering.'" *Social Problems* 44:324–41.

Nichols, Lawrence T. (1995). "Cold Wars, Evil Empires, Treacherous Japanese: Effects of International Context on Problem Construction." Pp. 313–36 in *Images of Issues: Typifying Contemporary Social Problems* (2d ed.), edited by Joel Best. Hawthorne, NY: Aldine de Gruyter.

Nolan, James L., Jr. (2002). "Drug Court Stories: Transforming American Jurisprudence." Pp. 149–78 in *Stories of Change: Narrative and Social Movements*, edited by Joseph E. Davis. Albany: State University of New York Press.

O'Toole, Richard, Patrick Turbett, and Claire Naepka (1993). "Theories, Professional Knowledge, and the Diagnosis of Child Abuse." Pp. 349–62 in *The Dark Side of Families*, edited by David Finkelhor, Richard J. Gelles, Gerald Hotaling, and Murray A. Straus. Beverly Hills: Sage.

Paterniti, Debora A. (2000). "The Micropolitics of Identity in Adverse Circumstance: A Study of Identity Making in a Total Institution." *Journal of Contemporary Ethnography* 29:93–119.

Paul, Ellen Frankel (1994). "Sexual Harassment: A Defining Moment and Its Repercussions." Pp. 67–97 in *The Politics of Problem Definition: Shaping the Policy Agenda*, edited by David A. Rochefort and Roger W. Cobb. Lawrence: University of Kansas Press.

Pawluch, Dorothy (1996). *The New Pediatrics: A Profession in Transition*. Hawthorne, NY: Aldine de Gruyter.

Peffley, Mark, Jon Hurwitz, and Paul M. Sniderman (1997). "Racial Stereotypes and Whites' Political Views of Blacks in the Context of Welfare and Crime." *American Journal of Political Science* 41:30–61.

Petonito, Gina (1992). "Constructing 'Americans': 'Becoming American,' 'Loyalty,' and Japanese Internment during World War II." Pp. 93–108 in *Perspectives on Social Problems* (Volume 4), edited by James A. Holstein and Gale Miller. Greenwich, CT: JAI.

Peyrot, Mark (1982). "Caseload Management: Choosing Suitable Clients in a Community Mental Health Agency." *Social Problems* 30:157–67.

Pfoul, Stephen (1977). "The 'Discovery' of Child Abuse." *Social Problems* 24:310–23.

Pfoul, Stephen (1978). *Predicting Dangerousness: The Social Construction of Psychiatric Reality.* Lexington, MA: Lexington.

Plummer, Ken (1995). *Sexual Stories: Power, Change and Social Worlds.* New York: Routledge.

Polkinghorne, Donald E. (1988). *Narrative Knowing and the Human Sciences.* Albany: State University of New York Press.

Polletta, Francesca (1997). "Culture and Its Discontents: Recent Theorizing on the Cultural Dimensions of Protest." *Sociological Inquiry* 67:431–50.

Pollner, Melvin and Jill Stein (1996). "Narrative Mapping of Social Worlds: The Voice of Experience in Alcoholics Anonymous." *Symbolic Interaction* 19:203–23.

Ponticelli, Christy M. (1999). "Crafting Stories of Sexual Identity Reconstruction." *Social Psychological Quarterly* 62:157–72.

Press, Andrea L. (1991). *Women Watching Television: Gender, Class, and Generation in the American Television Experience.* Philadelphia: University of Pennsylvania Press.

Quadagno, Jill (1994). *The Color of Welfare: How Racism Undermined the War on Poverty.* New York: Oxford University Press.

Radway, Janice A. (1984). *Reading the Romance: Women, Patriarchy, and Popular Literature.* Chapel Hill: University of North Carolina Press.

Reinarman, Craig and Harry G. Levine (1995). "The Crack Attack: America's Latest Drug Scare, 1986–1992." Pp. 147–90 in *Images of Issues: Typifying Contemporary Social Problems* (2d ed.), edited by Joel Best. Hawthorne, NY: Aldine de Gruyter.

Rice, John Steadman (1992). "Discursive Formation, Life Stories, and the Emergence of Co-Dependency: 'Power/Knowledge' and the Search for Identity." *Sociological Quarterly* 33:337–64.

Rice, John Steadman (2002). "Getting Our Histories Straight: Culture, Narrative and Identity in the Self-Help Movement." Pp. 79–100 in *Stories of Change: Narrative and Social Movements*, edited by Joseph E. Davis. Albany: State University of New York Press.

Richardson, Laurel (1990). "Narrative and Sociology." *Journal of Contemporary Ethnography* 19:116–35.

Riessman, Catherine (1989) "From Victim to Survivor: A Woman's Narrative Reconstruction of Marital Sexual Abuse." *Smith College Studies in Social Work* 59:232–51.

Riessman, Catherine (1990). *Divorce Talk: Women and Men Make Sense of Personal Relationships.* New Brunswick, NJ: Rutgers University Press.

Rios, Delia M. (1997). "A Bogus Statistic That Won't Go Away." *American Journalism Review* 19:12–14.

Rist, Ray C. (1970). "Student Social Class and Teacher Expectations: The Self-Fulfilling Prophecy in Ghetto Education." *Harvard Educational Review* 40:411–51.

Rittenhouse, C. Amanda (1991). "The Emergence of Premenstrual Syndrome as a Social Problem." *Social Problems* 38:412–25.

Rochefort, David A. (1986). *American Social Welfare Policy: Dynamics of Formulation and Change.* Bolder, CO: Westview.

Rochefort, David and Roger Cobb (1993). "Problem Definition, Agenda Access, and Policy Choice." *Policy Studies Journal* 21: 56–71.

Rochefort, David and Roger Cobb (1994). "Problem Definition: An Emerging Perspective." Pp. 1–31 in *The Politics of Problem Definition: Shaping the Policy Agenda,* edited by David A. Rochefort and Roger W. Cobb. Lawrence: University of Kansas Press.

Rochon, Thomas R. and Daniel A. Mazmanian (1993). "Social Movements and the Policy Process." *Annals of the American Academy of Political and Social Science* 528:75–87.

Rodriguez, Luis J. (1998). "The Color of Skin is the Color of Crime." Pp. 130–33 in *Images of Color, Images of Crime: Readings,* edited by Coramae Richey Mann and Marjorie S. Zatz. Los Angeles: Roxbury.

Rogers, Theresa, Eleanor Singer, and Jennifer Imperio (1993). "Poll Trends: AIDS-an Update." *Public Opinion Quarterly* 57:92–114.

Rose, Vicki McNickle (1977). "Rape as a Social Problem: A Byproduct of the Feminist Movement." *Social Problems* 25:75–89.

Rosenau, Pauline Marie (1992). *Post-Modernism and the Social Sciences: Insights, Inroads, and Intrusions.* Princeton, NJ: Princeton University Press.

Rosencrance, John (1985). "Compulsive Gambling and the Medicalization of Deviance." *Social Problems* 32:275–84.

Roser, Connie and Margaret Thompson (1995). "Fear Appeals and the Formation of Active Publics." *Journal of Communication* 45:103–21.

Rossol, Josh (2001). "The Medicalization of Deviance as an Interactive Accomplishment: The Construction of Compulsive Gambling." *Symbolic Interaction* 24:315–42.

Roth, Andrew L. (1998). "Who Makes the News? Descriptions of Television News Interviewees' Public Personae." *Media, Culture & Society* 20:79–102.

Rothenberg, Bess (2002). "Movement Activists as Battered Women's Storytellers." Pp. 203–25 in *Stories of Change: Narrative and Social Movements,* edited by Joseph E. Davis. Albany: State University of New York Press.

Sanders, William B. (1980). *Rape and Woman's Identity.* Beverly Hills: Sage.

Santiago-Irizarry, Vilma (2001). *Medicalizing Ethnicity: The Construction of Latino Identity in a Psychiatric Setting.* Ithaca, NY: Cornell University Press.

Sasson, Theodore (1995). *Crime Talk: How Citizens Construct a Social Problem.* Hawthorne, NY: Aldine de Gruyter.

Sawyers, Traci M. and David S. Meyer (1999). "Missed Opportunities: Social Movement Abeyance and Public Policy." *Social Problems* 46:187–206.

Scheingold, Stuart (1995). "Politics, Public Policy, and Street Crime." *Annals of the American Academy of Politics and Social Science* 539:155–68.

Schneider, Anne and Helen Ingram (1990). "Behavioral Assumptions of Policy Tools." *Journal of Politics* 52:510–29.

Schneider, Anne and Helen Ingram (1993). "Social Construction of Target Populations: Implications for Politics and Policy." *American Political Science Review* 87:334–37.

Schneider, Joseph (1978). "Deviant Drinking as Disease: Alcoholism as a Social Accomplishment." *Social Problems* 25:361–72.

Schneider, Joseph (1984). "Morality, Social Problems, and Everyday Life." Pp. 180–206 in *Studies in the Sociology of Social Problems*, edited by Joseph W. Schneider and John I. Kitsuse. Norwood, NJ: Ablex.

Schneider, Joseph (1985). "Social Problems Theory: The Constructionist View." *Annual Review of Sociology* 11:209–29. Palo Alto, CA: Annual Reviews.

Schram, Sanford F. (1995). *Words of Welfare: The Poverty of Social Science and the Social Science of Poverty*. Minneapolis: University of Minnesota Press.

Scott, Robert A. (1969). *The Making of Blind Men: A Study of Adult Socialization*. New York: Russell Sage Foundation.

Scott, Wilbur J. (1993) *The Politics of Readjustment: Vietnam Veterans Since the War*. Hawthorne, NY: Aldine de Gruyter.

Seccombe, Karen, Delores James, and Kimberly Battle Walters (1998). "'They Think You Ain't Much of Nothing': The Social Construction of the Welfare Mother." *Journal of Marriage and the Family* 60:849–65.

Seidman, Steven (1994). "Introduction." Pp. 1–26 in *The Postmodern Turn: New Perspectives on Social Theory*, edited by Steven Seidman. Cambridge: University of Cambridge Press.

Smith, Dorothy (1984). "Textually Mediated Social Organization." *International Social Science Journal* 36:59–75.

Smith, Ralph R. and Russel R. Windes (1997). "The Progay and Antigay Issue Culture: Interpretation, Influence and Dissent." *Quarterly Journal of Speech* 83:28–48.

Snow, David A. and Leon Anderson (1993). *Down on Their Luck: A Study of Homeless Street People*. Berkeley: University of California Press.

Snow, David and Robert Benford (1988). "Ideology, Frame Resonance, and Participant Mobilization." Pp. 197–217 in *International Social Movement Research* (Volume 1), edited by Bert Klandermans, Hanspeter Kriesi, and Sidney Tarrow. Greenwich, CT: JAI.

Snow, David and Robert Benford (1992). "Master Frames and Cycles of Protest." Pp. 133–55 in *Frontiers in Social Movement Theory*, edited by Carol McClung Mueller and Aldon D. Morris. New Haven, CT: Yale University Press.

Sobal, Jeffery (1999). "The Size Acceptance Movement and the Social Construction of Body Weight." Pp. 231–50 in *Weighty Issues: Fatness and Thinness as Social Problems*, edited by Jeffery Sobal and Donna Maurer. Hawthorne, NY: Aldine de Gruyter.

Socall, Daniel W. and Thomas Holtgraves (1992). "Attitudes Toward the Mentally Ill: The Effects of Label and Beliefs." *Sociological Quarterly* 33:435–46.

Soesilo, Arie and Philo C. Wasburn (1994). "Constructing a Political Spectacle: American and Indonesian Media Accounts of the 'Crisis in the Gulf.'" *Sociological Quarterly* 35:367–81.

Spector, Malcolm and John I. Kitsuse ([1977] 1987). *Constructing Social Problems.* Hawthorne, NY: Aldine de Gruyter.

Spencer, J. William (1994). "Homeless in River City: Client Work in Human Service Encounters." Pp. 29–45 in *Perspectives on Social Problems* (Volume 6), edited by James A. Holstein and Gale Miller. Greenwich, CT: JAI.

Stacey, Judith (1999). "Virtual Truth with a Vengeance." *Contemporary Sociology* 28:18–23.

Stafford, Mark C. and Mark Warr (1985). "Public Perceptions of Social Problems: Some Propositions and a Test." *Journal of Applied Behavioral Science* 21:307–16.

Stallings, Robert A. (1995). *Promoting Risk: Constructing the Earthquake Threat.* Hawthorne, NY: Aldine de Gruyter.

Staudenmeier, William. (1989). "Urine Testing: The Battle for Privatized Social Control During the 1986 War on Drugs." Pp. 207–22 in *Images of Issues: Typifying Contemporary Social Problems,* edited by Joel Best. Hawthorne, NY: Aldine de Gruyter.

Stein, Arlene (2001). *The Stranger Next Door: The Story of a Small Community's Battle Over Sex, Faith, and Civil Rights.* Boston: Beacon Press.

Stone, Deborah (1989). "Causal Stories and the Formation of Policy Agendas." *Political Science Quarterly* 104:281–300.

Stone, Deborah (1997). *Policy Paradox: The Art of Political Decision Making.* New York: W. W. Norton.

Stryker, Sheldon, Timothy Owens, and Robert W. White (2000). *Self, Identity, and Social Movements.* Minneapolis: University of Minnesota Press.

Sudnow, David (1965). "Normal Crimes: Sociological Features of the Penal Code in a Public Defender Office." *Social Problems* 12:255–70.

Sutton, John R. (1988). *Stubborn Children: Controlling Delinquency in the United States, 1640–1981.* Berkeley: University of California Press.

Suzuki, Tadashi (2001). "Frame Diffusion from the U.S. to Japan: Japanese Arguments Against Pornocomics, 1989–1992." Pp. 129–46 in *How Claims Spread: Cross-National Diffusion of Social Problems,* edited by Joel Best. Hawthorne, NY: Aldine de Gruyter.

Swift, Karen J. (1995). *Manufacturing 'Bad Mothers': A Critical Perspective on Child Neglect.* Toronto: University of Toronto Press.

Taylor, Verta and Nancy E. Whittier (1992). "Collective Identity in Social Movement Communities." Pp. 104–30 in *Frontiers in Social Movement Theory,* edited by Carol McClung Mueller and Aldon D. Morris. New Haven, CT: Yale University Press.

Thayer, Millie (1997). "Identity, Revolution, and Democracy: Lesbian Movements in Central America." *Social Problems* 44:386–407.

Tierney, Kathleen (1982). "The Battered Women Movement and the Creation of the Wife Beating Problem." *Social Problems* 29:207–20.

Toulmin, Stephen (1958). *The Uses of Argument.* Cambridge: Cambridge University Press.

Trent, James W., Jr. (1994). *Inventing the Feeble Mind: A History of Mental Retardation in the United States.* Berkeley: University of California Press.

Trethewey, Angela (1997). "Resistance, Identity, and Empowerment: A Postmodern Feminist Analysis of Clients in a Human Service Organization." *Communication Monographs* 64:281–301.

Troyer, Ronald J. (1993). "Revised Social Constructionism: Traditional Social Science More Than a Postmodernist Analysis." Pp. 117–28 in *Reconsidering Social Constructionism: Debates in Social Problems Theory,* edited by James A. Holstein and Gale Miller. Hawthorne, NY: Aldine de Gruyter.

Troyer, Ronald J. and Gerald E. Markle (1983). *Cigarettes: The Battle Over Smoking.* New Brunswick, NJ: Rutgers University Press.

Tuchman, Gaye (1993). "Realism and Romance: The Study of Media Effects." *Journal of Communication* 43:36–41.

Ungar, Sheldon (1990). "Moral Panics, the Military-Industrial Complex, and the Arms Race." *Sociological Quarterly* 33:483–501.

Ungar, Sheldon (1992). "The Rise and (Relative) Decline of Global Warming as a Social Problem." *Sociological Quarterly* 33:483–502.

Vanderford, Marsha (1989). "Vilification and Social Movements: A Case Study of Pro-Life and Pro-Choice Rhetoric." *Quarterly Journal of Speech* 75:166–83.

Waddell, Craig (1990). "The Role of Pathos in the Decision-Making Process: A Study in the Rhetoric of Science Policy." *Quarterly Journal of Speech* 76:381–400.

Wagner, David (1997). *The New Temperance: The American Obsession with Sin and Vice.* Boulder, CO: Westview.

Waller, Willard (1936). "Social Problems and the Mores." *American Sociological Review* 42:922–32.

Warr, Mark (1995). "Poll Trends: Public Opinion on Crime and Punishment." *Public Opinion Quarterly* 59:296–310.

Weinburg, Darin (2000). "Out There: The Ecology of Addiction in Drug Abuse Treatment Discourse." *Social Problems* 47:606–21.

Weiss, Janet (1989). "The Powers of Problem Definition: The Case of Government Paperwork." *Policy Sciences* 22:97–121.

Welch, Michael (2000). *Flag Burning: Moral Panic and the Criminalization of Protest.* Hawthorne, NY: Aldine de Gruyter.

Werthman, Carl and Irving Piliavin (1967). "Gang Members and the Police." Pp. 72–94 in *The Police: Six Sociological Essays,* edited by David Bordua. New York: John Wiley and Sons.

Westervelt, Saundra Davis (1998). *Shifting the Blame: How Victimization Became a Criminal Defense.* New Brunswick, NJ: Rutgers University Press.

Wexler, Richard (1990). *Wounded Innocents: The Real Victims of the War Against Child Abuse.* New York: Prometheus.

Williams, Gwyneth I. and Rhys H. Williams (1995). "'All We Want Is Equality': Rhetorical Framing in the Fathers' Rights Movement." Pp. 191–212 in *Images of Issues: Typifying Contemporary Social Problems* (2d ed.), edited by Joel Best. Hawthorne, NY: Aldine de Gruyter.

Williams, Rhys H. (1995). "Constructing the Public Good: Social Movements and Cultural Resources." *Social Problems* 42:124–44.

Wiseman, Jacqueline P. (1979). *Stations of the Lost: The Treatment of Skid Row Alcoholics.* Chicago: University of Chicago Press.

Wolkomir, Michelle (2001). "Emotion Work, Commitment, and the Authentication of the Self." *Journal of Contemporary Ethnography* 30:305–34.

Wood, Linda and Heather Rennie (1994). "Formulating Rape: The Discursive Construction of Victims and Villains." *Discourse and Society* 5:125–48.

Woolgar, Steven and Dorothy Pawluch (1985). "Ontological Gerrymandering: The Anatomy of Social Problems Explanations." *Social Problems* 32:214–27.

Yamazaki, Atsushi (1994). "The Medicalization and Demedicalization of School Refusal: Constructing an Educational Problem in Japan." Pp. 201–20 in *Troubling Children: Studies of Children and Social Problems,* edited by Joel Best. Hawthorne, NY: Aldine de Gruyter.

Zatz, Marjorie S. (1987). "Chicago Youth Gangs and Crime: The Creation of a Moral Panic." *Contemporary Crisis* 11:129–58.

Index

activists. *See* social (problems) activists
audience carrying capacity, 52, 174
audience(s), 20, 22, 25, 27–31, 35, 41, 51, 54, 56, 59, 64, 69, 76, 92, 98, 107, 110–112, 127, 153, 165, 166, 177, 179, 181

blame, 83, 84, 86

categories, categorization, 15–17, 132, 143, 145, 146, 169, 170. *See also* frames; typification(s)
claims-making, claims-makers, 20–22, 25–27, 30, 43, 45, 51, 53, 54, 59, 105, 107, 109, 110, 112, 113, 115, 116, 121–127, 132, 135, 152–154, 165, 178–180, 187, 190, 191
  and social activists, 37
  credibility, 36, 168
  mass media and, 40–43
  motives, 33–35
  primary *versus* secondary, 41
  strategies, 56, 57, 61, 64, 66–68, 79, 82, 85, 88
  successful claims, 139–141, 158, 169, 172–175, 191, 192
  timing of claims, 58
collective identity. *See under* identity

collective representations, 190
competition, 52–54, 98, 100, 128
conflict perspectives, 164, 165
consequences, 99
  as claims-making strategy, 57
constructionists, constructionist perspective. *See* social constructionism, constructionist(s)
contextual constructionism, 198–200
credibility. *See* hierarchy of credibility
crime, 53, 80
cultural (social) constructions, 18, 103–105
cultural change, 113, 115, 124. *See also* social change
cultural feeling rules, 30, 77, 79, 83, 129, 146, 147, 149, 191
cultural themes, 30, 63–67, 75, 76, 99, 100, 102, 106, 112, 129, 132, 134, 141, 146, 147, 149, 150, 156, 158, 165

deviance, 164
  medicalization of, 86, 87
  positive, 157
  primary, 155
  secondary, 155, 156